V-BOMBERS

Other books by the same author . . .

The Vulcan Story
RAF Fighter Pilot
Tiger Squadrons
Swing Wings
Fight's On
The Royal Air Force Manual
C-130 Hercules

As part of our ongoing market research we are always pleased to receive comments about our books, suggestions for new titles, or requests for catalogues. Please write to: The Editorial Director, Patrick Stephens Limited, Sparkford, Near Yeovil, Somerset BA22 7JJ.

V-BOMBERS

VULCAN, VICTOR AND VALIANT - BRITAIN'S AIRBORNE NUCLEAR DETERRENT

Tim Laming

Patrick Stephens Limited

First published in 1997

British Library Cataloguing in Publication data
A catalogue record of this book is available from the British Library

ISBN 1 85260 529 4

Library of Congress catalog card no. 96-78558

Patrick Stephens Limited is an imprint of Haynes Publishing, Sparkford, Nr Yeovil, Somerset BA22 7JJ

Designed and typeset by J. H. Haynes & Co. Ltd
Printed in Hong Kong

Contents

Introduction		7
Acknowledgements		10
Chapter 1	Britain's Bomb	11
Chapter 2	Britain's Bombers	22
Chapter 3	The Valiant	37
Chapter 4	The Vulcan	53
Chapter 5	The Victor	77
Chapter 6	Bigger Bombs	94
V-Bombers in Colour		97
Chapter 7	Into Service	115
Chapter 8	More Power	129
Chapter 9	Second Generation	144
Chapter 10	The Final Years	163
Chapter 11	Conclusions	177
Appendix	Valiant, Victor and Vulcan squadrons	196
Index		198

V- BOMBER BASES AND OPERATIONAL
CONCERSION UNITS

THOR LOCATIONS

0 10 20 30 40 50mls

0 20 40 60 80kms

Carnaby
Full Sutton Driffield
  Catfoss
Breighton

Caistor
Finningley Ludford Magna
Hemswell
Scampton Bardney
Waddington Coningsby
Coleby Grange
  Folkingham
Cottesmore Wittering Marham
Melton Mowbray North Pickenham
North Luffenham Feltwell
Polebrook Mepal Honington
Harrington Wyton
Gaydon Shepherds Grove
  Tuddenham

Introduction

When writing a history of the RAF's V-Force in 1996, it is difficult to remember how very different the world political situation was in the 1950s, when Britain first developed the capability to manufacture nuclear weapons. Nearly 50 years later it seems incredible that a British Government would sanction the production of three different aircraft types, in substantial numbers, to perform just one specific task; namely, to deliver an atomic bomb to a target somewhere in the Soviet Union. There is no doubt that Britain's financial situation was no better then than it is now, yet huge resources were poured into the development of atomic bombs and the aircraft to carry them.

The reason for such effort may seem unclear to younger generations, but after emerging from the horrors of the Second World War it had quickly become clear that the Third World War was by no means an abstract nightmare for the distant future. It seemed very likely that Russian tanks might well be rolling across West Germany before the end of the 1950s and, when it was realized that Russia possessed a nuclear capability, the prospect of a Soviet invasion was regarded as a very serious possibility.

As hindsight has illustrated, the only defence against a nuclear bomb is another nuclear bomb — the infamous concept of Mutually Assured Destruction — and the British Government recognized this fact at a very early stage. America, with significant British support, had invented the atomic bomb and, having done so, it was impossible to 'uninvent' it. The weapon was a reality, and Britain believed that to be without an atomic capability would be dangerous at best and politically foolish at worst. Reliance upon America as a 'nuclear umbrella' was an easy option, but by no means a certain one. Thus it was agreed that Britain would not allow America to become the West's nuclear monopoly, and that Britain should also join the 'nuclear club'.

Surprisingly, even though the American Government had relied upon British scientific knowledge in order to develop their nation's first atomic weapons, they were more than reluctant to allow Britain to produce her own weapons. The US Government believed that atomic weapons should be placed under international control, and that until such a situation could be achieved the USA should remain as an independent nuclear power. Of course, international control never became a practical proposition, but America did not relish the prospect of Britain being armed with nuclear bombs when it could be overrun by Russian forces at any time (at least in their opinion). More practically, the

Four Vulcans from the Waddington Wing climbing away from Finningley, following a scramble demonstration, September 1982. (Tim Laming)

ongoing discoveries of Russian spies within the British scientific and political spheres simply served to strengthen American resolve to keep atomic know-how a closely guarded secret.

However, having worked so closely with the USA during the development of the first nuclear bombs, Britain already had a fundamental knowledge of atomic weapon design, and when it was established beyond any doubt that America would not share her secrets, Britain simply decided to go it alone and develop independently-designed weapons, not only as a means of assuring Britain's security, but also to ensure that Britain remained at the forefront of international politics. A country which possessed the capability to annihilate virtually any other country had to be taken seriously.

When the first British atomic devices had been tested, the USA quickly changed course and made great efforts to foster close co-operation between the two countries; almost as if the 'Special Relationship' forged in the Second World War had never gone away, but had simply been put on hold until Britain could catch up with the USA. Having done so, the ties between Britain and America became stronger than ever, with the supply of American aircraft, atomic bombs, missiles and technological information, enabling Britain to secure a position as the world's third largest nuclear power.

The story of the V-Force emphasizes just how much the British Government relied upon the US Government to make nuclear deterrence a practical possibility. The Special Relationship was a bargain deal for Britain, but in return the USA obtained a means of maintaining a fortified position within striking range of the Soviet Union. The Royal Air Force and the United States Air Force co-ordinated their strategies and planned for the doomsday scenario in which their combined forces would, in response to a Soviet attack, launch a massive retaliatory strike against Russian airfields, command centres and cities, delivering a decisive nuclear blow which would effectively destroy the Soviet Union. The RAF, situated so close to the East–West border, would be at the forefront of this almost unimaginable strike force and, had the plans been put into practice, the RAF's bombers would already have been returning to whatever remained of the United Kingdom as hundreds of USAF bombers continued their deadly journey across the Atlantic.

Thankfully, the battle plans were never put into action, but the very fact that Britain and the USA were prepared to take such action was enough to convince the Soviet Union that military adventurism beyond Eastern Europe was not a practical proposition. As if proof were needed of this fact, the concept of Mutually Assured Destruction was put to the test in 1962, when Soviet missiles

were shipped to Cuba, positioning them within striking range of the North American continent. Kennedy could not allow Kruschev to do what America had effectively done in Britain, and the stand-off between the Soviets and Americans intensified until both countries reached the very edge of nuclear confrontation. If the missiles were not removed, a war would ensue which neither side could confidently expect to win. Consequently, Kruschev, in distinctly untypical fashion, backed down.

More recent history reveals how the thaw in East–West relations was precipitated by the realization that the constant updating of each country's weapon capability was creating an artificial 'technology war' that the Soviet Union could never hope to win. Thus USA effectively bought her victory in the Cold War, and the Soviet Union accepted that the arms race was inevitably going to be won by the more affluent country. Once that vital fact had been

Vulcan K.2 XM571 taxying to No. 50 Squadron's dispersal, Waddington 1982. (Tim Laming)

digested, the Soviet Union crumbled.

As for the United Kingdom, the independent nuclear deterrent remains, both as a guarantee that Britain will remain secure under her own 'nuclear umbrella', no matter how American policy might change, and as a guarantee that, even without an Empire, the British Government will still be afforded a Very Important status within the international community. The nuclear deterrent has long since been transferred from the RAF to the Royal Navy, but this book traces the history of how Britain first developed her nuclear capability, during an era of great uncertainty and austerity, with more than a little help from her friends across the Atlantic.

Acknowledgements

This book has only been possible with the assistance of many individuals and organizations, and the author would particularly like to thank Mark Swann, Ken Billingham, John Hale, Terry Wong-Lane, B. Hulme, Roger and Heather Brooks, Andy Stulpa, Paul Jackson, Mick Coombes, Harry Homes, David Walton, David Thomas, David Haller and Mike Harries.

CHAPTER ONE

Britain's Bomb

Although nuclear weapons are often regarded as a relatively new aspect of warfare, the origins of Britain's strategic nuclear bomber force can be traced back as far as 1938, when three German scientists, Otto Hahn, Lise Meitner, and Fritz Strassmann, first discovered the principle of nuclear fission. Three other scientists (Yakov Frenkel in the Soviet Union, John Wheeler in the USA, and Niels Bohr in Denmark) had already produced reports describing the theory of how nuclear fission took place, and in 1940 Otto Frisch and Rudolph Peierls, while working at the University of Birmingham, produced a report which concluded that uranium 235 could be separated from uranium 238, thus initiating a 'chain reaction' which would produce a devastating explosive force.

Their calculations indicated that a bomb could be developed which would

An unusual head-on view of a Vulcan B.1, illustrating the type's clean lines which at the time, were unusual for a bomber aircraft. (British Aerospace)

possess awesome destructive power.

The British Government were not slow to understand the significance of this discovery, not least because Nazi Germany was already believed to be pursuing similar studies. The government commissioned a group of British scientists to study the possibilities of producing a 'uranium bomb' under wartime conditions, and the group became established as the Maud Committee, the peculiar cryptonym being derived from a telegram sent by Niels Bohr to Otto Frisch when Germany invaded Denmark. The telegram closed with the words: 'Tell Cockcroft and Maud Ray Kent'. British intelligence interpreted the last three words as an anagram meaning 'radium taken', which fuelled speculation that Germany was making significant scientific progress. Years later it transpired that the message was simply intended for Maud Ray, the Bohr children's former governess, who lived in Kent.

The Maud Committee spent 15 months studying available scientific evidence, and concluded that an effective bomb could be manufactured and that it would be 'a very powerful weapon of war'. It was estimated that a bomb could be completed by the end of 1943 at an estimated cost of £5 million. The cost and time predictions were decidedly optimistic, but the committee's belief that an atomic bomb would probably create an explosive force equivalent to 1,800 tons of TNT was fairly accurate, as was their estimation that radioactive fall-out would be produced as a result of an atomic explosion, rendering large areas of land totally uninhabitable for very long periods.

Although it was accepted that the war in Europe might end before an atomic bomb was produced, the committee stated that 'effort would not be wasted, since no nation would care to risk being caught without a weapon of such decisive possibilities'. It was also recommended that work on the new weapon should be conducted in co-operation with the USA. Transatlantic exchanges of scientific data had begun in 1940, following the visit to Washington, D.C., of Sir Henry Tizard, the British Government's chief advisor on weapons research, who carried a 'black box' of weapons-related secrets which were openly divulged to the United States. Tizard negotiated agreements for the exchange of weapon design data by offering details of British breakthroughs in the development of radar, underwater detection devices, jet engines, and magnetrons, among other things, and Britain's information contributed greatly to the massive rearmament programme then under way in the USA prior to that nation's entry into the Second World War.

The Maud Report was also given to the USA, and Dr Vannevar Bush, Chairman of the National Defense Research Council, used it to secure President Roosevelt's support for full-scale atomic research. Roosevelt wrote to British Prime Minister Winston Churchill during October 1942, suggesting that British and American production efforts should be 'co-ordinated or even jointly conducted'. Churchill's response was rather muted, and after waiting two months he only offered his general willingness to co-operate. The British Government's lack of enthusiasm was prompted by a gross miscalculation of the ultimate cost of atomic weapon research, leading to a belief that Britain could easily 'go it alone', and a reluctance to become too closely tied to a relatively slow-paced peacetime project when Britain was keen to pursue a high-priority wartime development programme. Additionally, it was believed that America might be unable or unwilling to 'keep nuclear secrets', and that the USA was adopting a distinctly neutral position in relation to the war in Europe.

Following the Japanese attack on Pearl

Harbor and the USA's inevitable entry into the war, the situation changed drastically, and huge resources were poured into their atomic weapon programme. In July 1942 Roosevelt committed virtually unlimited funds to the new Manhattan Project, and the British Government realized that it would be foolish to continue atomic weapon development in isolation from the USA. Churchill agreed to the acceptance of Roosevelt's co-operation offer, but by this time the Americans were no longer interested, chiefly because they could not see what contributions the British could now make to their programme.

Dr Vannevar Bush and his colleagues persuaded the President to impose a 'use in this war' principle on Britain, which meant that transatlantic co-operation would be confined to the exchange of information relevant to weaponry designed for use only during the war. Britain was forced to face the prospect of independent atomic development, but Roosevelt was privately inclined to foster greater co-operation with Britain, recognizing that his advisors were chiefly concerned with Britain's post-war commercial atomic intentions rather than the rather more immediate wartime considerations. Churchill understood their anxiety too, and convinced the Americans that Britain did not have any interest in obtaining nuclear power production data, thus removing all of America's reservations. Consequently, the Quebec Agreement of 19 August 1943 established transatlantic co-operation, stating that:

- neither state would use atomic weapons against the other
- neither would use them against third parties except with the other's consent
- neither would transfer relevant data to third parties except with the other's

consent
- the transfer of commercially relevant data to Britain would be subject to presidential discretion
- a Combined Policy Committee (CPC) would be established to administer co-operation and allocate resources.

British scientists quickly joined the Manhattan Project in substantial numbers, working in close co-operation with their American counterparts, although information was still exchanged on a strictly compartmentalized 'need-to-know' basis (not because of the British presence, but simply as part of the project's high-security status, which restricted specific areas of knowledge to individuals who actually required the information as part of their work). Subsequently a second agreement, the Hyde Park 'aide memoire', was signed by Roosevelt and Churchill late in 1944, committing both countries to continued industrial and military atomic energy co-operation even after the war, unless the agreement was terminated by either party. Peculiarly, Roosevelt never informed his officials of this agreement, and the American copy disappeared into his files for several years.

As work on the Manhattan Project progressed, the British Chiefs of Staff asked their Joint Technical Warfare Committee (JTWC) to consider future British defence options. Under the chairmanship of Sir Henry Tizard the committee studied the latest develop-ments in weapon technology, although they were given no information concerning atom bomb production. Despite this, the Tizard Report of 13 July 1945 urged that the Government should encourage more research into atomic energy, envisioning the development of both atomic weapons and jet bombers capable of cruising at 500 mph at 40,000 ft, carrying a bomb load equivalent to that of the wartime Lancaster. The report also stated: 'The only answer that we can see to the atomic bomb is to be prepared to use it ourselves in retaliation. A knowledge that we were prepared, in the last resort, to do this might well deter an aggressive nation'. Thus, in this brief paragraph, the genesis of the V-Force was identified and established.

At 05:29 on 16 July 1945 the Manhattan Project's efforts reached fruition when the world's first atomic device was successfully detonated. The Trinity site where this historic event took place is situated within the White Sands Missile Range in the New Mexico desert, north of Alamogordo. The unwieldy 'bomb' was actually a rather crude contraption (which certainly could not have been dropped from an aircraft) assembled on a 100 ft tower to avoid sucking up large amounts of desert floor which would later descend to earth as radioactive fall-out. The blinding flash was seen for hundreds of miles, many people reporting that the sun had mysteriously risen and gone down again. The blast wave was felt as far afield as Arizona and Texas, and reports of shattered windows were received from as far as 200 miles away. Having proved the concept, on 6 August a second and more compact device was detonated at 09:16, just 1,900 ft above the Shima Hospital in Hiroshima, Japan. It had been dropped in a huge bomb casing from a United States Army Air Force (USAAF) Boeing B-29 bomber flying at 32,000 ft.

The power of the bomb was later assessed at 12,500 tons of TNT, of which 35 per cent was released as thermal radiation, 17 per cent as radioactive radiation, and the remainder as blast energy. Dubbed 'Little Boy', the bomb was a 4-ton uranium device, built around an artillery gun barrel which fired one piece of fissionable material at another, initiating the 'chain reaction' explosion.

Three days later at 11:03 a third bomb was detonated, this time at 1,650 ft above the Urakami district of Nagasaki in Japan, with an explosive yield equivalent to 22,000 tons of TNT. Unlike the Hiroshima weapon, 'Fat Man' was a 4.5-ton plutonium 'implosion' bomb. Japan quickly surrendered, and the Second World War was over.

Without Britain's contribution to the Manhattan Project it is very unlikely that any atomic bombs would have been completed before the end of the war. A million American casualties were expected to result from the scheduled invasion of Japan, and Gen Groves, who masterminded the Manhattan Project, later commented that there probably would not have been an atomic bomb to drop on Hiroshima without 'active and continuing British interest'. America had clearly benefited tremendously from Britain's contribution to the development of atomic bombs, and in return British scientists established the basic theory and technical knowledge of how such bombs could be produced, as well as gaining some fundamental knowledge of how thermonuclear weapons could be designed. As Lord Chadwick, Chairman of the atomic weaponry committee which reported to the Ministry of Supply (MoS), commented, British scientists could not be expected 'to take amnesia tablets before returning home'.

Although the Anglo-American nuclear relationship suffered many blows during the war, it survived intact, but it was almost inevitable that it would not continue in peacetime. Britain had justifiable claims to American technical data and resources, and President Harry Truman's administration was prepared to recognize this fact. But by 1946 American political opinion had grown suspicious of Britain's new socialist government, and the USA's position moved towards isolationism and a nuclear monopoly which the administration could not realistically challenge, especially when it was revealed in April 1946 that a British nuclear physicist had been passing US nuclear information to Soviet agents.

Co-operation effectively ended in August, following the imposition of the Atomic Energy Act, more commonly known as the McMahon Act after its proposer. The act ignored the wartime Quebec and Hyde Park agreements, stipulating that the transfer of any nuclear information to any foreign country was illegal under penalty of imprisonment or even death. Senator McMahon subsequently stated:

> The British contributed heavily to our own wartime atomic project, but due to a series of unfortunate circum-stances, the nature of the agreements which made this contribution possible was not disclosed to me or my colleagues on the Senate Special Atomic Energy Committee at the time we framed the law in 1946.

Despite his comments, it is unlikely that even a full statement of Britain's wartime involvement would have significantly changed American attitudes during 1946.
British Prime Minister Clement Attlee was astonished when the McMahon Bill was passed through Congress, and he sent a telegram to Truman stating:

> Our continuing co-operation over raw material shall be balanced by an exchange of information which will give us, with all proper precautions with regard to security, that full information to which we believe we are entitled, both by the documents and by the history of our common efforts in the past.

Truman did not even acknowledge receipt of the communication, and Britain's immediate reaction to the USA's shift towards isolationism was to secure her own supply of raw uranium (which is separated into fissionable U-235) from joint Anglo-American uranium stocks which had first been established during the war. The US Government believed that Britain had favourable relations with Portugal, South Africa, Belgium, and other Commonwealth countries who possessed uranium mines in numerous locations, but in reality Britain would not have been able to compete with the purchasing power of the mighty Dollar. However, Britain's interest in securing a good supply of uranium emphasized to the USA that, if necessary, Britain was willing to 'go it alone' and develop her own atomic weapons.

In retrospect, Britain's decision to develop atomic weapons independently was regarded as inevitable, even if US co-operation had been available. Attlee later recalled:

> We had to hold up our position vis-à-vis the Americans. We couldn't allow ourselves to be wholly in their hands and the position wasn't awfully clear always. There was the possibility of their withdrawing and becoming isolationist again. The manufacture of a British bomb was therefore at this stage essential to our defence.

Towards the end of 1947, co-operation between the two countries began to improve in both the foreign policy and defence spheres. A growing American belief that commitments to Britain had not been honoured was compounded by a very real, and growing, uranium shortage, while Britain enjoyed on-going production from sources such as the Belgian Congo. Consequently, negotiations between the two countries began, and the talks were concluded successfully during January 1948, the USA being granted access to British uranium stocks in exchange for technical co-operation. Alas, the new agreements did not last long, and continued Congressional pressure led to yet another breakdown in the fragile Anglo–American relationship. By 1949 the situation had deteriorated to such an extent that Truman commented: 'We have got to protect our information and we must certainly try and see that the British do not have the information to build atomic weapons in England because they might be captured'.

Having now decided to begin construction of two atomic piles at Windscale, Britain had clearly indicated that production of atomic weapons would go ahead, regardless of American support. The continuing 'monopoly mentality' in the USA encouraged congressional reluctance to supply technological 'know-how' to the UK despite the rather ironic development of collaborative agreements between the RAF and the United States Air Force (USAF). By this stage some 60 American Boeing B-29 Superfortresses had been deployed to Britain, having been accepted by Attlee in 1948 (they were reconfigured to carry atomic weapons during 1950), and although their presence suggested a new 'special relationship' with regard to nuclear know-how, the new capacity for joint planning between the RAF and the USAF's Strategic Air Command (SAC) was severely restricted because of the continuing American refusal to discuss atomic technology and weaponry.

The absurdity of this situation finally led to an attempt to make a 'fresh start' with Britain, and in September 1949 a new proposal was made which would have effectively restored a complete exchange of nuclear information. Once again, however, the transatlantic consensus was very fragile, and the continuing espionage stories surrounding the likes of Fuchs, Maclean, and Burgess did nothing to ease America's doubts, so negotiations eventually broke down yet again. The British Government believed that America could not be relied upon to confront an enemy which did not threaten the USA directly. Likewise, British Chiefs of Staff believed that atomic bombs would be essential to ensure the country's international position. One report commented: 'We feel that to have no share in what is recognized as the main deterrent in the Cold War would mean that in war the United Kingdom would have no claim to share in the policy or planning of the offensive'.

However, despite the continuing political setbacks, behind the scenes a transatlantic collective common sense slowly began to prevail. The rapidly-emerging conceptual problems of thermonuclear weapon (hydrogen bomb) development were already beginning to concern American scientists, and in June 1950 North Korean forces crossed the 38th Parallel. Britain was becoming increasingly concerned by the emergence of the Soviet Union as an embryonic nuclear power (it detonated its first atomic device in September 1949) and, having taken the decision to produce her own atomic bombs, Britain had effectively declared her nuclear independence, regardless of any subsequent deliberations over the means of weapon delivery which might take place with the USA. The path was now laid for true co-operation, but the US Congress stubbornly tried to maintain what was rapidly becoming a nuclear duopoly (the other power being the Soviet Union), and the situation remained essentially stagnant until 2 October 1952, when Britain's first atomic device was successfully detonated and America finally realized that Britain could, and would, remain as independent as ever.

The aforementioned 1945 Tizard Committee Report had made only hypothetical references to nuclear weapons, and in the light of the Hiroshima and Nagasaki attacks the Chiefs of Staff requested during September 1945 that the report be suitably amended. This resulted in a revised version which was issued on 1 July 1946, with relevant comments as follows:

a) Given sufficient accumulation in peace and adequate means of delivery, atomic and biological weapons might achieve decisive results with relatively small effort against the civil population of a nation without a clash between the major military forces and too rapidly to permit either the building-up of military forces or the exercise of sea power.

b) Some five or ten atomic bombs landed on the target, with the prospect of more to follow, might well cause the evacuation of cities to an extent sufficient seriously to sap the power of waging war by conventional means of any country physically and psychologically unorganized to meet such action. Without the moral backing of adequate military power in being, with which to limit or repel invasion, or to launch an effective counteroffensive, such attack might well lead to collapse. On the other hand, some hundreds of atomic weapons might fail to cause the collapse of a country suitably organized physically and psychologically, and morally reinforced by adequate military power in being. Although biological weapons have not yet been used in war, we consider that the number of atomic weapons required would be materially reduced if biological weapons were simultaneously used.

c) There is no firm basis on which to assess the quantities of atomic and biological weapons required by any nation to bring about the collapse of another, and many of the factors involved are imponderable. Nevertheless, our estimate, based on such information as is at present available, leads us to believe that some 30–120 atomic bombs accurately delivered by the USSR might cause the collapse of the United Kingdom without invasion, whereas several hundred bombs might be required by the United States or the United Kingdom to bring about the collapse of the USSR. The number of bombs required to cause a similar collapse in the United States would probably be somewhat greater than for this country, but the problem of landing them accurately in the United States at the ranges involved is much greater.

d) The percentage of bombs despatched which could be accurately delivered depends on future developments in the technique of attack and defence, the ranges involved and the relative concentration of targets. Unless defensive weapons and methods can be developed more rapidly and to a far greater extent than the methods of attack already envisaged, there seems to be little possibility of preventing the accurate delivery of a substantial proportion of the weapons launched — perhaps 50 per cent or more. The most promising form of defence so far conceived is the Guided Anti-Aircraft Projectile; and the importance and urgency of its development cannot be over-emphasized. The Chiefs of Staff also agreed that 'the following conclusions, substantially as reached by Sir Henry Tizard's Committee', remained valid, as follows:

a) Until fighters using controlled or guided weapons and reliable ground-controlled weapons are available, the strategic bomber capable of speeds approaching the speed of sound will have a great advantage. In contrast, once the defensive weapons mentioned above are in being, provided the expected advances have been made in radar, deep strategic bombing with ordinary explosives as exploited in the last war is likely to be too costly to be sustained over a long period. Heavy precision attacks on important targets will still be possible despite the loss rate.

b) Anti-aircraft fire of conventional but improved kind will remain a necessary defensive supplement on land and sea to supersonic fighters. Particular importance attaches to anti-aircraft fire as the defence against fast low–flying aircraft, since against these all forms of wire barrage may well be ineffective, and supersonic aircraft may be unable to intercept in the time available.

c) The rocket will remain a very difficult form of bombardment to counter and will be effective at ranges up to perhaps as much as 400 miles, the more so since it can be used in the sustained 'dribble' attack uninterrupted by weather and independent of the defender's fighter superiority. Much the same remarks apply to pilotless aircraft, but we think that they are likely to be inferior to rockets at medium ranges. It is thus of importance, in view of the difficulty of intercepting rockets, that no potential enemy should possess bases within 400 miles of ours.

d) Sources of uranium, thorium and other relevant elements will be of great strategic importance. Natural sources of oil will also remain equally important.

e) It is of first importance that a reduction in the time interval between research and development, on the one hand, and the availability in quantity of weapons, such as aircraft, can and must be achieved in this country.

f) The continued and indeed improved integration of military and scientific thought at all levels remains an essential defence requirement, and must ensure in the immediate future that much emphasis is placed on long-term research, and the improvement of the level of technical education in the Services, and indeed in the country as a whole.

g) The effect of the changes we foresee in weapons may have a great impact on the men who operate them and therefore on their selection and training.

A long annex entitled 'Main Problems for Defence Research' explored atomic and biological weapons, together with possible high–performance manned aircraft capable of carrying them. On 8 July the Chiefs of Staff recommended that the Cabinet Defence Committee should accept the conclusions of the revised Tizard Report, and the ensuing Cabinet-level decision to set up a joint–Service group to study future developments in weapons and warfare enabled the Air Staff to issue a requirement for an atomic bomb, OR.1001 dated 9 August 1946, for the 'development of a bomb employing the principle of nuclear fission'. The weapon, which was not to exceed 10,000 lb in weight, 24 ft 2 in in length, and 5 ft in diameter, was to be capable of release at all heights between 20,000 ft and 50,000 ft at speeds of between 150 kt and 500 kt.

Despite the Air Staff's new requirement, official governmental approval for the development of atomic weapons did not materialize until early 1947. Lord Portal, the Controller of Production of Atomic Energy, brought matters to a conclusion during a meeting at No. 10 Downing Street on 8 January, via a memo presented by the Minister of Supply. Lord Portal stated:

I submit that a decision is required about the development of atomic weapons in this country. The Service Departments are beginning to move in the matter and certain sections of the Press are showing interest in it.

My organization is charged solely with the production of 'fissile material', i.e. the 'filling' that would go into any bomb that it was decided to develop. Apart altogether from producing the 'filling', development of the bomb mechanism is a complex problem of nuclear physics and precision engineering on which some years of research and development would be necessary.

I suggest that there are broadly three courses of action to choose from: a) Not to develop the atomic weapon at all, b) To develop the weapon by means of ordinary agencies in the Ministry of Supply and Service Departments, or c) To develop the weapon under special arrangements conducive to the utmost secrecy.

I imagine that course a) above would not be favoured by HM Government in the absence of an international agreement on the subject. If course b) is adopted it will be impossible to conceal for long the fact that this development is taking place. Many interests are involved and the need for constant consultation with my organization (which is the sole repository of the knowledge of atomic energy and atomic weapons derived from our wartime collaboration with the United States) would result in very many people, including scientists, knowing what was going on.

Moreover, it would certainly not be long before the American authorities heard that we were developing the weapon 'through the normal channels' and this might well seem to them another reason for reticence over technical matters, not only in the field of military uses of atomic energy, but also in the general 'know-how' of the production of fissile material.

After making further comments concerning possible courses of action, Lord Portal continued: 'I therefore ask for direction on two points: first, whether research and development on atomic weapons is to be undertaken; and if so, whether the arrangements outlined are to be adopted'. He then spoke to the Ministers during the afternoon of 8 January, emphasizing that the Chiefs of Staff were anxious that Britain should not be without atomic weapons if other countries possessed them. The Foreign Secretary agreed with this view, and also commented that Britain could not afford to acquiesce in an American atomic monopoly. The Minister of Defence also believed that Britain had to develop the bomb unless an effective international system of control could be developed.

Consequently, the meeting agreed that research and development work on atomic weapons should be undertaken, and one of the most momentous British governmental decisions was made.

Development work was led by Dr William Penney, a hitherto relatively unknown scientist who, after having conducted useful explosives research during the war, went on to become a leading member of the British team involved with the Manhattan Project. Penney was an expert on blast and shock effects, and the American scientists made numerous attempts to retain his skills, but after assisting with America's early atomic bomb tests in 1946 he returned to Britain to work on his native country's nuclear programme.

As the 'iron curtain' descended over Europe and the Cold War was unofficially declared, the first Soviet atomic bomb was detonated in August 1949, but production of the first British bomb was still some time away, largely because of the delay in producing plutonium. Production of this fissile material (which is more efficient than uranium) began at Windscale in 1941, and the first supplies became available in March 1952, just a few weeks before the first bomb was tested.

Long before the bomb was complete, there was still the question of where the detonation could take place. The obvious location was in the state of Nevada, where American tests were proceeding, but the continual problems over technological secrecy made this option unworkable. Britain's scientists felt it would be pointless to be effectively duplicating America's efforts, but the absurdity of the situation was evidently not so obvious to the US Government. The British Joint Services Mission in Washington reported:

When the British team arrived over here they would be subjected to so many petty restrictions and there would be so much red tape that in effect the Americans would explode our weapon for us and let us have only those results which they felt they could safely divulge.

Canada was considered, and a site in Manitoba was investigated, but although it would have provided an area devoid of habitation for more than 100 miles downwind of detonation, the coastal area was too shallow to enable ships to reach the shore, and Penney was anxious to test Britain's bomb in shallow water. Surprisingly, even Britain was considered as a possible test site, and an area around Wick in north-east Scotland was evaluated, but the final choice was the Monte Bello Islands, some 50 miles off the north-west coast of Australia. These uninhabited islands had a six-fathom channel close to their shorelines, where a shipborne test could be conducted.

Governmental advisors chose this shallow-water detonation set-up so that the possible damage caused by an atomic device secretly housed on board a ship could be investigated. Some commentators have remarked that the experiment was intended to impress the Americans, who had no technical information on seaborne detonations, but such a consideration was obviously more important to an island nation like Britain (which could easily be attacked by sea) than it was to the Americans, and rather than being seen as an alternative to Nevada, the Monte Bello Islands became Britain's first choice as an atomic test site.

As part of Operation Hurricane, the naval frigate HMS *Plym* departed the Thames Estuary in June 1952, loaded with an unusual array of TV aerials (because a naval intelligence officer decided to disguise the ship as a 'television vessel') and a rather more serious cargo of two prototype warheads. Two months later the plutonium was delivered from Windscale to Aldermaston, from where it was transported in two green furniture vans to RAF Lyneham in Wiltshire. The plutonium was then flown by Hastings transport aircraft to Seletar in Singapore, from where the journey continued by Sunderland flying boat.

On board the ships of the 'special squadron', the trip to Australia was far from happy, even though Air Vice-Marshal Davis, a member of the planning committee, had previously said: 'Any right-minded man would regard these trials as a grand experience combined with the fun of a picnic'. The scientists on board the flagship, HMS *Campania*, infuriated senior naval officers by continually fraternizing with stewards and seamen, even though they had been made honorary members of the wardroom. Protocol pettiness culminated during a Sunday evening film show, when a first lieutenant announced that ties should be worn. The 'boffins' responded by wearing ties but no shirts.

More seriously, one member of the special squadron recalls that, during one briefing on board his ship, the scientists said: 'they did not have a clue exactly what would happen and they could not say what would happen to future generations. As a result, one person tried to get off.' Another seaman remembers being told: 'we would all be sterile for the next ten years as a result of the test. No-one complained because we were young and reckless then.' After arriving on 8 August, work continued on the construction of roads, buildings and communication links. On Alpha Island, MoS photographers built a remote-control camera installation to record the event, while on Trimouille the Army's Mechanical Effects Division planted a variety of measuring devices to record the effects of the blast, including 200 petrol cans and toothpaste tubes in the bizarre collection. Paint samples, clothing, and thermometers were positioned to record heat effects, and the Radiation Hazard Division constructed a variety of air samplers, some built from household vacuum cleaners.

Final assembly of the bomb then took place, and during the early hours of 2 October the weapon's initiator and neutron source were installed, after which the scientific staff retired to the control centre on Hermite or to HMS *Campania,* a former aircraft carrier. At 09:30 next morning the device was successfully detonated by cable from nearby Trimouille. HMS *Plym* was vaporized and the detonation was a great success, much to the surprise of some of the scientists, who had become increasingly pessimistic during the two months of frantic preparation. Ten seconds after detonation the team's photographers stepped out from their cover to take a look at the results of Penney's efforts. They expected to see the 'mushroom cloud' effect that was already becoming a familiar sight in the world's newspapers, but the Hurricane device produced a rather different sight. The ground-positioned bomb had sucked up millions of tons of mud, and this had developed into a peculiar cauliflower shape which was billowing upwards and sideways. Many of the uninformed observers assumed that it was a new type of bomb which Penney had secretly developed.

Seamen on board some of the ships were positioned on the decks, about five miles from the bomb. One man recalls:

There was a blinding electric-blue light, of such intensity I had not seen before or since. I pressed my hands hard to my eyes, then realized my hands were covering my eyes and this terrific light was actually passing through the tarpaulin, through the towel and through my head and body.

The pressure wave passed over the observers a few seconds later, and the assembled spectators heard the deafening thump of the distant detonation.

Prime Minister Winston Churchill made an official announcement to the House of Commons on 23 October, stating: 'The weapon was exploded in the morning of 3 October. Thousands of tons of water and mud and rock from the sea bottom were thrown many thousands of feet into the air and a high tidal wave was caused.' A simultaneous announcement was made by No. 10 Downing Street that Dr Penney had been appointed Knight Commander of the Order of the British Empire.

CHAPTER TWO

Britain's Bombers

Although in retrospect it seems obvious that Britain's atomic bombs would be carried by long-range bombers, the means of delivery for these weapons was by no means certain in the early 1940s. Sir Arthur Harris speculated that an 'atomic exploder' could be brought into an enemy country piece by piece, to be assembled and detonated in almost any location where suitable cover could be found. Others offered the proposition that atomic weapons could be housed on board ships and detonated in enemy ports, a suggestion which was considered so seriously that Britain's first atomic bomb was tested aboard a frigate in shallow water. However, a more obvious means of delivery was a strategic missile, something which Nazi Germany had clearly been considering during the latter stages of the Second World War.

Germany launched more than 4,000 V-2 rockets during the latter part of 1944 and early 1945. More than 1,000 were targeted on London, following the onslaught of V-1 weapons, of which more than 8,000 reached south–east England. Clearly, Germany had achieved considerable success with a weapon system which had progressed far beyond the experimental stage. Britain also had some rocketry experience, having first developed guided missiles during the First World War, but scientific interest had largely centred around small solid-fuel rockets, rather than large liquid-fuel missiles as developed by the Germans. However, Britain did conduct a relatively low-key test of captured German V-2s during 1945, with the co-operation of captured rocket scientists. Operation Backfire was based on the site of a former Krupp naval gunnery range at Altenwalde, where three rockets were eventually launched as part of the test programme.

Following the division of Germany into Allied areas of responsibility, the tests were halted when America requested that the German rocket scientists should be transferred to their military control. By this stage the British research scientists had learned a great deal about the V-2, and it was clear that rocket technology would not be able to offer a means of delivering atomic weapons, at least not for a very long time. The V-2's maximum payload was a mere 2,150 lb, compared to the massive 9,000 lb and 10,000 lb bombs dropped on Hiroshima and Nagasaki respectively. Likewise, the V-2's range was woefully inadequate, even if an improved weapon could have been launched from British bases in Germany. Even its designer, the legendary Wernher von Braun (whom the British did not even invite to the Operation Backfire tests), believed that the V-2 was no more than a high-altitude research vehicle, and could only be regarded as a useful stepping stone on the way to more ambitious projects.

Thanks to a combined lack of funds, resources, and manpower the MoS ended all research into long-range rocket development in 1948, leaving America to build upon this early experience and ultimately put a man on the Moon little more than 20 years later. British interest subsequently concentrated entirely on the manned bomber aircraft, a delivery system which had been proved successfully by both America and Britain during the Second World War. The outstanding Avro Lancaster was developed into the more capable Lincoln, but this was almost obsolete when it entered RAF service. With a range of 2,250 miles it was an impressive aircraft, but by no means a match for the Soviet jet fighters which were already being developed. It was supplemented in 1950 by 87 Boeing B-29s, named Washington

in RAF service, which were supplied by America as part of the post-war Military Assistance Program. With a maximum range of more than 4,000 miles the Washington was clearly nuclear-capable, but no official announcement was made to indicate whether the aircraft did carry such (American) weapons, and although the Air Staff devoted plenty of discussion to the possibility of equipping Washingtons with atomic bombs, no practical efforts were made in this direction.

The B-29s remained in front-line service, based at Coningsby and Marham, until the end of 1954, when deliveries of the first English Electric Canberra medium-range bombers had begun. Officially, the B-29s were procured to bridge the 'bomber gap' between the dwindling number of Lincolns and the arrival of the Canberra, whereas in reality it was the prospect of receiving the aircraft free which persuaded the British Government to accept them, as it had just

An early photograph of a Boeing B-29 Washington touching-down 'somewhere in the UK'. (Boeing)

The Boeing B-29 Washington, the Royal Air Force's 'stop-gap' bomber. (Boeing)

introduced post-1949 financial crisis austerity measures. The piston–engined aircraft were merely regarded as stop–gap tactical bombers which could only be used effectively at night, operating alongside the Lincolns, until the first 'interim' jet bombers were delivered. More importantly, they provided a political presence which placated both the Conservative Party, who were concerned about the situation in Korea, and the RAF, who were worried about their 'bomber gap'.

It is interesting to note that a British requirement for a bomber capable of carrying an atomic weapon was established long before any decision was made to produce British nuclear bombs. Lord Tedder (Marshal of the RAF, 1946–50) wrote early in 1948:

In the furtherance of the supreme aim of our defence policy – namely, to prevent war – the air striking force will play a role of such paramount importance that I am sure my colleagues will wish to be informed of the present programme for its development and of the earliest date at which we can expect it to constitute an effective deterrent to a potential aggressor.

It has been appreciated that the risk of war between now and 1952 must be accepted and that, if war comes, we must fight as best we can with what we have got. Thereafter the risk will greatly increase until about 1957, by and after which date it will become really serious. As stated by the Minister of Defence, we must place emphasis on 'those sections of our Armed Forces which have an obviously deterrent effect', and 'the RAF must provide a striking force equipped with strategic bombers capable of reaching and hitting all the principal targets in Russia, and the gravity of the risk in 1957 may be materially reduced if we can build up a strong deterrent force before that date'.

Early in 1952, even before Britain had tested her first atomic device, Sir John Slessor (Marshal of the RAF, 1950-54) said:

I have always been sceptical about the popular conception of World War III. I believe the supreme need is to prevent it, and that we can prevent it. But if it came, I do not believe the Red Army could be stopped by the Divisions and Tactical Air Forces which Nato can in fact build up without busting Europe and the UK economically — which may well be the Russian game. I believe the only really sound course would be to build up a completely overwhelming British/American bomber force with the A-bomb, capable of pulverizing Russia itself and eliminating the Red Air Force at its bases.

Until the end of the Second World War, Air Ministry thinking had been firmly attached to the concept of heavily-armed bombers which relied on armour plating and gun turrets to ensure survivability over hostile territory. It was only with the arrival of de Havilland's famous Mosquito that speed and altitude were first recognized as a potential defence against enemy fighters. The Mosquito was unarmed, yet its survivability rate was impressive when compared with slower and heavier armed bombers. During the Second World War the Mosquito flew a total of 39,795 operational missions for the loss of 254 aircraft, while the Vickers-Armstrongs Wellington flew 47,409 missions for the loss of 1,332 aircraft. Clearly, the Mosquito, which could be confidently flown over Germany in daylight, demonstrated that armament did not necessarily guarantee protection.

However, there was no question of building a Mosquito-sized nuclear bomber. In 1945 it was widely accepted that the first-generation atomic bombs would weigh approximately 10,000 lb and would be roughly 10 ft in diameter and possibly 30 ft long. Additionally, the aircraft would have to be capable of completing a round trip of over 3,000 miles. Consequently, a completely new generation of bomber aircraft was required, able to fly strategic distances with a heavy bomb load, at altitude. The traditional gun armament, together with the associated gun crews, armour plating, and other associated equipment, would not be incorporated in the design, and the emphasis would be on speed and altitude performance, reflecting the success of the Mosquito and the recognized surviv-ability of high-altitude photographic aircraft such as the Spitfire.

In retrospect it seems foolish to have assumed that performance alone would ensure survivability, when anti-aircraft missiles were already being developed. But at the time it was believed that guided weapons were an abstract futuristic concept, and that all other means of anti-aircraft fire were unlikely to be effective at altitudes above 35,000 ft. The Head of the Guided Weapons Department at Farnborough (1948-53) later commented:

There was a heck of a problem getting those missiles to fly, and those V-bombers would have had a free run for a long time. It was a long haul to set up a complex guided missile system, though most advanced countries have done it now, and we could build V-bombers and get them operational years before there was a hope in hell of anyone saying they knew for sure that they could cope with them.

The Germans had developed a

surface-to-air missile. The Wasserfall (Waterfall) rocket was capable of hitting a target at 45,000 ft, over a distance of 25 miles. Its radar guidance system was fairly crude, and the missile had to be visually guided by joystick on the ground and detonated remotely. Later missiles such as the Schmetterling (Butterfly) suffered from the same difficulties, but well over 100 missiles were tested and launching sites were constructed around cities and other strategic targets. However, there is little doubt that these early and imaginative surface-to-air missile (SAM) systems were reaching far beyond the technological capability available at the time. In 1945 the concept of manufacturing a long-range bomber which carried no defensive armament was revolutionary, and by contrast the USAF did not abandon defensive armament until the Northrop B-2 Spirit was introduced in the 1990s.

Early in 1946 the Air Staff drafted a formal requirement for a new long-range bomber which would be completely devoid of defensive armament. Operational Requirement 230 (OR.230) specified a landplane capable of carrying one 10,000 lb bomb, with a range of 4,000 nm, a cruising speed of about 500 kt, manoeuvrability at high speed and a cruising altitude of between 35,000 ft and 50,000 ft. Its maximum all-up weight was not to exceed 200,000 lb. Issued in December 1946, OR.230 was initially refused by the MoS because they believed that the specifications were beyond the capabilities of Britain's aircraft manufacturers (and partly because such a heavy aircraft would require a runway at least 6,000 ft long), and the requirement was effectively held in abeyance until September 1952, when it was cancelled. The Air Staff's faith in Britain's aircraft designers was possibly over-optimistic, but the concept of a long-range, high-speed and high-altitude

jet bomber had been firmly established.

At the time OR.230 was issued nobody believed that a war was imminent, and in August 1947 the Minister of Defence issued a directive stating that the risk of a major war within the next five years could be ruled out, and that the risk would only increase gradually over the next five years. This was almost a repeat of a 'ten-year rule' imposed in 1919 in order to cut back on military expenditure. This time, however, there was little opposition to it, especially from the Chiefs of Staff, who were still digesting the lessons learned in Hiroshima and Nagasaki. Likewise, Britain's aviation industry was attempting to grasp new technologies in the shape of jet power and high-speed flight, while the Treasury was trying to find ways of financing it.

The first report by the newly formed Defence Research Policy Committee (DRPC) set up in January 1947 under the chairmanship of Sir Henry Tizard stated: 'For atomic weapons to be a useful deterrent, we must hold a stock, of the order of 1,000, of such bombs, and we must have the means of delivering them immediately on the outbreak of war'. This statement was based on a Home Office estimate that 25 atom bombs would be sufficient to effectively destroy the United Kingdom, although it was refined a few months later when both Tizard and the Chiefs of Staff accepted that the British bombs would form part of an overall Western deterrent which would require approximately 600 bombs by 1957, two-thirds of which would be American, leaving Britain to produce 200.

The DRPC report continued:

We consider therefore that the main operational requirement in this field is a fast subsonic manned bomber capable of high-altitude flying and delivering atomic and other bombs at a radius of the order of 2,500 miles. Whether such a radius is practicable remains doubtful at present and a radius of the order of 2,000 miles would be acceptable as an intermediate aim. Full advantage should be taken of the increasing bias in favour of the Offence and we thus regard it as reasonable to accept an unarmed bomber for this purpose, a decision which would probably be forced upon us in any case by reason of the range/load requirements.

The report also stated that a big advance in bombing accuracy would be required over wartime standards in order to achieve an economy of force, and that:

. . . the main emphasis of R&D [research and development] should be directed to improving navigation methods and instruments, bomb-sights, high–altitude ballistics, and bomb control, the aim being that by 1957 a bridge will be considered a suitable target for individual blind bombing from high altitude.

Having digested the varying political, scientific, and military viewpoints, the government accepted that a long-range, high-speed jet bomber should be developed, which would be ready for production towards the end of the ten-year period during which Soviet power and influence was expected to increase dramatically. This relatively long development period would enable the design teams to produce an aircraft which was equal, if not superior, to any other bomber being manufactured by either America or the Soviets. The Air Staff issued a new requirement, OR.229, which was first circulated in draft form on 7 November 1946. It bore a strong resemblance to the earlier OR.230, except for the aircraft's projected range and weight, which had been reduced to more realistic figures. The Air Staff specified that they required a 'medium-range bomber landplane, capable of carrying one 10,000 lb bomb to a target 1,500 nm from a base which may be anywhere in the world', and that 'it must be possible to operate this bomber from existing heavy bomber type airfields and the maximum weight when fully loaded ought, therefore, not to exceed 100,000 lb. The Air Staff is to be informed if this weight will be exceeded'.

The OR also specified that, as the new aircraft was destined to replace the Avro Lincoln, it should have a conventional bombing capability in addition to the primary nuclear role, and that it should be capable of carrying a 20,000 lb load of high-explosive bombs in 10,000 lb, 6,000 lb and 1,000 lb sizes. However, the physical dimensions of its bomb bay would be dictated by the 10,000 lb 'special', which would have a maximum diameter of 5 ft, compared with the high-explosive equivalent's 3 ft 4 in, both bombs being 24 ft 2 in long. Following a consultation period, during which the MoS discussed the project with Britain's aircraft manufacturers, the Air Ministry issued Specification B.35/46, sending invitations to tender to Handley Page, Short Brothers, Armstrong Whitworth, Bristol, Avro, Vickers-Armstrongs and English Electric on 8 January 1947. By coincidence, this was the same day that Ministers authorised the development of atomic bombs.

During discussions on 17 December 1946 the representative of the MoS, Mr S. Scott-Hall, said:

The conclusion had been reached that the long-range bomber (OR.230), the all-up weight of which would be in the region of 200,000 lb, and have swept-back wings [although OR.230 did not specifically mention this feature] represented too great an advance in design to be entertained at the present juncture. Considerable research and development would be necessary, including, in all probability, the construction of half-scale flying models.

He recommended that consideration be given to a medium-range aircraft (OR.229), and that the long-range design should be put 'on hold' for the time being.

Scott-Hall also commented that his views applied to the medium-range bomber, and that a more conventional straight-winged aircraft should be designed, albeit with less ambitious performance figures, as an 'insurance' against the possible failure of attempts to develop aircraft in accordance with OR.229. He envisaged a three-stage programme comprising an 'insurance bomber' to replace the Lincoln, a medium-range bomber, and a long-range bomber which would be regarded purely as a 'very long term project'. His comments led to Specification B.14/46, issued by the MoS on 11 August 1947 and based on Air Staff Operational Requirement OR.239, issued in January 1947, as follows:

The Air Staff have set out in their Requirement No. OR.229 the details of a medium-range bomber which they would like to have. This requirement, however, is a severe one and will necessitate an aircraft with swept-back wings and other features which are at present somewhat unconventional and not proved. The Air Staff therefore require an additional aircraft built as nearly as possible to Requirement No. OR.229 but constructed on more or less conventional lines, so that it could go into service in the event of the more exacting requirement being held up or

delayed an undue length of time.

This requirement for an 'insurance' aircraft should therefore be read in conjunction with OR.229, which provisions should be met in all respects except as follows . . .

The exceptions were the weight fully loaded, which was to be kept down to 140,000 lb or even 120,000 lb if possible, enabling the aircraft to operate comfortably from unmodified bomber airfields; the speed, which was specified as a maximum continuous cruise of 390 kt at heights between 35,000 ft and 45,000 ft; and both the climb rate and ceiling, which were scaled down accordingly.

Meanwhile, a Tender Design Conference was held on 28 July and it was recommended that, from the six designs submitted to Specification B.35/46, the Avro submission should be accepted, and that both a prototype and a flying model should be ordered. Additionally, it was recommended that the Handley Page and Armstrong Whitworth submissions should be investigated by the Royal Aircraft Establishment (RAE) at Farnborough, including wind tunnel tests, after which a choice would be made between the two designs before placing an order for a prototype and flying model in the same way as the Avro design had been chosen. The English Electric design was considered to be relatively unimaginative (and in any case, the company was expected to be heavily committed to the development of its Canberra bomber), as was the Vickers-Armstrongs submission, whilst the Short and (after further investigation) Armstrong Whitworth designs were believed to be too ambitious. They offered the possibility of a good cruising altitude and a relatively low weight, but they also offered the risks of major developmental problems, not least in terms of longitudinal stability.

The Advanced Bomber Project Group (ABPG), a team of aerodynamicists and structural engineers briefed to choose between the various submissions, believed that the Short and Armstrong Whitworth designs would only be useful as unmanned expendable bombers. Bearing in mind the huge cost of production, which would have to include sophisticated navigation and bombing equipment, their fate was consequently sealed. All-up-weight considerations became less of a concern when the ABPG studied the projected performance of the jet engines being developed at the time. The B.35/46 specification was therefore broadened to accept a maximum weight of 115,000 lb. However, Handley Page's design, for example, was unlikely to reach an altitude above 50,000 ft if the specified weight restriction was enforced, whereas nearly 54,000 ft could be achieved with a larger wing (and therefore a reduction in wing loading) and an increase in weight to 158,000 lb. The Air Staff agreed that the improvement in performance anticipated by both the Handley Page and Avro designers would be worth the expense of longer and stronger runways, effectively returning to the terms of the now–defunct OR.230.

Having ruled out the English Electric, Armstrong Whitworth, Short, and Vickers-Armstrongs submissions for Specification B.35/46, the ABPG accepted another submission from Short Brothers to fulfil the requirements of Specification B.14/46 for a less ambitious 'insurance' bomber. The Short S.A.4 was undoubtedly a fairly unimaginative design, retaining the same fuselage as outlined in the company's B.35/46 submission (albeit with a conventional tail unit), but with a straight wing in place of the advanced swept wing. Even in August 1947 there was some doubt as to whether the S.A.4 could

even meet the OR.239 requirements, as expressed by the Director of Military Aircraft Research and Development:

It has been apparent for some months now that the Short B.14/46 design will not quite meet the performance requirements written by DOR in OR.239 and incorporated by us as the Appendix B in Specification B.14/46. The advisory design conference on this aeroplane was held on 10 July and we are now fairly clear on the probable extent of the deficiency.

He continued: 'I consider that Shorts have made the best job they can of this design, and it is no discredit to them that they have fallen a little short on performance'. No matter how Shorts refined its design, the S.A.4 was essentially a Second World War bomber fitted with jet engines, while the Handley Page and Avro designs were radical solutions to the requirements of the nuclear age. Further investigation of both B.35/46 designs had revealed that although the two aircraft were very different in terms of construction and layout, their projected performance figures were remarkably similar, and in true British 'belt and braces' tradition it was decided that both designs should be pursued further.

Instruction to Proceed (ITP) contracts covering the development of both the Avro and Handley Page aircraft were issued in December 1947, although MoS confidence appears to have been reserved for Avro's submission, as official approval for financial cover was not granted to Handley Page until 23 December, support for Avro having been approved more than a month previously. However, while work progressed on the B.35/46 designs, attention had moved to Vickers-Armstrongs, where chief designer George Edwards was busy convincing

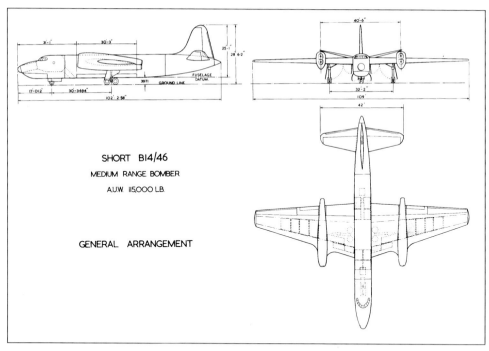

Short Sperrin general arrangement drawing.

MoS officials that there was more than a little merit in his Type 660 design, submitted to Specification B.35/46, which had been rejected as not being sufficiently advanced. S. Scott-Hall, the Principal Director of Technical Development, reported:

> In preliminary discussions DOR(A) [Director of Research (Aircraft)] and I had agreed that inasmuch as the long-range bomber is by far the most important item in our future programme, we should re-examine the possibility of proceeding with interim types to Spec. B.35/46 to take a place in the programme between the Short B.14/46 and the advanced types envisaged, such as the HP crescent wing and the Avro delta wing B.35/46.

He continued:

> We accordingly discussed with Edwards, who considers the

difficulties of a delta or crescent wing will be very great. Vickers have now made an examination of such a project and their work fully endorses Edwards' views.

The Vickers submission was accordingly revised to incorporate a variety of changes, as follows:

1. The incorporation of Rolls-Royce Avon or Metropolitan-Vickers (Metrovick) F.9 (which later became the Armstrong Siddeley Sapphire) engines in place of the Napier T.2/46, which was unlikely to be developed in time for the construction of an 'interim' bomber.
2. An all-up weight of 115,000 lb, but with a tandem-wheel undercarriage which would enable the aircraft to operate from existing (unmodified) bomber airfields.
3. A total bomb load of 10,000 lb, effectively eliminating a third 6,000 lb bomb.

4. The requirement for a jettisonable crew cabin to be dropped.
5. The removal of unnecessary equipment such as cloud and collision warning radar.

English Electric was also advised of the revised criteria and invited to resubmit its B.35/46 design based on these considerations. As a result, the Air Staff were effectively presented with no fewer than three different aircraft, all being procured to meet B.35/46, while a fourth design was being produced to meet B.14/46. Not surprisingly, they were somewhat unhappy with the situation, as reflected in a long summary issued by Air Marshal Sir William Dickson in September 1947:

The first is a long-term replacement for the Lincoln, a bomber which will have the approximate performance of 3,350 nm range at 45,000 ft at 500 kt. In our specification we have said that it is desirable that the all-up weight of this type should not exceed 100,000 lb and we have stressed that this aircraft should be able to operate from existing heavy bomber airfields. To meet these requirements it is inevitable that we must venture into revolutionary changes in aerodynamics. In other words the delta wing. At the current rate of research and development it is unlikely that an aircraft of this performance will be ready for production inside eight years.

He continued:

As an insurance against the possibility that the firms in question will not be able to solve the aerodynamical problems involved in the production of this new type of bomber, we have asked the Ministry of Supply to build a bomber of conventional design with a reduced performance of not less than 3,350 nm at a height of 40,000 ft and a speed of 435 kt. While this reduced requirement is less than we think to be essential, we cannot afford not to have a replacement for the Lincoln which is already obsolescent if not obsolete. To meet our requirements for this 'insurance' bomber, the Ministry of Supply have already placed an order with Shorts. We are not at all happy about this, because from what we know, the Shorts design is very unimaginative and its estimated performance is already dropping below the Air Staff figures I have quoted above. It is probable that the performance will drop still further which is very serious bearing in mind that we do not expect to get even this 'insurance' type into production inside 6-7 years. We also know that since the Ministry of Supply have placed this order, two further designs have been submitted for this 'insurance' specification. From what the Air Staff know these designs are superior to that of Shorts. On the other hand, these two alternative designs are based on a new jet engine, which is still on the drawing board, whereas the Shorts design employs an engine which is much further advanced in design.

During the early months of 1948 the Vickers proposal was firmly incorporated into the Air Staff's plans, as reflected by a report from the Air Ministry which stated:

It has been decided that another type of bomber should be built to bridge the gap between the conventional medium-range bomber — the Short B.14/46 — and the two more advanced types which have been ordered from Handley Page and Avro — the B.35/46. Design studies were received from a number of firms and that of Vickers has been judged to be the most promising and a contract is about to be placed for prototypes of this aircraft. The Vickers medium-range bomber will have a still-air range of 3,350 nm carrying a bomb load of 10,000 lb at a speed of about 465 kt and height of about 45,000 ft. It will weigh approximately 110,000 lb and this will be distributed on a multi-wheel undercarriage. The aircraft will be powered by four Rolls-Royce Avon engines and will start with an initial sweep-back of 20 degrees on the outer-plane with the possibility of increasing this in future to 30 degrees and later 42 degrees. The inner section of the wing is swept back to 42 degrees initially.

The MoS gave Vickers an ITP notice in April 1948, followed in February 1949 by a contract for two prototypes of its Type 660, which were to be delivered to the RAF 'as early as possible'. Meanwhile, in Belfast, work on the Short S.A.4 was already under way. Shorts based much of its original design work on hydraulic analogy tests performed in the company's seaplane tank at Rochester, not having the luxury of its own wind tunnel. (The company normally relied on access to RAE and National Physical Laboratory (NPL) facilities, but by the mid-1940s the waiting times had become prohibitive.) The resulting S.A.4 was extremely simple in terms of layout, having a uniformly-tapered wing with constant dihedral from root to tip. Likewise, the fuselage was of straightforward construction, featuring a large Sunderland-style tail unit.

Conversely, the engine layout was rather less orthodox, with a pair of Rolls-Royce Avon turbojets mounted above and below each wing in huge nacelles which, despite their bulky appearance, caused surprisingly little drag. The advantage of this arrangement was that servicing access was made easy, and the wing construction could remain simple and therefore relatively light weight. The wing comprised two spars with spanwise channel-section stringers supporting the skin between widely-spaced box ribs. The fuselage was a three-section construction comprising a large centre section, a nose unit butt-joined just aft of the pressure cabin, and a rear portion incorporating the tail unit.

The main four-wheel-bogie under-carriage, built by Messier, was hinged on the wing spars and retracted sideways and inwards to lie flat within the inner wing, and had two doors attached to the oleo leg and lower wing root. The twin-wheel nose gear retracted rearwards.

The crew entry door was aft of the nosewheel bay, just ahead of the bomb cell. Entry to the main cabin was gained via a sloping tunnel and an airlock door which also served as the emergency exit.

Three production jigs were set up in Belfast, one for each prototype and a third for a structural test specimen, and the first aircraft, VX158, was completed early in 1951. By this time, however, the S.A.4's future had already been dealt a fatal blow. The aircraft's fate had effectively been sealed towards the end of 1949, when the Air Staff compared the predicted performance of the S.A.4 with that of the Vickers Type 660 being built to Specification B.9/48 to meet OR.229. Air Vice-Marshal Pelly commented:

At a meeting held at the Ministry of Supply on 11 October, I said that we could do without the B.14[/46] for the following reasons. If the long-term planning dates to which the whole of our programme is aimed are still valid, there is every reason to hope that one of the B.35[/46] designs will be available in time. We still need one earlier type with which to re-equip

The Short S.A.4 Sperrin, illustrating the unusual engine configuration, and the relatively conventional airframe design. (Shorts)

Bomber Command, to practise the techniques involved in long-range operations at such high altitudes and to be ready at the same time as the special bomb. Nevertheless, only one type of aircraft would be required, and I feel sure that the B.9[/48], in view of its performance, offers a far better solution to our problem, the only disadvantage being that it is six months behind the B.14. Although the B.9 is of more advanced design than the B.14, the increased knowledge gained lately on swept-back wings and other high-speed complications leads to the belief that no major troubles need to be expected with the B.9 and, therefore, production of that aircraft could start early in 1953 if need be and would, I understand, match up with the production of the special bomb.

Subsequently, it was decided not to order the S.A.4 into production, but it was agreed that the two prototypes should be completed and used as R&D aircraft for the on-going bomber programme. Ground running and taxying of the prototype began in the spring of 1951, and VX158 made its maiden flight from Aldergrove (the company airfield at Sydenham was considered too small for a first flight) in the hands of Tom Brooke-Smith on 10 August 1951, some three months after the Vickers design had successfully taken to the air for the first time. After completing a mandatory 10 hours of test flying, the aircraft made its public debut at the 1951 Society of British Aircraft Companies' (SBAC) display at Farnborough, resplendent in a red, grey and black paint scheme. During the show week Brooke-Smith performed a series of spirited displays in VX158 (including numerous ultra-low-level passes over the runway), demonstrating the aircraft's manoeuvrability and his own flying skills. The S.A.4 also had a good short-landing capability, aided by Maxaret wheel brakes and twin braking parachutes, but the appearance of Vickers' sleek and shiny natural-metal 660, now named the Valiant, effectively stole the show from the rather clumsy-looking S.A.4. After Farnborough the prototype returned to Aldergrove to begin an important career which was to be completed in relative obscurity.

In July 1952 the second prototype S.A.4, VX161, was transported like her predecessor by road to Aldergrove, and made a successful first flight on 12 August. Manufacturer's trials were subsequently conducted by both aircraft from Sydenham (after the completion of a runway extension) until 1953, when VX158 went to the RAE at Farnborough to begin radar navigation and bombing trials, taking over from Avro Ashton WB492. The aircraft remained at Farnborough until the end of 1953, when it was returned to Shorts and placed in storage. The second aircraft, which did not have a radar system, moved to Woodbridge during April 1953 to begin bomb loading and release trials on behalf of the MoS. The Armament and Instrument Experimental Unit was based at nearby Martlesham Heath, but larger and heavier aircraft were normally operated from Woodbridge, taking advantage of the huge runway available there. When the base was handed over to the USAF in 1952 the S.A.4 programme continued in between the operational activities of the 20th Fighter-Bomber Wing (FBW), flying Republic F-84Gs.

Various bomb shapes were carried by the aircraft, mostly relating to the development of the early Blue Danube weapon, although trials were also undertaken with dummy representations of the Blue Boar guided bomb which was to have equipped the B.35/46 bombers. Developed by Vickers, Blue Boar was to have carried a 5,000 lb kiloton-range warhead, but after several years of work

the Air Staff turned their attention to all-weather stand-off bombs, ultimately resulting in Blue Steel. Shortly before the trials at Woodbridge were completed the S.A.4 was named Sperrin, in line with Short's alliterative system of nomenclature and in reference to the mountain range across the Tyrone and Londonderry border area. After being moved to Farnborough, VX161 was returned to Sydenham in July 1956, where it was placed in storage, never to fly again.

Sperrin VX158 was also nearing the end of a useful career, but jet engine developments provided the prototype with another important task. de Havilland was working on the Gyron, a new axial-flow engine producing 15,000 lb static thrust. The Sperrin's unique engine arrangement made the aircraft an ideal test bed for the new powerplant, so VX158's port lower engine bay was strengthened and enlarged to accommodate the bigger and more powerful Gyron. The first test flight took place on 7 July 1955, and it was quickly established that the Gyron's power effectively balanced the output of both Avons on the starboard wing. Most of the test programme was conducted from Hatfield, and in March 1956 the aircraft returned to Sydenham to be fitted with a matching starboard lower nacelle so that the aircraft could test-fly a pair of 20,000 lb Gyron D.Gy.2 engines, in which form it flew on 26 June 1956. During this test flight the port outer undercarriage door fell loose and, rather than manufacture a new one, a similar unit was removed from the stored VX161, which then became a 'hangar queen' spares source before being scrapped two years later.

The first prototype's test career continued, however, and after making a show-stopping appearance at the 1956 SBAC Farnborough show, where the noise of its 53,000 lb thrust powerplant certainly captured the spectator's attention, the aircraft remained active until the latter months of 1957. By this time the infamous defence White Paper had been published, cancelling OR.239, for which Hawker was designing the supersonic P.1121. This aircraft was to have been powered by the Gyron, and without this programme the engine no longer appeared to have a useful future, although a scaled-down version, the Gyron Junior, was subsequently developed for the Buccaneer. Without a test programme to perform, VX158's flights were reduced, but funding for the aircraft (which had been purchased by de Havilland by this stage) could no longer be justified, so after a series of Gyron infra-red radiation trials the aircraft was withdrawn, being scrapped at Hatfield late in 1959.

Whether the Sperrin could have been developed to match the predicted performance of the Vickers Type 660 will never be known, but there was no doubt that, at least 'on paper', the Vickers design was certain to be a better option for the Air Staff. For example, the Type 660 was expected to have a cruising speed of 445 kt, a still-air range of 3,350 nm, and a height over target of 43,700 ft, compared with the Sperrin's 430 kt, 2,900 nm, and 40,000 ft. However, it must be borne in mind that the S.A.4 was designed to be relatively modest in terms of performance, to guarantee that the aircraft could be produced should the much more advanced B.35/46 design fail. The Sperrin did provide a great deal of data for the new bombers in terms of navigation and radar bombing equipment research, bomb design, engine development, and in the production of an effective four-wheeled landing gear which was later used on the Bristol Britannia airliner, and, in the final analysis, it can be judged to have been a great success, even though it was effectively redundant even before it was built.

Interestingly, Short Brothers persisted with their design which had first been submitted to meet the B.35/46 specification. Like Avro and Handley Page, who both produced piloted flying scale models of their new bomber designs, Shorts decided to adopt a similar policy under the company designation P.D.1, covering the development of what was essentially a swept-wing version of the S.A.4 Sperrin. The MoS refused to supply funding for the project, having long since regarded the Shorts B.35/46 proposal as too advanced, so Shorts opted to finance its own one-third-scale glider.

Some properties of swept-wing design were already well established, including trailing-edge control surface flutter, which prompted Shorts chief designer David Keith-Lucas to choose a pivoting-wing layout which would require the incorporation of a fin and rudder. Swept wings also have a tendency to twist under load, altering aerodynamic shape to such an extent that their lift properties are seriously affected. In a tight turn wingtip lift diminishes, while a greater load is absorbed by the rest of the wing. The resulting aeroelastic effect pulls the tips upwards towards each other.

However, by moving the wing structure's torsional box further aft, the wing's torsional and flexural axes coincide, so that when the wing flexes, the twisting moment is eliminated. Conversely, when the wing twists, the wing incidence is not affected. This new design was first described by Professor Geoffrey Hill of Westland, who dubbed it the 'isoclinic' wing. The glider model, designated S.B.1, was completed early in 1951 and made its maiden flight, launched by winch, from Aldergrove on 14 July that year, with Tom Brooke-Smith at the controls.

The S.B.1 was a relatively cheap and

simple aircraft, manufactured mostly from spruce and featuring a shoulder-mounted 38 ft-span wing with a leading-edge sweep of 42.5°. However, the wing trailing edge began with a straight inboard portion, was swept back 30° at mid-span, then decreased to just 18° on the outer section. More than a third of the wing on each side comprised a pivoted tip, these tips acting as ailerons when moved in opposition or as elevators when moved in unison.

Painted silver with black and yellow bands, the sole S.B.1 was given the B conditions marking G-14-1, and after two test flights preparations were made for the first launches from towed flight. Fortunately Shorts already had a company-owned tug aircraft in the shape of Sturgeon TT.2 prototype VR363, which had been retained by the company after production of 24 Sturgeons for the Fleet Air Arm. On 20 July the S.B.1 was launched from the Sturgeon's tow cable at 10,000 ft and performed perfectly. The only problem encountered by Brooke-Smith was the severe turbulence generated by the prop-wash from the two huge six-bladed contrarotating propellers driven by the Sturgeon's 2,080 hp Merlin 140 engines. Brooke-Smith suggested that the towline be extended to keep the glider well away from the Sturgeon, but on the next flight, on 14 October, the problem was found to be even worse and Brooke-Smith was forced to cut the glider from the towline at low altitude, causing it to hit the runway in a nose-down attitude at more than 80 mph. He was injured quite severely and, although the S.B.1 escaped relatively unscathed, he was less than keen to fly the glider-and-Sturgeon combination again.

Having taken note of their chief test pilot's views, the Shorts team decided to build a redesigned fuselage to which the S.B.1's wing and tail could be fitted. The new design, designated S.B.4, was slightly longer than the glider and was to incorporate a pair of Turbomeca Palas turbojets, each developing 353 lb static thrust. On 4 October 1953 the isoclinic wing took to the air again. Test flying was undertaken from both Aldergrove and Sydenham, and although the decidedly underpowered S.B.4 was limited to a top speed of 250 mph and an altitude of 5,000 ft, it was a very useful research tool, indicating an impressive performance for the full-scale P.D.1, which was to have a wing span of 114 ft and a top speed of about Mach 0.87.

The S.B.4 was named Sherpa before appearing at the 1954 SBAC display, where the little aircraft generated a great deal of interest. However, the MoS still saw little point in developing the project any further, not least because a variety of rather less exotic solutions to high-speed flight were being discovered. When Shorts had completed its research the Sherpa was given to the College of Aeronautics at Cranfield, where further research was conducted on a fairly low-key basis until 1964, when the Sherpa's engines reached the end of their fatigue life.

Although the Sherpa programme indicated that the full-scale P.D.1 would probably have been a very successful aircraft, there was never any great official interest in the isoclinic wing. The P.D.1 would probably have been as capable as both the Vulcan and the Victor, and it might well have had even better handling characteristics, especially at low speed. Tom Brooke-Smith certainly believed that the Sherpa could have been scaled up into a very impressive aircraft. But in the final analysis the Sherpa and the associated P.D.1 were way ahead of their time, especially when one considers that variable-camber wings are only now beginning to be treated with any degree of seriousness, some 40 years later.

CHAPTER THREE

The Valiant

The Sperrin's relatively poor performance was not the main reason behind the ABPG's decision to request a fourth medium-range bomber design. In reality, it was the fact that something better was readily available which turned attention away from the S.A.4, towards another 'insurance' aircraft. As the predicted performance of the S.A.4 emerged, George Edwards, chief designer at Vickers, continued to remind the MoS that his company had already submitted a design which would comfortably meet the performance figures specified in B.14/46, and that it would outperform the S.A.4. While Vickers' B.35/46 proposal might have been rejected as being 'too simple', the same design was ideal for the less-advanced B.14/46 requirement.

The company had plenty of experience in the design and construction of large bomber and transport aircraft. Having produced the revolutionary Wellesley high-altitude, long-range monoplane bomber before the outbreak of the Second World War, Vickers had also manufactured the famous Wellington bomber which later formed the basis for the Viking, Valetta and Varsity family of transport aircraft, eventually leading to the Viscount. George Edwards joined the company at the end of 1934 as an aircraft stressman, rising through the ranks to

become its chief designer at the age of just 37.

Edwards argued that the perceived disadvantages of the Vickers medium-range bomber design were in fact, its greatest assets, and that the bomber's projected performance would be almost as good as that of the Avro and Handley Page designs. More importantly, the Vickers aircraft would not be a 'design risk', and without the long periods of R&D (including the production of flying scale models) required for the B.35/46 aircraft it could be produced quickly.

Edwards even went so far as to guarantee a production timescale for the Vickers Type 660, promising that a flying prototype would be ready in 1951, followed by a production version before the end of 1953 and quantity deliveries at the beginning of 1955. The Air Staff, considering the wider political picture which then included Korea, the Berlin blockade, Russia's nuclear bomb programme and America's isolationist attitude, decided that the guarantee of an 'interim' bomber was just too good to refuse, and that the RAF could not afford to wait until the Avro and Handley Page designs were completed. Consequently, Specification B.9/48 was issued, together with an ITP, on 16 April 1948, based on the Vickers design and the delivery timescale promised by Edwards. A full contract was awarded to Vickers on 2 February 1949, covering a first prototype powered by four Rolls-Royce Avon RA.3 6,500-lb thrust turbojets, and a second prototype (Type 667) with four Armstrong Siddeley Sapphires.

Design continued through 1949, and components began to emerge in 1950. Assembly took place at Vickers' secure experimental shop at Fox Warren, chiefly because the Weybridge factory was heavily involved with Valetta, Viking, and Viscount production, but also because Fox Warren was much closer to Wisley Airfield, from where the prototype bomber would make its first flight. As with most modern designs (but unusually for the 1940s), the Type 660 was ordered directly 'off the drawing board', but prototypes were still required in order to explore what was still a distinctly experimental design. The urgency with which the bomber was developed is indicated by the fact that the airframe design was well established even before wind tunnel tests had been conducted.

After transporting the sections by road from Fox Warren, final assembly of the major components was completed at Wisley in less than six months, and on 18 May 1951 the Type 660 was flown from the grass airfield on a test flight lasting five minutes. The Vickers design had beaten the Short S.A.4 into the air by three months; a remarkable achievement and a rather ironic one, in view of the fact that the Type 660 was in essence a replacement for the S.A.4. The first flight was made by Vickers chief test pilot Joseph 'Mutt' Summers, who had already accumulated an impressive tally of maiden flights, including the legendary Spitfire. Not surprisingly, he was determined to fly the Type 660 before he retired, and his successor, Gabe 'Jock' Bryce, acted as co-pilot for this first flight, the aircraft, serialled WB210, being flown throughout with its landing gear extended.

Valiant B.1 WZ365 entered RAF service in September 1955, serving with No. 232 OCU, 199 Squadron and 18 Squadron before reaching premature retirement in 1963. (via Richard Caruana)

It had taken just 27 months from contract to first flight, and the Type 660 was right on schedule. Three more test sorties were made from Wisley before WB210 was transferred to Hurn (Bournemouth) Airport, from where flight trials continued in less-congested airspace while a concrete runway was laid at Wisley. Up to this stage it had been official policy to name RAF bombers after British and Commonwealth cities, but the new bomber was undoubtedly ushering in a new era of RAF operations, and the traditional system of nomenclature was finally dropped. Consequently, Vickers employees were invited to select a name for the Type 660 and, although Vimy was a popular suggestion, the final choice was Valiant, a name which had previously been applied to the Vickers Type 131 general-purpose biplane of 1931.

The Valiant had a shoulder-mounted wing with compound sweep on the leading edge, the four engines being buried within the wing root structure. Its large wing area gave the Valiant a comparatively low wing loading, which enabled the aircraft to meet its long-range requirements while retaining a respectable short-take-off performance. Indeed, the second prototype, WB215, undertook a series of trials in 1956 with de Havilland Super Sprite rocket-assisted take-off gear (RATOG) units attached to the lower wing, inboard of the main undercarriage, but the boosted performance was later deemed unnecessary, largely because of continued development of the Valiant's engines but also because the risks of a rocket failure, leading to a dangerous asymmetric take-off, were felt to be too high.

The wing's broad inboard chord allowed the Vickers designers to restrict the wing root thickness to no more than 12 per cent while still providing sufficient depth to incorporate the engines and associated systems. The wide root chord also permitted a greater acute angle of sweepback on the inner third of the span, thus raising the local critical Mach number in the area where airflow accelerating around the nose met the wings. The precise angle of sweepback was dictated by the need to co-locate the wing's aerodynamic centre with the aircraft's centre of gravity (c.g.), which gave the aeroplane good stability and enabled the designers to use a smaller, and therefore lighter, variable-incidence tailplane, which was positioned high on the fin, clear of the engine exhaust efflux. The engine intakes were simple rectangular slots in the wing root leading edge, although vertical airflow straighteners were fitted into the intakes before the prototype's first flight. The second prototype and all production Valiants featured bigger 'spectacle' intakes to provide a larger mass flow of air for the higher-powered Avon series RA.7, RA.14 and RA.28 engines.

With a mean sweep angle of 20°, the Valiant's wing was more sharply swept inboard than on the outer sections, where the sweepback angle was restricted by the need to prevent tip stalling. The greater inner-wing sweep compensated for this, maintaining the overall balance and creating a 'compound sweep' planform which was invented and patented by designer Elfyn Richards, a Vickers aerodynamicist.

The dimensions of the main fuselage were largely dictated by the bomb bay, the nose-mounted H2S radar scanner, and the pressurised cabin accommodating a crew of five. A massive backbone member ran along the top of the fuselage centreline, two right-angled branches forming the main wing spars which were joined at the centreline and attached to the outer wing spars, heavy channel-section booms extending and tapering towards the wingtips. These main spars were bifurcated and reinforced around the engine bays, while the main keel beam construction also provided the load-carrying 'roof' for the bomb bay, from which the Valiant's weapons were slung. Vickers introduced sculpture milling to manufacture this massive backbone structure, and the technique paved the way for succeeding Vickers and British Aircraft Corporation (BAC) designs.

Shortages of steel girder sections, largely due to the needs of the Korean War, led to the employment of pre-stressed concrete in the construction of the Valiant's main assembly jig pillars. Glassfibre plastic bonding was also introduced for the production of the various dielectric components, such as the huge nose radome and a number of suppressed aerial panels, and synthetic bonding was used for the production of control surface doubling plates and various skin reinforcements. The undercarriage comprised a huge twin-wheel bicycle main gear unit which retracted outwards to lie flat within the wing structure, covered by two large doors, while the nose gear was a simple twin-wheel unit which retracted rearwards into the forward fuselage,

behind the pressure cabin.

Although the Valiant's structure was fairly conventional, both in terms of constructional methods and materials used, the Valiant introduced a major innovation in having all-electric systems. The only exception was the hydraulic brake and steering system, but even the pumps for this were driven by electric motors. The high-voltage (112V) DC electrical system, chosen because a 28V system would have been heavier and AC design was not sufficiently advanced at the time, fed the avionics, the powered flying controls, power-activated components and the navigation and bomb-aiming equipment.

Because Vickers was already committed to a variety of other aircraft programmes, most importantly the Viscount airliner, many of the Valiant's components were subcontracted to nine other companies, including Saunders-Roe, which manufactured the aircraft's pressurised cabin in its Isle of Wight factory. This nose section had a concave diaphragm forward bulkhead with radial stiffening beams, and a convex (and unstiffened) rear shell. Specification B.35/46 had stated:

The complete pressure cabin must be

An impressive line-up of Valiant B.1s at Gaydon, circa 1956. (via Richard Caruana)

Although all three V-Bombers were equipped with pilot and co-pilot ejection seats, the rear crews were never afforded the luxury of a truly effective escape system. Martin Baker did conduct a series of trials with a Valiant, but ejection seats for the rear crews were never introduced. (Martin Baker)

jettisonable. Such a cabin must be provided with parachutes to reduce the falling speed to a value at which the occupants will be unhurt when hitting the ground while strapped in their seats. If such a jettisonable cabin cannot be provided, the seats must be jettisonable.

Unfortunately, Avro, Handley Page, and Vickers found that it was virtually impossible to provide such a facility, and George Edwards informed an advisory design conference that the structural difficulties in providing ejection seats for all of the crew were too great, and that the extra space required would prejudice the design of the cabin canopy. Consequently, Specification B.9/48 for the Valiant stated: 'A completely jettisonable cabin is desired. If this is not practicable, arrangements should be made for good emergency escape means for the crew.'

The need for an effective means of escape for the crew was highlighted by the tragic loss of Valiant prototype WB210 on 12 January 1952. Having made a sensational first appearance at the 1951 SBAC show, the aircraft had resumed test flying and was performing a series of engine shut-down and relight tests over the Hampshire coast as part of noise measurement trials associated with the V.1000, a proposed transport version of the Valiant which was subsequently abandoned. One of the Avon engines suffered a wet start, which led to a fire in a wing bay where a detection sensor had not been fitted, being thought unnecessary in this area. By the time the fire was discovered, the crew believed that the starboard wing was about to burn through, and the aircraft was abandoned over Bransgore, near Hurn. The crew survived with the exception of the copilot, Sqn Ldr Foster, who was killed when his ejection seat struck the aircraft's fin. Like the prototypes, production Valiants were fitted with ejection seats for both the pilot and copilot, but the rear crew were expected to escape via the cabin entrance.

Although it was realized that this was far from satisfactory, at least as far as the rear crews were concerned, the Valiant's

Valiant and Victor assisted take-off trials were conducted with DH Sprite and Spectre rocket packs. The risk of asymmetric take-off danger (should a rocket fail) and the very respectable performance of all three V-Bombers, prompted the abandonment of any ambitions to put the system into regular RAF service.
(Brooklands Museum)

excellent safety record suggests, in retrospect, that a more complicated (and hugely expensive) escape system would have been pointless.

The loss of WB210 was not critical to the Valiant development programme because the second prototype was already nearing completion at Wisley. Powered by four 7,500-lb thrust RA.7s, instead of Sapphires as originally planned, WB215 was first flown just three months after the loss of WB210, on 11 April 1952. Apart from the incorporation of the aforementioned larger mass-flow air intakes, the aircraft was virtually identical to the first prototype, reflecting

the soundness of the Valiant's design.

On 20 April the previous year, 1951, a production order for 25 aircraft had been placed, covering 5 pre-production Type 674s powered by 9,500 lb Avon RA.14s and 20 Type 706 Valiant B.1s with 10,050 lb Avon RA.28 204 or 205 engines (with slightly extended jetpipes). All of the production aircraft were delivered on or ahead of schedule, peaking at a rate of one per week and flying from the Vickers factory airfield at Brooklands, where the runway was only 3,600 ft long. As promised, Service deliveries began in 1955, when WP206 arrived at RAF Gaydon in Warwickshire, where 138

The Valiant's four Avon engines were semi-recessed within the inner wing section, with external fairings over the exhaust ducting pipes. (via Richard Caruana)

Squadron had been formed as the first Valiant squadron before moving to Wittering. The second production machine, WP207, arrived at Gaydon on 19 February, and 232 Operational Conversion Unit (OCU) was established two days later as the first V-bomber training unit, tasked with the conversion of crews on to the new type and intensive flying trials of the Valiant.

The term 'V-Bomber' had become established in October 1952, when it was decided that Avro's B.35/46 design should be named Vulcan, following the decision to name the Vickers Type 660 Valiant and prior to naming the Handley Page aircraft the Victor, thus forming a 'V' class of medium-range bombers. The term did not signify anything in particular, and in retrospect it is evident that it was merely derived from the adoption of the Valiant's name in June 1951.

Although the first V-Bomber unit to be formed was an operational squadron, its role was widened to include training and development flying before the establishment of the OCU. As more crews converted on to the Valiant, more squadrons were formed at Gaydon before being transferred to their operational bases. Further training was undertaken at the Bomber Command Bombing School (BCBS) at Lindholme, where crews were introduced to V-Bomber radar navigation and bombing equipment, flying numerous training sorties primarily in Vickers Varsities, and in later years in modified Handley Page Hastings transports (the training course was also modified to include elementary instruction in the use and effects of nuclear weapons). Pilots and copilots received initial flying training on Canberras at Bassingbourne before being posted to Gaydon.

During April 1955 138 Squadron received four more Valiant B.1s (WP213, WP212, WP211, and WP215), and in May the first dual-role reconnaissance and bomber Valiant B(PR).1 (Vickers Type 710) was delivered to Gaydon, being temporarily attached to 138 Squadron pending the formation of 543 Squadron on 1 June. Further B(PR).1s (WP219, WP223, and WP221) arrived in July. From the outset, unlike the Avro and Handley Page designs, the Valiant was developed as a dual-role bomber, with a strategic reconnaissance capability built into the design of a specific production batch. Reconnaissance cameras could be carried in a purpose-built crate in the Valiant's bomb bay, and a full complement of equipment could include up to eight F96 cameras with 48 in lenses and four F49 survey cameras, giving the Valiant an horizon-to-horizon coverage capability. The aircraft could quickly be prepared for the bomber role as and when required by removing the camera crate.

The Valiant was also destined to become the RAF's first flight-refuelling tanker, the new role emerging as aircraft were rolling off the Weybridge production line. Although a number of preliminary in-flight refuelling trials had been conducted with various aircraft types, especially during the pre-Second World War years, the RAF did not consider the concept a viable proposition. Finally, in 1954, after a great deal of persuasion by Sir Alan Cobham, the chairman and managing director of Flight Refuelling Ltd, the Air Staff decided that the entire fleet of V-Bombers should be capable of receiving fuel in flight. Later that same year the Air Staff concluded that it would also be 'desirable' for as many of the V-Bombers as possible to be capable of operating as both receiver and tanker aircraft.

On 15 March 1955 Air Marshal Sir George Mills, the Air Officer Commanding in Chief (AOC-in-C) of Bomber Command, stated that flight

WZ368, a Valiant B.1 which served with No. 232 OCU and No. 7 Squadron, ending its days at St Athan, where it was broken up in 1963. (R. L. Ward)

refuelling equipment would be fitted to 80 Valiants by the end of the first quarter of 1956. An Air Staff Requirement for a Flight Refuelling Electronic Positioning System was issued one month later, the specification including a reference which stated: 'It should be noted that, with the exception of some early Valiants, all V-class aircraft will have fixed fittings to enable them to be operated as either tankers or receivers. No aircraft will, therefore, be designed solely for use as tankers.'

Indeed, there was no provision to finance the production of dedicated tanker aircraft, so it was not possible to introduce a flight refuelling capability into the V-Force until sufficient Vulcans and Victors had been produced, thus enabling Valiants to be temporarily withdrawn for tanker modifications. The Treasury finally agreed to finance a Valiant tanker fleet in 1959, and 32 sets of fuel tanks were ordered to be delivered by March 1958, providing that no technical difficulties were encountered with the equipment. (The last Valiant had been completed at Weybridge in August 1957.) Tanks were also designed for the Vulcan B.1, but no order for them was ever placed.

Preparations for the flight refuelling role began in February 1958, when Controller, Aircraft (CA) Release was given to the Valiant B(K).1 and B(PR)K.1 aircraft, tanker conversions of the

Valiant B(PR).1 WP220 served with Nos 138 and 7 Squadrons, prior to being withdrawn from service use in October 1962. (R. L. Ward)

A nostalgic view of a 232 OCU Valiant B.1, with a second Valiant visible in the air, a Victor B1 to the right and a SAC B-47 to the left. (R. L. Ward)

bomber and dual-role reconnaissance/bomber respectively. Trials had been conducted by both Vickers and the Aeroplane and Armament Experimental Establishment (A&AEE) at Boscombe Down, and crews from 214 Squadron (which had formed at Gaydon early in 1956 before moving to Marham, the first aircraft transferring on 15 March) were detached to both Boscombe Down and Flight Refuelling Ltd's airfield at Tarrant Rushton for instruction and training. The squadron was divided into two Flights; 'B' Flight comprised B.1s, each equipped with a pair of 1,650 gal underwing tanks, while 'A' Flight converted to the tanker role, XD869 and XD870 becoming the first squadron aircraft so equipped.

In September 1958 the RAF gave its first public demonstrations of in-flight refuelling when 214 Squadron demonstrated Valiant-to-Valiant 'hook-ups' for the SBAC show spectators at Farnborough and at Battle of Britain displays at Cottesmore, Honington, Marham, and Upwood. However, the refuelling system was not yet operational, and it was not until 23, 26, and 27 January 1959 that the first 'wet' fuel transfers were completed, leading to the first long-range Valiant sortie, lasting 12 hours, on 23 February. At long last the RAF had regained a strategic bomber capability.

Yet another role assigned to the Valiant was electronic countermeasures (ECM), as outlined in a 1952 Air Ministry report:

It has now been agreed that a specialist RCM [radio countermeasures] aircraft is required to operate with, and in support of, bomber forces. Consideration is being given to the suitability of the Canberra or the Comet for this role as a short-term measure. It is proposed to meet the long-term requirement by a suitably-equipped Valiant.

On 1 October 1957, 199 Squadron, previously equipped with Lincolns, re-formed at Honington with seven Valiant B.1s assigned to the specialist RCM role, in support of both Fighter Command and Bomber Command. However, the squadron continued to remain active at Hemswell with a fleet of Lincolns, and to avoid confusion the Hemswell unit was designated 1321 Flight. It continued to operate Lincolns until 31 March 1958. Meanwhile, at Honington, the squadron

A Valiant B(PR).1 turning onto a (tight!) final approach to Wyton's runway. (R. L. Ward).

also acquired a single Canberra, and their Valiant fleet was gradually developed into a capable ECM force, equipped with APT-16A and ALT-7 jamming transmitters, Airborne Cigar and Carpet-4 jammers, APR-9 and APR-4 search receivers, and foil dispensers.

The Valiant's ECM role was described in a 1957 Air Ministry document, which stated:

RCM, radio countermeasures, are means of upsetting those elements of the enemy's defence system that are based on radar or radio devices. Radar detection depends on picking-up and isolating a very low-powered signal; RCM, by emitting a large number of random signals over a wide range of frequencies, prevents an accurate bearing being taken on the signal generated by the radar echo, thus seriously embarrassing the defenders. The RCM installation which is planned for the V-Bombers consists of a three-fold system to jam both active and passive radar systems, as well as disrupting the enemy communications

radio. It will be effective against radar-guided missiles as well as ground radar systems.

As the V-Force was gradually developed, sophisticated ECM equipment was incorporated into all three bombers, giving each aircraft type its own self-protection capability. However, 199 Squadron's Valiants (later absorbed into 18 Squadron at Finningley) pioneered the V-Bomber ECM systems, and although the Valiant was never designed to carry large amounts of electronic equipment it adapted to the role perfectly. As a refuelling tanker, another role for which it was not specifically designed, the aircraft became invaluable to the RAF, and 543 Squadron's strategic reconnaissance aircraft were also extremely capable machines. However, the Valiant was primarily designed as a bomber, and it was in this role that it was deployed in 1956, when Operation Musketeer began.

By 1956 a total of six Valiant squadrons had been formed: Nos 138 at Wittering,

Valiant BK.1 WZ403 (pictured landing at Marham) was operated exclusively by No. 207 Squadron before being withdrawn in March 1965. (Richard J. Caruana Archives)

148 at Marham, 207 at Marham, 214 at Marham, 49 at Wittering, and 543 at Wyton. (A seventh, appropriately 7 Squadron, formed at Honington in December.) Of these, Nos. 138, 148, 207, and 214 Squadrons were assigned to Operation Musketeer, the codename given to the RAF's participation in the Suez crisis, the other two units being assigned specialist roles. Canberra bombers were deployed to Cyprus and Malta, and the Valiant force of 24 aircraft was detached to RAF Luqa, Malta. Over a six-day period from 31 October to 5 November the aircraft flew 131 conventional bombing missions against targets in Egypt, in particular the airfields at Abu Sueir, Almaza, Cairo West, Fayid, Kabrit, Kasfareet, and Luxor.

Despite the very serious nature of the operation there was great excitement among the Valiant crews at the prospect of performing a series of 'live' bombing missions. Surprisingly, the crews were not even sure where their targets would be until they were briefed at Luqa, as 214 Squadron's records indicate:

> The looks and expressions of surprise can only be imagined when, within two hours of landing at Luqa, all crews gathered in the Bomber Wing Operations briefing room for the first operational briefing and the curtains were drawn aside to reveal Egyptian airfields as targets.

Number 138 Squadron deployed its entire complement of eight Valiants to Luqa, while 148 and 207 Squadrons each sent six aircraft and 214 Squadron supplied four. The first attack, against Almaza airfield, was led by 148 Squadron and, as with subsequent bombing missions, little opposition was encountered. Cairo West was another important target, and to minimise civilian casualties British radio stations broadcast positions of the bomber's targets in advance of the raids. The crews were briefed to aim for runway intersections, and to avoid areas of possible population. The first raid on

Cairo West was abandoned shortly before the combined Valiant and Canberra force entered Egyptian airspace. News was received that 15 USAF transport aircraft were busily evacuating American civilians via the airport, and the RAF's bombers were recalled. A total of 942 tons of bombs was dropped during the offensive, but the operation was later judged to have been less than successful.

It was accepted that the Valiant force had been intended for a 'radar' war in Western Europe, and that the Canberras were only equipped with Gee-H blind bombing equipment, which required ground-based beacons in order to function. As it had been decided to launch the first attacks at night, because Egyptian early-warning radars were thought to be unserviceable and defending fighters were unlikely to attempt visual interceptions in darkness, the bombers were forced to revert to Second World War-style target marking techniques. Many of the Valiants had yet to be fully equipped with navigation and

bombing equipment, and had to rely on hastily-installed sighting heads from Second World War bombsights. Had the RAF's Lincolns not been withdrawn a year previously, it was felt that they would have been used more effectively, even though they would have been more vulnerable to Egyptian fighters.

The Valiant's navigation and bombing system (NBS) was reported to have suffered a high unserviceability rate, and on the first raid against Almaza two of the five Valiants reported that their NBS was not functioning. The Valiants were not cleared for the carriage of high-explosive (HE) bombs, and without a reliable navigation system they could not be recovered to Luqa without first arriving overhead the airfield to establish their position. Consequently, getting the bomber force back on to the ground was a time-consuming process, further hampered by frequent bad weather.

The Suez operation prompted the RAF seriously to re-think almost every aspect of Bomber Command's

No. 7 Squadron Valiant B(PR).1, displaying the unit's blue circle (with white stars) insignia on the tail unit. (R. L. Ward)

operations. Although the V-Force was primarily assigned to a nuclear strike, it was clear that the bombers' crews would also need to be proficient in conventional bombing techniques, and be capable of long-range overseas deployments. It was recommended that an all-weather bombing and navigation capability be established, and that overseas reinforcement squadrons should make regular deployments to, and train in, areas where they might be required to operate. The rather half-hearted operation had yielded few useful results, and only three of the seven main Egyptian airfields had been put out of action, the rest requiring minimal repairs. Ironically, the only airfield to be totally disabled was Cairo West, after the Egyptians detonated demolition charges on the runways to prevent French and American landings. However, Operation Musketeer was the only occasion when Valiants were ever required to operate 'in anger', even though the aircraft was assigned to other, much more violent duties.

Having successfully proved the concept of atomic weaponry, and having ordered a fleet of medium-range and high-speed bombers to carry the weapons, the next task was to mate the atomic bomb with its carrier aircraft. Early ballistic trials of various bomb casings were undertaken using an Avro Lincoln (as mentioned previously, later casings were dropped from the Sperrin). The Lincoln was an appropriate choice, not only because the aircraft was readily available, but because the type was to be modified to carry operational atomic bombs if the V-Bomber programme failed.

In 1948 Lord Tedder suggested to the Chiefs of Staff that the RAF should begin training for the handling and storage of nuclear weapons, and subsequently a committee was set up to explore all matters relating to this subject. It was known as the Herod Committee, an acronym of High Explosives Research Operational Distribution, and the first meeting took place on 22 November. During a meeting on 24 January the committee established that planning for the acceptance of nuclear weapons at Wittering and Marham should be initiated, and at a later meeting they agreed that the first in-service bombs should be designed for in-flight fusing, enabling the tube containing the fissile components and corresponding outer layers of the bomb to be inserted after take-off, as a safety measure.

In November 1951 the Herod Committee decided that the RAF Atomic Weapons School should be located at the first RAF station where nuclear weapons would be stored (Wittering), and it was agreed that the Armament Training School should also be based there, after having considered Honington, which was originally scheduled to be the first Valiant station. The first operational Valiant squadron, No. 138, would also be at Wittering, and as it also housed the co-located Valiant Trials Flight, No. 1321, the station was at the very heart of the RAF's V-Force build-up.

Development work on the first atomic bombs progressed well, and it was unclear if the bomb would be completed before the first Valiants or vice versa. Doctor Penney commented:

My philosophy is that the RAF has handled aircraft for a long time and can fly Valiants as soon as they come off the production line. But the RAF has not yet handled atomic weapons. Therefore, we must get some bombs to the RAF at the earliest possible moment, so that the handling and servicing can be practised and fully worked out.

Looking rather weather-worn, WZ363 served with Nos 138 and 148 Squadrons before crashing near Market Rasen during May 1964. This accident was particularly significant as it marked the beginning of the Valiant's fatigue problems which ultimately led to the type's premature withdrawal from service. (R. L. Ward)

He added that these first weapons would be essentially the same as later developed versions, but that they might require modifications to the In-Flight Insertion (IFI) cartridge and, if these first bombs had to be used, the cartridge might have to be loaded just before take-off, rather than in flight.

During 1953 plans had been laid for the storage of atomic weapons at Wittering, Marham, Honington, and Waddington, and for a bomb depot to be completed at Barnham in Norfolk. The first atomic bombs were delivered to the RAF (the Bomber Command Armament School) on the nights of 7 and 14 November 1953, when convoys arrived at Wittering. Trials with the Valiant were to begin during 1954, but the first aircraft could not be delivered to Wittering until the following year, and it was not until 15 June that WP201 arrived. The MoS had formed No. 1321 Flight during 1954, specifically for the dropping trials, and the unit completed some bomb delivery and handling training with Vickers at Wisley. It was decided that bombs would only be dropped by operational units, so, following the initial drop trials, No. 1321 Flight became 'C' Flight of 138 Squadron in February 1956, changing to

49 Squadron on 1 May 1956.

With the arrival of Valiant WP201 the MoS flight trials began, the first ballistic store being dropped from 12,000 ft at 330 kt over Orfordness on 6 July. Progress was satisfactory, but a setback occurred on 29 July when 138 Squadron's WP222 crashed shortly after taking off on a cross-country training flight. The Valiant entered a left-hand turn which continued through 300° until the aircraft impacted at about 300 kt just three minutes after take-off, killing the entire crew. Subsequent investigations revealed that a runaway actuator had fixed an aileron tab in the 'up' position, causing the uncontrollable roll. Fixing the potentially fatal flaw was simple, but the crash raised more concerns about the ability of aircrew to abandon the V-Bombers in emergencies. In fact, this controversial subject was never properly addressed, partly because of cost considerations, but also because of the RAF's belief that the V-Bombers were remarkably safe aircraft, which was proved correct.

As the Blue Danube bomb-dropping trials continued, it became clear that the RAE designers had produced a near-perfect ballistic casing for the atomic warhead. When the instrumented test specimens were released they often 'flew' beneath the Valiant's rear fuselage before falling clear – drops were tracked visually by theodolite. To counter this potentially dangerous tendency the Valiant was equipped with strakes forward of the bomb bay which created an airflow disturbance to push the bomb downwards, away from the fuselage.

Equipped with six Valiant B.1s, 49 Squadron was quickly assigned to Operation Buffalo, which would culminate in the the first air drop of a live British nuclear weapon. While other Valiant squadrons became involved with Operation Musketeer, 49 Squadron's specialized tasks continued at Wittering until two Valiant B.1s, WZ366 and WZ367, departed for Australia on 5 August. Further training was to have been conducted from Wittering, but poor weather and difficulty in obtaining sufficient weapons-range access meant that the crews could operate more effectively by using the Maralinga and Woomera ranges.

The work-up towards Operation Buffalo did not proceed smoothly, as a report by Gp Capt Menaul, the Commander of the Air Task Group, indicates:

The Valiants arrived at [RAAF] Edinburgh having completed part of a bombing training programme in the UK. It was planned to complete their training in Australia using the range facilities at Maralinga or Woomera as required. The main reason for the non-completion of training in the UK was the late delivery of aircraft and the lack of flight clearance for certain items of equipment, notably the bombing system, the automatic pilot and the radar altimeter. Unsuitable weather and difficulties in obtaining bombing ranges also added to the delays.

Both aircraft were fitted with a T.4 bombsight which had been modified by the incorporation of drift smoothing. The system had never been tested in a Valiant type aircraft however, until 5 June 1955. A&AEE gave temporary clearance for the installation after a six-bomb detail had been completed from 19,000 ft. During the training which followed, ten practice 10,000 lb bombs and 60 x 100 lb bombs were dropped in the UK by the two Valiant aircraft. The 10,000 lb bombs were primarily to prove the weapon and aircraft systems and the 100-pounders to prove the accuracy of the T.4 bombsight, particularly in the hands of inexperienced crews. On completion of this training programme in the UK, the results of which were not entirely satisfactory, it was decided that the standard obtained, considering the time available, was adequate and the aircraft and crews were prepared to fly out to Australia. Technical defects discovered during the UK training phase were corrected, and modifications to the bombsight sighting head and the Green Satin output improved the system and gave considerably better bombing results at a later date. The whole of the training programme in the UK could have been considerably improved if more emphasis had been placed on overseas operations.

The report by the Operation Buffalo Air Task Commander also includes a description of the historic sortie during which the first air drop took place:

Valiant WZ366 took off from Maralinga airfield with the live nuclear weapon on board. The crew consisted of Sqn Ldr Flavell (captain), Gp Capt Menaul, Flt Lts Ledger and Stacey,

Flg Off Spencer and Plt Off Ford. The aircraft climbed to 38,000 ft in a wide arc, avoiding the range area until it reached the emergency holding area. The bombsight was levelled, contact was established with the air controller on the ground by VHF and HF, and the aircraft then descended to 30,000 ft ready to begin the fly-over sequences, using precisely the same drills and procedures as in the concrete and HE drops. At 14:25 the first fly-over, Type 'A' was successfully completed, with all equipment, both in the air and on the ground, working satisfactorily. Types 'B' and 'C' fly-overs were then completed in turn, and by 15:00 all was in readiness for the final Type 'D' fly-over and the release of the nuclear weapon. The final 'D' type fly-over was completed according to plan with all equipment functioning perfectly, and the weapon was released at 15:27. Immediately after release a steep turn to starboard on to a heading of 240° true was executed in order to position the aircraft correctly for the thermal measuring equipment to function. During this turn 1.9G was applied. The weapon exploded correctly and the aircraft, after observing the formation of the mushroom cloud, set course for base, where it landed at 15:35. The operation had gone

smoothly and exactly according to the plans drawn up during training. The bombing error was afterwards assessed at 100 yd overshoot and 40 ft right.

The Blue Danube's explosive yield had been fixed at 40 kilotons, but for this drop the figure had been reduced to 3 kiloton in order to avoid the risks of extensive radioactive fallout, which would have been created if the bomb's barometric fusing had failed and the airburst had become a groundburst. This was mentioned in a report sent to the Secretary of State for Air by Air Marshal Tuttle, which said:

The weapon, a Blue Danube round with modified fusing, in-flight loading and with the yield reduced to 3-4 Kilotons, was dropped from the Valiant aircraft at 30,000 ft. The weapon was set to burst at 500 ft and telemetry confirmed that the burst occurred between 500 and 600 ft. The bomb was aimed visually after a radar-controlled run-up.

This first 'live' air drop demonstrated to the world that Britain not only possessed nuclear know-how, but that the RAF now had a practical means of delivering nuclear weapons to their targets. The British nuclear deterrent had been created.

CHAPTER FOUR

The Vulcan

Formal tenders to Specification B.35/46 were submitted to the MoS in May 1947. To examine the merits of each design, the MoS referred the subject to the RAE at Farnborough, where the ABPG was set up under the chairmanship of Morien Morgan, the head of Farnborough's Aerodynamic Flight Section. Eighteen aerodynamicists and structural engineers were appointed to the group, and together they considered each submission. In essence, the performance requirements of Specification B.35/46 were almost mutually exclusive. High speed could be achieved, but only at the expense of either range or payload capability. Conversely, a long-range bomber could easily be developed, but speed and payload performance would be reduced accordingly. Long range was the most important factor. The Advanced Bomber Group believed that a suitable payload could be carried at 50,000 ft and 500 kt, but to achieve a range of 3,000 miles as well seemed an insurmountable problem.

Weight was another problem. A bigger wing would enable the aircraft to fly at higher altitudes owing to lower wing loading, but it would increase the aircraft's weight beyond the 115,000 lb limit. As mentioned previously, this problem was conveniently bypassed when the RAF finally accepted that it would be easier to extend and strengthen the medium bomber force's runways, rather than add another restriction to the design specification. From the range of submissions at their disposal, the group decided that the Handley Page design offered the best chance of success, especially in terms of altitude, but Avro's submission appeared to offer much better manoeuvrability, and there did not appear to be any major reason to prefer one design over the other.

In view of the fact that very little aerodynamic data was available at the time, the group considered that either of the designs could later reveal a basic flaw which would render the submission useless, and, rather than risk choosing the wrong one, they opted to select both designs for further development. They also decided that a 'design intermediate' should be produced, to guarantee the RAF a more conventional (and therefore less capable) bomber, in case both the Handley Page and Avro aircraft failed to reach production status. This 'insurance' aircraft became the Short S.A.4 Sperrin, which, as recounted earlier, was later abandoned in favour of the Vickers Valiant.

Design work on the Avro 698 began in January 1947 at the company's Projects Department offices at Chadderton, Manchester. A six-man design team was led by chief designer Stuart Davies and technical director Roy Chadwick. At the time the company was heavily committed to the continuing development of the Avro Anson, the maritime derivative of the Lincoln (which became the Shackleton), and the Tudor airliner. Additionally, the company factory at Yeadon had just closed, and the ensuing merger with the Manchester plant created even more disruption for a very busy team.

Bob Lindley, later to became vice-president of McDonnell, was in charge of the Project Office, and his team were already well acquainted with German Second World War research on swept-wing design. In Bonn, Walter and Reimar Horten had produced a variety of swept-wing tailless aircraft, beginning in 1932 with their H-1 glider and culminating in the Ho 9 fighter-bomber, which would have become the Go 229 in its production version had the war in Europe continued. It was estimated that the Go 229 would have been capable of almost 600 mph at sea level and a ceiling of 52,000 ft, carrying a 4,400 lb bomb load and four 30 mm cannon. Most of the Horten research and design data was destroyed before the Allies arrived, but some research papers were recovered and the Avro team studied all of the available data.

Doctor Alexander Lippisch was another leading German designer whose work influenced Avro's thinking. Famous for the creation of the rocket-powered Messerschmitt Me 163 interceptor, Lippisch developed an interest in triangular, delta-wing designs which he subjected to supersonic wind tunnel analysis, a facility that only the Germans had at the time. At the war's end the Allies captured his factory at Wiener Wald and his DM-1 glider was taken to the USA, where the design was developed by Lippisch and the Convair

company into the XF-92A, the world's first delta-winged jet aircraft, and subsequently led to the F-102 Delta Dagger interceptor. Avro maintained an interest in his work too, and also in Armstrong Whitworth's tentative steps into 'flying wing' research. That company had produced an all-wing research glider, the A.W.52G, in 1945, and two examples of a powered version, the A.W.52. One of the latter crashed during 1949, its pilot, Jo Lancaster, becoming the first British pilot to use an ejection seat to abandon an aircraft. (A German pilot had ejected from the Heinkel He 280 V1 on 13 January 1942, using a compressed-air ejection seat.)

Further pioneering flying-wing work was carried out by Northrop in the USA, which produced the huge XB-35 flying wing later redeveloped as a the jet-powered YB-49 bomber. An astonishing 40 years later, Northrop's all-wing design interests re-emerged in the shape of the USAF's Northrop Grumman B-2 Spirit stealth bomber.

Unfortunately for Britain, most of the captured German research data on swept wings and tailless aircraft went to America, owing to the route taken across Germany by the advancing American forces. Moving across central and southern Germany, they captured many research facilities, which were mostly located in this part of the country. However, a considerable amount of research material was gathered by Britain, including a significant number of captured German airframes which were investigated at Farnborough. Reports compiled by the RAE, together with translations of German papers, were circulated to British aircraft manufacturers as soon as they became available.

Roy Chadwick was a great believer in the flying-wing concept, and it is very likely that he had already planted the seeds of this idea in the minds of his designers before he was taken ill towards the end of 1946. While he was away the design team drew up the preliminary Avro 698 design. To save weight, the team opted for a swept-wing tailless configuration, but the wing was far too big and much heavier than required. Reducing the span exacerbated the problems by affecting the wing area, wing loading and other factors. Consequently, the team experimented by removing wing area from the tips and replacing it between the wing trailing edge and the fuselage. The logical result was a delta wing, and when Chadwick returned from his convalescence he was delighted to find that the design team had produced a configuration which, either by accident or design, closely matched his own preliminary sketches.

The delta design offered a near-perfect solution to the team's problems. The 45° wing sweep could be retained, and by increasing inboard wing chord the wing's thickness could also be increased while still maintaining a good thickness-to-chord ratio. The thicker wing would enable the engines, landing gear and weapons bays to be buried inside, keeping the external aerodynamic shape clean. With small twin fins and rudders attached to the wingtips, the flying wing quickly took shape and was well established by May, when the Type 698 design was submitted to the MoS.

Further development led to a series of revisions to the original design. Initially the wingtip vertical surfaces were moved slightly inboard, where they would house the actuators for all-moving wingtips, a concept which Shorts had also incorporated into its Sherpa. However, this idea had been abandoned by September, after it was realized that individual ailerons and elevators could be fitted to the wing trailing edge. Furthermore, there was some doubt as to

whether the tailless design would be longitudinally stable, so the wing-mounted rudders were replaced by a conventional fin and rudder on to which a tailplane could be mounted should it prove necessary. With its huge circular air intakes at the wing-to-fuselage joint the design looked remarkably like a scaled-up Gloster Javelin fighter, but the intakes were redesigned and emerged as 'letterbox' slots in the wing leading edge, similar to those of the Valiant.

The undercarriage layout had originally been similar to the bicycle arrangement used on Boeing's B-47, with small outrigger wheels at the wingtips. Once the wing had been deepened, however, a more conventional tricycle gear could be fitted, and the mainwheel units were to be housed in bays either side of the two bomb bays. The early design incorporated two bays; one to carry either a nuclear bomb or a number of smaller conventional weapons, and another to carry either more bombs or fuel tanks. The aircraft's centre section incorporated the engines together with their associated intakes and exhausts, which were to be 'stacked' in pairs, Lightning fashion.

After a series of wind tunnel tests at Farnborough, the RAE suggested that the wing's thickness-to-chord ratio should be reduced in order to raise the predicted cruising speed. After much debate the Avro team agreed, and when the wing layout had been revised there was only sufficient space to bury the engines and undercarriage units, necessitating relocation of the bomb bays to a single space on the centreline. The crew compartment was moved forward from the wing leading edge to form a more pronounced nose section, housing the crew, the radar system, and fuel tanks, as well as the nose landing gear unit.

The complications of the Type 698's

design process were clearly illustrated in a paper written in 1956 by J. R. Ewans, Avro's chief aerodynamicist during the bomber's developmental period:

So far as can be ascertained, the idea of using a triangular planform for aircraft wings, now known as the delta wing, was first put forward in 1943 by Professor Lippisch, who will be remembered for his association with the Messerschmitt Company. His studies had led him to think that this planform was most suited for flight at speeds in the region of the speed of sound, where conventional aircraft designs were already known to be in trouble. By the end of the war he had a number of delta wing projects in hand, including an unpowered wooden glider which was intended to explore the low-speed properties of the delta wing. This was by then partially built, and was later completed under United States orders.

The idea of the delta wing was studied by many other aeronautical experts and a strong recommendation for its use was given, for instance, by Prof von Karman of the USA, at the 1947 Anglo-American Aeronautical Conference in London. At the time of writing, three British delta aircraft and two American are known to have flown, and it is pretty certain that others are on the way. In the date order of their first flight, these are the Consolidated-Vultee XF-92, Avro 707, Boulton Paul P.111, Douglas XF-3D and the Fairey FD.1. With the exception of the last named, which is fitted with a small fixed tailplane for the first flights, all the above aircraft are tailless.

Right at the beginning, it must be said that the delta wing is of value only for very high speed aircraft, and at the present stage of engine development,

this implies the use of jet engines. When projecting his high-speed aircraft, the designer will attempt to produce an aircraft carrying the greatest payload for the greatest distance, at the highest speed, and for the least expenditure of power (i.e. using the least amount of fuel). This applies to all types of aircraft, whether bombers in which the payload is bombs, or civil aircraft in which the payload is passengers or cargo, or fighters, in which the payload is guns and ammunition.

It has been shown in theory, and found in practice, that the speed of sound occupies a fundamental position in the speed range of aircraft. The speed of sound is actually 760 mph at sea level, and falls off to a value of 660 mph at heights above 30,000 ft. Because the speed of sound is of such importance, aeronautical engineers relate aircraft speeds to the speed of sound, using the term "Mach number", defined as the ratio of the speed of an aircraft to the speed of sound at the same height. As an aircraft approaches the speed of sound — in fact for conventional aircraft when a speed of about 70 per cent of the speed of sound (i.e. a Mach number of 0.7) is reached — the effects of compressibility become important and the characteristics of the airflow around the aircraft change fundamentally. There is a very large increase in the air resistance or drag, and an excessive expenditure of power becomes necessary to increase the speed any further.

For transport and bomber aircraft the speed at which the drag starts to increase (known as the 'drag rise' Mach number) becomes the maximum cruising speed, since if the aircraft is flown at higher speeds, the disproportionally higher thrust required from the engine means excessive fuel consumption and loss of range. At a rather higher Mach number there will be changes in the stability of the aircraft and in its response to the pilot's control — leading possibly even to complete loss of control.

In order to progress along the speed range to higher speeds it is therefore necessary to design aircraft so as to postpone and/or overcome these effects. We have noted that with an 'old fashioned' type of aircraft design (i.e. that of jet propelled aircraft current in 1945) the limiting speed in steady cruising flight is likely to be a Mach number of 0.7 (higher speeds have, of course, already been achieved and a number of aircraft have exceeded the speed of sound, but only for short periods, either by diving or by use of rocket power). From the knowledge available, however, it appears possible by careful aerodynamic design of an aircraft, to postpone the rise in drag until a Mach number in the region of 0.9 is reached, and this figure is likely to be the practical limit of cruising speed for transport aircraft of all types for many years to come. The designer of a civil aircraft, a bomber, or a long-range fighter will, therefore, bend all his energies to achieving a Mach number of this order without any drag rise. In addition he must pay attention to the changes of stability or lack of control which might occur in this region, and this will occupy his attention to the same extent as the purely performance aspect of the drag rise.

It is quite easy to design a fuselage shape which is relatively immune from Mach number effects. It is the design of wings which is difficult, particularly since a wing that is suitable for high speed must also give satisfactory flying properties at low speeds, e.g. for take-off and landing. As the air flows past a wing its speed is increased over the upper surface to a considerable extent and over the lower surface to a lesser extent so that there is greater suction on the upper surface than on the lower surface. This difference gives rise to the lift which enables the wing to sustain the weight of the aircraft. Thus, whatever speed an aircraft is flying, the speed of the air around the wing will, in fact, be higher. In the case of an aircraft flying at Mach 0.8 the speed around its upper surface will be equal to, or may easily exceed the speed of sound. At this stage, the airflow pattern around the wing will be considerably changed, and it is, in fact, this change which gives rise to the drag and stability effects mentioned above. It is essential, therefore, to keep the velocity above the wing as little in excess of the speed of the aircraft as possible. There are four ways of improving the high Mach number behaviour of the wings. They are different methods, all of which can be applied simultaneously, of keeping down the air velocities round the wing. They are: a) Sweepback, b) Thinness, c) Low wing loading, d) Low aspect ratio. We will consider each of these effects in turn.

The amount of sweepback is measured by the angle by which the tip of the wing lies behind the centreline. The extent of the gains possible from sweepback is very considerable, and sweeping a wing back may easily lead to a postponement of the compressibility effects by a Mach number of 0.1. The drag rise of the former occurs at 0.7 and the latter is 0.83. Keeping a wing thin leads to a reduction in the amount of air that must be pushed out of the way by the wing. This helps the passage of the wing through the air. The thickness of a wing is measured by the thickness/chord ratio, which is the maximum depth of a wing divided by its length in the line of flight. In the past, the thickness/chord ratios of an aircraft wing have ranged from 21 per cent down to perhaps 12 per cent. Now values of 10 per cent down to 7 per cent are becoming common.

The wing loading is the weight of an aircraft carried by a unit area of wing, measured in pounds per square foot. Mach number effects are postponed by keeping the wing loading as low as possible, i.e. by supporting the weight of the aircraft with a large wing area. This is particularly important for flight at high altitudes, where the low air density puts a premium on keeping the wing loading low. In fact, flight at high altitude becomes virtually impossible unless this is done.

Aspect ratio is the ratio of the span of a wing to the average chord. For moderate speeds, a high aspect ratio, i.e. a large span relative to the chord, gives greatest efficiency. At high Mach numbers this consideration is no longer important, in fact some alleviation of compressibility effects is given by reducing aspect ratio. There is another reason for choosing a low aspect ratio. One of the disadvantages of sweeping a wing back is that the flying characteristics at low speed become worse. A typical symptom is that the wing of a swept-back wing stalls, giving violent behaviour if the speed is allowed to fall too low.

Research has, however, shown that this bad characteristic of highly swept back wings may be overcome relatively easily. Although almost any aspect ratio can be accepted with an unswept wing, for wings of 45° sweepback an aspect ratio of little over 3 is the most satisfactory. There is a third reason for choosing a low aspect ratio – the behaviour (as regards stability, etc.) in the high Mach number region. For reasons which it is not possible to go into here, compressibility effects are minimised and a transition from speeds below that of sound to the speed of sound and above is much more readily accomplished if the aspect ratio is low, say in the order of 2 to 4.

Put the above requirements together and the result is an aircraft with a highly swept-back, thin wing, a moderately large wing area and a low aspect ratio. A little consideration of geometrical properties and possible planform of wings leads to the conclusion that the delta wing is the only form which satisfies these requirements. It possesses high sweepback and low aspect ratio. The wing area will, of necessity, be generous for the size of the aircraft and, for reasons which will be detailed later, it is easy to build it with a low thickness/chord ratio. We must see how the delta planform, indicated from considerations of aerodynamic performance, lines up with practical design requirements, and in particular the overriding necessity for keeping weight and drag low in order to obtain a maximum performance. A preliminary question is whether a tailplane is necessary.

From the earliest days of flying, the question has been raised as to whether aircraft can be flown satisfactorily without a tailplane. Confining our attention to the case of high-speed jet aircraft, we will examine each of the functions of a tailplane in turn, in relation to a delta-wing aircraft. A tailplane performs the following functions:

a) To trim out changes of c.g. position according to the load carried and the consumption of fuel. Investigation shows that a control surface at the trailing edge of the wing, provided that the latter has a large root (as has the delta) can cater for all but the most extreme c.g. movements.

b) To deal with trim changes due to landing flaps, etc. With the low wing loading associated with the delta wing, take-off and landing speeds are moderate without the use of flaps, and this question does not, therefore arise.

c) To provide damping of pitching oscillations. The reduction of damping of the pitching oscillation has led to some difficulty on some tailless aircraft, but it does not arise on the delta since the large chord near the root gives adequate damping.

d) To deal with loss of stability or control power consequent on distortion of the wing structure (Aerolastic Distortion). At very high speeds all aircraft structures distort to a greater or lesser extent under the high loads imposed, and this distortion alters the aerodynamic form. In extreme cases this leads to a loss of stability or control power, making the aircraft dangerous or impossible to fly at high speeds. An aircraft with a high-aspect-ratio sweptback wing would need a tailplane to deal with this, but the shape of the delta wing makes it extremely stiff both in bending and in torsion, and a tailplane does not appear necessary.

e) To provide for spin recovery. Although this point has not been proved, it is expected that the controls

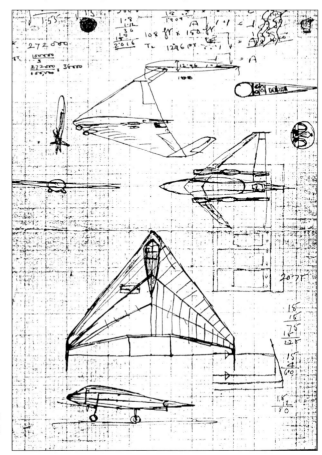

Roy Chadwick's initial sketches of the Avro 698 design. (via British Aerospace)

on a tailless delta wing would not be powerful enough to ensure recovery from a fully developed spin. A tailplane appears to be the only way of dealing with this. The restriction is of no significance for transport or bomber-type aircraft for which spinning does not arise, but on fighter or trainer aircraft a tailplane would appear to be a necessity. It is therefore concluded that, for a delta wing aircraft of the transport or bomber type, a tailplane is unnecessary. Its deletion leads immediately to a considerable saving of weight and drag, and to a major gain in performance.

Compared with a conventional aircraft, the delta wing aircraft will therefore be simpler by the omission of the following items: the tailplane, the rear fuselage necessary to carry the tailplane, wing flaps and other high–lift devices such as the drooped leading edge. There is a considerable saving of weight, of design and manufacturing effort, and of maintenance when the aircraft is in service. These economies will have considerable bearing on the initial cost and the manpower necessary to produce and maintain a number of aircraft.

Because of its shape and the large root chord, the delta wing provides a large internal volume in relation to its surface area, even when using the thin wing sections which, as we have seen above, are essential for high–speed aircraft. Simple calculations show that for the same wing area, the delta wing has 33 per cent more internal volume than an untapered wing, while if the inboard half of the wing only is considered, as this presents a more practical case from the point of view of the aircraft designer, the internal volume of the delta wing is more than

twice that of the corresponding untapered wing. It is found that without exceeding a wing thickness of as little as 8 per cent to 10 per cent it is possible on a moderate sized delta-wing aircraft to completely bury the engines, undercarriage and sufficient fuel tanks for a very considerable range. The fuselage also has a tendency to disappear into the wing at the root. The result is the attainment of an aircraft consisting only of a wing, a fin and a rudimentary fuselage, representing a degree of aerodynamic cleanliness which has never before been reached. In fairness, it must be pointed out that this is achieved at the expense of a rather larger area than usual, but investigation shows that the drag of this is considerably less than that due to a conglomeration of items such as engine nacelles, tailplane, etc.

From the design point of view, the shape of the delta wing leads to an extremely stiff structure without the use of thick wing skins, and strength becomes the determining feature rather than structural stiffness. This avoids the inefficiency of conventional sweptback wings where the wing has to be made stronger than necessary in order that it shall be stiff enough. It is found that the delta wing lends itself to conventional design techniques, and to conventional methods of construction. Summarising the above, we have seen that in order to meet the requirements of large loads for long range, at high speeds, the high-performance transport or military aircraft of the future will cruise at a considerable altitude, at a speed not much below that of sound. The delta wing provides the only satisfactory solution to these requirements, for the following reasons:

1) It meets the four features necessary for avoiding the drag rise near the

speed of sound, i.e. it is highly swept back, it can be made very thin, the wing loading is low, and the aspect ratio is low.

2) Extensive wind tunnel and flight tests have shown that the low-aspect-ratio delta wing gives minimum change in stability and control characteristics at speeds near the speed of sound.

3) In spite of being thin, the internal volume is large, so that the engines, undercarriage, fuel and all the necessary equipment can be contained within the wing and a rudimentary fuselage.

4) Adequate control can be obtained by control surfaces on the wing, thus eliminating the need for a conventional tailplane. Together with item 3, this leads to a considerable reduction in the drag of the aircraft and, therefore, to high performance.

5) Auxiliary devices such as flaps, nose flaps, slots and the all-moving tailplane are unnecessary, thereby saving weight and design effort, and simplifying manufacture and maintenance.

6) The delta wing is very stiff and free from distortion troubles.

This extensive and detailed paper illustrates Avro's enthusiasm for simplicity both in terms of aerodynamics and manufacturing processes. The Type 698's straightforward and clean design offered much greater manoeuvrability than could ever be attained by the H.P.80, but the Handley Page design was capable of carrying a heavier bomb load at a higher altitude. However, Avro always managed to compensate for this shortfall thanks to the continuing development of the Bristol Olympus engine, which had increased to 13,400-lb thrust by 1958, whereas Handley Page was restricted to the 11,000-lb thrust of the Armstrong Siddeley Sapphire. Stuart Davies later

commented: 'There is no question that, if high altitude was the only requirement, the Victor was best. For the same power it could always go higher, but it never had the same power so the Vulcan cheated.'

Chadwick was convinced that the delta-winged bomber would be a huge success, and he put a great deal of effort into his 'salesmanship' with the MoS, often taking scale models of the aircraft to meetings, where he dismissed George Edwards's comments concerning the unpredictability of both the Avro and Handley Page designs. In fact, the MoS were more than a little uneasy about the situation, but a man with Chadwick's track record had to be taken very seriously. Chief designer Stuart Davies commented: 'It is one thing for a junior technician to push an unconventional idea, but for a designer with Mr Chadwick's past history of success to risk his reputation on such a venture was an act of high courage which was not perhaps sufficiently recognized'. Tragically, Chadwick was killed on 23 August 1947 when the Avro Tudor 2 prototype crashed on take-off from the company's airfield at Woodford. It was later revealed that the aileron controls had been reversed.

Avro's shock at the loss of Chadwick was compounded by the fear that the Type 698 might not survive the MoS's scrutiny without his backing. However, the position of technical director was taken by W. S. 'Bill' Farren, a former director of the RAE, who had a reputation almost as formidable as Chadwick's. He immediately put his support behind the project, and in January 1948 the MoS placed an order for two prototypes, although the official go-ahead had been given to both the Handley Page and Avro projects during the previous November, as outlined in a report by Air Cdre H. V. Slatterly, which stated:

The Tender Design Conference was held on 28 July. This conference recommended that an order for the prototype of the Avro version of the B.35/46, and a flying model, should be placed. Additionally, either the Handley Page or the Armstrong Whitworth should be ordered with a flying model, after further investigation by the RAE. Nothing much happened until a meeting of the Ministry of Supply in November 1947. This meeting recommended that financial cover should be given to A. V. Roe's. An ADC [advisory design conference] was held on the Handley Page version on 23 December, and by 9 January 1948 we were advised that token sums of money had been granted to cover ITP's issued to A. V. Roe's and Handley Page. In the same month it was forecast that A. V. Roe's could start production by mid-1955 and Handley Page's by mid-1956.

At this stage there was still a considerable lack of information on the flying characteristics of the delta wing, both in high-speed and low-speed configurations. The Avro design team had agreed during 1947 that a delta-winged glider model would be a useful tool with which to gather data, but by the time the order was placed for the Avro 698 prototypes the MoS had accepted that a one-third-scale piloted powered flying model should be constructed. Powered by a single Rolls-Royce Derwent, the Avro 707 would be used to investigate the low-speed handling characteristics of the delta wing. Additionally, a high-speed research aircraft, the Avro 710, would also be built, powered by two Rolls-Royce Avons, to explore the flight envelope up to 60,000 ft and Mach 0.95.

By September 1948 Avro's confidence in the basic Type 698 design had grown considerably. The airframe construction had already been established, and it was agreed that time and resources spent on the 710 would simply delay work on the 698 rather than contribute towards its success. Avro therefore decided to abandon the 710 and construct one high-speed 707, two low-speed 707s and a full-scale Type 698 which would be stripped of all but the most basic equipment, simply to gather flight data. However, the

Avro 707 prototype VX784 pictured shortly after the type's first flight. (British Aerospace)

WZ736 pictured at Avro's Woodford facility. (British Aerospace)

'stripped' Type 698 was also dropped later, as the 707s were adjudged capable of gathering sufficient data, especially when news of Convair's successful XF-92A was received.

The Avro 707 was a relatively simple and inexpensive aircraft, built around Specification E.15/48, created for it. With a modest 400 kt maximum speed, the aircraft was to have been built of wood, but it was later decided to use a simple pressed sheet metal construction with two supporting spars. The first 707 was fitted with the canopy and nose landing gear unit of a Gloster Meteor, and an Avro Athena advanced trainer's main undercarriage units. The flying controls were conventional and non-powered, and the simple fuselage housed only fuel and test monitoring equipment, together with the Derwent engine. After completion in August 1949, the first Avro 707, VX784, performed a series of engine runs and taxying trials at Woodford before being dismantled and transported by road to Boscombe Down on 26 August.

The 707 was reassembled in time for a planned first flight on 3 September, but on that day a 20 kt crosswind prevented the flight from taking place, and it was at 19:30 on 4 September that Flt Lt Eric Esler, chief test pilot at the A&AEE, gently lifted the diminutive 707 into the air for a perfect maiden flight. Two more flights totalling 2.5 hr were made over the next couple of days, after which Esler flew VX784 to Farnborough for static exhibition at the SBAC show. After the display, the 707 returned to Boscombe Down to continue test flying. Its handling characteristics were reported to be very good and, in most respects, very similar to those of more conventional aircraft, apart from the considerably lengthened take-off run needed to reach a comfortable unstick speed.

The success of the 707 programme was marred by the sudden loss of VX784 on 30 September. The aircraft crashed near Blackbushe during a test flight, killing Esler, and the post-accident investigation revealed that the 707 appeared to have stalled at low speed. This news served to confirm the gloomy predictions from various commentators who still believed that the delta-wing design would be lethal at low speeds. However, further investigation suggested that the true cause of the crash had been the failure of a control circuit, which had locked the airbrakes in the fully extended position, and Esler had been unable to recover the aircraft. This news came as a relief to Avro, and, reassured by the knowledge that the design was still safe, the company quickly completed the second 707, VX790, the airbrakes and elevators being suitably modified. It was also decided that an ejection seat should be fitted. The design revision for this installation, which required a larger nose section, was already in hand for the high-speed 707 to Specification E.10/49, so Avro accelerated the design of this portion of the high-speed aircraft and fitted it to VX790.

As with the first prototype, the 707B, as it was designated, had an Athena main undercarriage, but this time the nose gear came from the Hawker P.1052. The first flight was made from Woodford by Avro's recently-appointed chief test pilot, Wg Cdr R. J. 'Roly' Falk, who had previously been a test pilot at Vickers and chief test pilot at RAE Farnborough. The maiden flight was scheduled for 5 September 1950, but after spending most of the day on pre-flight tests Falk decided to limit the day's activities to some taxying trials and a 'hop' along the runway. He made the 15 min first flight the following day.

Immediately after this flight, Falk telephoned Avro managing director Roy Dobson and Air Marshal J. N. Boothman, the Controller of Supplies — Air, to obtain permission to take the 707B to the SBAC show. It duly appeared at Farnborough the same day, flying in to join the static display during the late afternoon. After the SBAC show VX790 began test flying, up to the aircraft's top speed of 350 kt, limited by the intake's air starvation at high speed. The intake was

suitably modified, and minor oscillations in the pitching plane were simply ignored, as the cause, out-of-phase movement of the elevators, was not relevant to the Type 698, which would have powered flying controls. The only other significant modification was the lengthening of the nosewheel leg by 9 in to increase the wing's angle of attack during take-off, enabling the elevators to become effective at a lower speed and shortening the take-off run. In all other respects VX790 was a delight to fly, and was capable of performing aerobatics and flying at 30° angle of attack without stalling. When conventional aircraft could not even achieve 15° this was quite a feat, especially for an aircraft which many believed would have poor low-speed-handling.

Although the 707B completed approximately 100 hr of research flying for Avro before being handed over to the A&AEE for further research, much of the flight data it yielded was of little value, as by May 1950 the first detail drawings of the Type 698 had been finalized. Some information was found to be relevant, however, not least the discovery that the Type 698's fin could be reduced in size, thanks to an increase in longitudinal stability caused by angling the engine exhaust pipes outwards. Although it was much less important than the gathering of test data, the 707 flights also served to satisfy the MoS that the delta-wing design would work.

There was a great deal of discussion about the future of the 'high-speed' 707A, WD280, which had been robbed of its nose section to provide the 707B with an ejection seat. Completing the aircraft seemed pointless now that so much work on the Type 698 had already been completed, but it was eventually agreed that the aircraft could contribute some data which would guide the planning of the bomber's flight test programme. In

An unusual view of VX790, illustrating the type's early intake configuration and the wing's pure delta planform. (British Aerospace)

WD280 was retro fitted with a revised wing leading edge, representative of the configuration adopted by the Vulcan B.1A. (Denis O'Brien)

Avro 707C WZ744 was assembled at Bracebridge Heath, flying for the first time (from nearby Waddington) on 1 July 1953. (British Aerospace)

fact, WD280 proved the effectiveness of both the rectangular air intake design and the elevator and aileron layout which would be incorporated in the Type 698's wing. Its first flight was made from Woodford on 14 July 1951, by which time metal was being cut on the Type 698 prototype, which indicates just how little influence the 707A had on the design.

Although the 707 programme did serve a useful purpose, there can be no doubt that the idea was compromised by a lack of synchronization with the Type 698 programme, and that, in devoting a lot of time and resources to the 707s, attention was diverted from the Type 698. In some instances the designers often had to revise the 707 layout to keep pace with the Type 698, rather than the other way round, but it would be unfair to suggest that the 707 programme was a waste of time. In fact, it was the incredible speed and success of the bomber programme that created the

confusion. The 707A did eventually have a more direct influence on the Type 698 design, when it was discovered that the airframe 'buzzed' (a high-frequency vibration) at high speed and high altitude. The problem was partly rectified by installing wing fences, but eventually the wing leading edge was redesigned, reducing the angle of sweep inboard before increasing it again towards the wingtip, thereby producing a 'kinked' effect. Unfortunately, the first Type 698s were being manufactured by the time this solution had been found, and the first 16 leading-edge units had to be scrapped; an expensive waste which could have been avoided if the two programmes had been better co-ordinated.

Air Marshal Boothman flew the 707B during September 1951, and such was his delight in the handling and performance of the aircraft that he commented: 'Twenty-five selected pilots must fly it at once'. The 707 was demonstrating that the Type 698 was going to be a practical proposition.

A second 707A, WZ736, was also constructed, but this aircraft was produced specifically for the RAE and was operated on a series of research programmes, including automatic throttle development. Unlike the earlier 707s it was assembled at Avro's Bracebridge Heath factory, being towed along the A15 to make its maiden flight from Waddington on 20 February 1953. The final 707 to be manufactured was 707C WZ744, a two-seat version designed in anticipation of a requirement for dual-control conversion trainers for the bomber. When it was established that the Type 698 was surprisingly safe and easy to handle, the need for a specific trainer aircraft disappeared, and WZ744 was assigned to various research programmes with the RAE, following its maiden flight at Waddington on 1 July 1953.

While the 707 programme continued, construction of the bomber began in 1951, after a three-month delay during which the design altered quite significantly. Avro had effectively fixed the Type 698 design when the RAE at Farnborough notified the company of some rather disturbing results of model tests in their wind tunnel. The shape of the Type 698's fuselage was affecting air pressure distribution over the wing surfaces and engine intakes in ways which Avro had not predicted. The results were not conclusive, but they suggested that the onset of compressibility drag rise, which would effectively be the Type 698's maximum speed limit, would take place at a lower speed and altitude than previously envisaged.

Clearly, the design would have to be modified, and the Avro team worked furiously from December 1949 until May 1950 to revise the wing layout completely, so that the thickest section would be close to the leading edge, instead of being at a more traditional position near the root chord centre. This produced a wing root nearly as deep as the fuselage to which it was attached, resulting in a 'flying-wing' appearance which seemed to revert to the shape evolved during the preliminary design stage. The Avro designers were not entirely convinced by the RAE's evidence, but the deeper wing provided additional space for more efficient air intakes and bigger engines, and it was the projected need for larger and more powerful engines that finally persuaded Avro to redesign the wing. Some 190 draughtsmen worked on the Type 698, plus thousands of engineers with Avro and sub-contractors around the country.

Construction of the massive wing sections began at Woodford, while the rest of the airframe took shape at Chadderton, and in June 1952 notification was received that a contract for 25 production aircraft would be placed. Although this was good news for Avro, the company's delight was tempered by the news that Handley Page had also been awarded a contract for 25 aircraft, and that its H.P.80 had already been delivered to Boscombe Down in preparation for a first flight. It had been widely anticipated that just one design would be selected, and it was later revealed that the original plan had indeed been to select either the Avro or Handley Page design and then award a contract for a first batch of 50, but nobody could guarantee which aircraft would prove to be the superior design. Of course, another possible cause for this state of indecision was the unenviable prospect of telling either Sir Frederick Handley Page or Sir Roy Dobson that his company's submission had been rejected.

Spurred on by the news of Handley Page's progress, the Avro team worked around the clock in the hope of achieving a first flight of the Type 698 in time for the 1952 SBAC show. The huge centre-section components were transported by road from Chadderton, necessitating the modification of some lamp posts in Greater Manchester so that they hinged sideways to enable the convoys, with their bulky tarpaulin-covered loads, to pass through during the early hours. After a 17-mile journey to Woodford the prototype was fully assembled during August, and engine runs began. The new Bristol B.E.10, later named Olympus, which it was estimated would deliver 11,000-lb thrust, had been selected to power the Type 698, but as it was not expected to be available until 1953 the 6,500-lb thrust Rolls-Royce Avon was selected for the prototype.

On 30 August Roly Falk taxied the Type 698, VX770, on to Woodford's runway and made just one fast taxying run to determine the speed at which the nosewheel would unstick from the runway. Falk decided that further runs were unnecessary, and that they might simply overheat the braking units, so he positioned the aircraft for take-off. After a flock of seagulls had been cleared from the area, clearance for the historic first flight was given, and the four Avon RA.3s were opened up to full power. With a mighty roar the gloss-white bomber lurched forward and, after a surprisingly short take-off run, lifted smartly into the air. Once it was comfortably clear of the ground its undercarriage was retracted and a steady climb to 10,000 ft was made. Falk then performed a series of gentle manoeuvres to establish a 'feel' for the aircraft's controls, and once he was satisfied he turned the aircraft back to Woodford to land.

Almost 30 min later VX770 appeared overhead Woodford, and Falk lowered the undercarriage. At this stage, watchers in Woodford's control tower noticed something falling away from the aircraft

This historic view shows VX770 embarking on her maiden flight, 30 August 1952. (British Aerospace)

An evocative shot of the Avro 698 prototype, emphasizing the pure delta layout of the pre-production Vulcan. (British Aerospace)

and reported this to Falk, who replied that everything was functioning as normal. Observers quickly took off in both a Vampire and an Avro 707 to investigate at close quarters while Falk orbited the airfield with the undercarriage locked down. Closer inspection revealed that both rear main undercarriage doors had broken loose, but that everything else appeared to be in order. Duly assured that a safe landing could be made, Falk turned on to final approach and gently touched down, after which he streamed the prototype's big braking parachute. Falk later commented that, despite the drama of the undercarriage doors, the first flight had been a great success, and that even without a second pilot's seat, cockpit pressurization or a wing fuel system the Type 698 was clearly going to be a great aeroplane. Just two more test flights were made from Woodford before the aircraft was ferried to Boscombe Down.

Three hours of flying were completed at Boscombe Down, after which VX770 made daily appearances at the 1952 SBAC show. For security reasons it was agreed that the aircraft should not land at Farnborough, so it operated directly from Boscombe Down each day. The missing undercarriage doors were not replaced in time for the show, and after each day's display the exposed microswitches and other associated components were strengthened in response to Falk's display, which grew a little faster each day. After Farnborough, VX770 was fitted with a second-pilot's seat, and although there was some media speculation that the second seat was crammed into the flight deck as an afterthought, this was not the case, the aircraft being designed for a two-pilot crew from the outset. A large and heavy nuclear bomber was never intended to be entrusted to just one pilot, but Falk did feel it appropriate to emphasize the fighter-like handling qualities of the aircraft. He did this by insisting that the control column should be a fighter-type stick rather than the more conventional 'spectacles' column fitted to other heavy bombers, and the light feel of the stick reflected the bomber's manoeuvrability, which was superior to that of many contemporary fighters.

During the following month Sir John Slessor announced his 'V-Class' nomenclature decision, and after considering names such as Albion and, most appropriately, Avenger, Vulcan was adopted. Gilbert Whitehead, the project engineer on the Type 698, later commented: 'I never liked the name. After it was announced I went to look it up in a mythology book and the definition of Vulcan was "misshapen god of war thrown out of heaven".' By the end of January 1953 VX770 had completed 32 hr of test flying, and further modifications had been made to the aircraft. These included installing fuel cells in the wings (up to that time a temporary system had been fitted in the bomb bay), making the cockpit pressurization operative, and replacing the four Avon engines with Armstrong Siddeley Sapphire ASSa.6s, each rated at 7,500-lb thrust. This gave the Vulcan the same thrust as the prototype H.P.80, which had been named Victor, and flying resumed in June 1953.

By now the second prototype, VX777, was nearing completion, and although ground running trials were completed with Bristol Olympus Mk.99s, it made its maiden flight on 3 September 1953 with four 9,750-lb thrust Olympus 100 engines. The first prototype's nose gear leg had been lengthened during construction in response to data gathered

A classic photograph of both Avro 698 prototypes and four 707s, presenting a delta formation for the 1953 SBAC show. (British Aerospace)

from the 707 trials, and to allow the longer nose gear to fit into the forward undercarriage bay, it was designed to telescope during retraction. On VX777 the undercarriage bay was lengthened to avoid this complication, and as a result the entire nose section was slightly longer. This machine also incorporated a visual bomb-aiming blister under the nose. Less than a week after its first flight the aircraft appeared in the 1953 SBAC show, and to create an even greater spectacle than the previous year's display, VX777 was joined by VX770 and four Avro 707s to form a huge delta formation which brought Farnborough to a standstill.

Both Vulcan prototypes then continued their test flying programmes until 27 July 1954, when VX777 suffered a heavy landing while operating from Farnborough, sustaining extensive and serious damage to the airframe. The accident was a major setback for Avro, not least in terms of powerplant progress, and the aircraft remained grounded for six months, during which time it was fitted with Olympus 101 engines rated at

10,000-lb thrust. The airframe was reworked using data from a static-test specimen, while the first prototype, VX770, continued to fly a variety of test profiles within its rather more limited flight envelope. When VX777 resumed flying in 1955, the exploration of high-speed and high-altitude flight quickly confirmed the mild buffeting (when pulling 'g' at speeds around Mach 0.8) experienced in the Avro 707 programme. With early 9,000-lb thrust engines this phenomenon was of little importance, but when projected thrust improvements were taken into account it became clear that this high-speed and high-altitude threshold would be reached with only the smallest applications of power. There would be problems maintaining accuracy when flying bombing runs, and a risk that the outer wing structure would eventually fail. A solution was clearly needed.

The result was the Phase Two wing with a revised 'kinked' leading edge, as described previously. Having tried a variety of remedies on the 707, including wing fences, vortex generators, and

The second Avro 698 prototype, VX777, climbing over Farnborough, the port main gear door still retracting. (British Aerospace).

notches, the Avro team still could not
come up with a cure. Finally, the
difficulty was solved by Farnborough's
High Speed Tunnel Section, whose
representative calmly suggested that the
wing leading edge be swept back at an
angle of 52° inboard, the sweep then
reducing by 10° before increasing again
to 52° towards the tips, where the wing
leading edge was slightly drooped. This
redesign would give the outer wing a 20
per cent increase in chord, enabling 'g' to
be pulled at any height without
adverse effects. By this stage the first
production Vulcan B.Mk.1, XA889, was
nearing completion, and although the
second prototype was retrofitted with
a Phase Two wing, flying in this form on
5 October, the new wing leading edge
was not fitted to XA889 when it was
rolled out at Woodford in January 1955.
Resplendent in an overall silver
paint scheme, with a black fibre-
glass/Hycar sandwich dielectric nose

radome, the aircraft made its first
flight on 4 February, some 12 months
ahead of Handley Page's Victor, and a
year later was fitted with a Phase Two
wing and vortex generators, designed to
speed up boundary layer airflow over
the wing.

On 30 September 1954 Avro received
an order for a further 37 Vulcans, fitted
with Olympus 104 engines (which were
retrofitted to earlier Vulcans). The second
production Vulcan, XA890, joined the
test programme in 1955, and although it
did not have a Phase Two wing it was
equipped with radio and radar, and
undertook a variety of trials with these
systems. Roly Falk flew XA890 to the
SBAC show in September, and on the
first day of the show he put the aircraft
through its paces, culminating in a slow
upward barrel roll which graphically
demonstrated the strength and
manoeuvrability of the Vulcan's airframe.
Falk's aerobatics astonished the SBAC's

The Vulcan's unusual wing leading edge 'reversed' jig into which sheet metal was formed. (British
Aerospace)

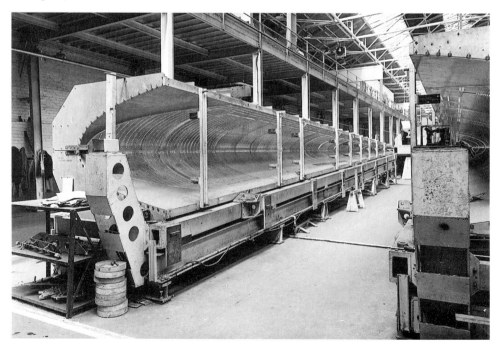

president, Sir Arnold Hall, who forbade Falk to repeat the manoeuvre on subsequent days, even though Avro personnel assured him that a steady 1g roll was perfectly safe and well within the Vulcan's capabilities. Unconvinced, Hall replied that it would set a bad example for future RAF Vulcan pilots.

On 7 September XA890 again made the news when Prime Minister Anthony Eden arrived at Farnborough in a Central Flying School Dragonfly helicopter and, after watching Falk's magnificent display, was invited to climb aboard for a short demonstration flight during which he occupied the copilot's seat and took the controls for a while. The Vulcan landed at Blackbushe, and Falk later received a handwritten note from Eden which said:

Thank you so much for piloting me so well yesterday. I enjoyed my flight very much and I was most impressed by the way in which the Vulcan manoeuvred in your skilled hands. I am also grateful for the generous things you said about my part in the flight, which was really 'nil'. Be careful of that roll!

The first production Vulcan was delivered to Boscombe Down in March 1956 to begin acceptance trials with the RAF. The second prototype had also spent some time with the A&AEE, and the conclusions reached by the test pilots were less than enthusiastic, as their report illustrates:

A preliminary flight assessment has been made on the second prototype Vulcan in 17 sorties totalling 27 flying hours. During these tests the aircraft was flown at a mid c.g. position and take-off weights of 119,000 lb and 130,000 lb. The expected operational take-off weight of production aircraft is about 165,000 lb.

The expected cruising Mach number is 0.87M (500 kt) and the design Mach number is 0.95M. Above 0.6M a nose-down change of trim occurred, which became pronounced with increase of Mach number towards the limit, making the aircraft difficult to fly accurately and requiring great care on the part of the pilot to avoid exceeding the maximum permitted Mach number. This characteristic is unacceptable; the Firm propose to eliminate it in production aircraft by the introduction of an artificial stability device (a Mach trimmer).

With increase of Mach number above 0.89 the damping in pitch decreased to an unacceptably low level, particularly near the maximum permitted Mach number, and the aircraft was difficult to fly steadily. The Firm propose installing a pitch damper in production aircraft. As tested, the Mach number/buffet characteristics were unacceptable for a high-altitude bomber, but considerable improvement is hoped for with the drooped leading edge and vortex generators. Associated with the buffet were oscillating aileron hinge movements which in these tests imposed severe limitations from considerations of structural safety.

Making due allowances for the differences in engine thrust and aircraft weight between the aircraft as tested and the production version, the performance, in terms of attainable altitude, was not outstanding. The likely target height with a 10,000 lb bomb will only be about 43,000 ft with 11,000-lb thrust engines, and the high-altitude turning performance will be poor. The level of performance is considered to be inadequate for an unarmed subsonic bomber, even under cover of darkness. In summary, although the aircraft has certain

The third pre-production Vulcan, XA891, which later crashed during July 1969. (British Aerospace)

After serving with Nos 83 and 44 Squadrons, XA896 was partially converted into a test bed for the Hawker P.1124. When the latter design was abandoned, the Vulcan's conversion was terminated and the aircraft was scrapped at Patchway. (British Aerospace).

VX770 was destroyed during September 1958, when the aircraft broke-up during a flying demonstration at Syerston. Later investigations revealed that the aircraft had been flown beyond the airframe's design limits. (British Aerospace).

Vulcan production underway at Chadderton, 1951.
(British Aerospace)

outstanding features, serious deficiencies are present, particularly in and above the cruising Mach number range, and until these are rectified the Vulcan cannot be considered satisfactory for Service use.

This rather sober appraisal of the second prototype's capabilities contrasts with the initial CA release, which was made on 29 May 1956:

Tests have been made on the first production Vulcan B.Mk.1 to assess the type for use by the Royal Air Force, in the medium bomber role. The trials programme was completed in 26 sorties, totalling 48 hr 15 min flying time. During these tests the aircraft was flown over the full c.g. range, and at take-off weights up to a maximum of 165,220 lb.

The first production Vulcan, XA889, was representative of Service aircraft in all respects save those of operational equipment, automatic pilot, the rear crew stations and certain items of cockpit layout. The aircraft incorporated the drooped leading edge outer wing with vortex generators, the longitudinal auto–Mach trimmer, the pitch damper and revised airbrake configuration. These modifications have successfully overcome the unacceptable flying characteristics exhibited by the second prototype in the preliminary assessment carried out by this Establishment, and when all stability aids are functioning, the Vulcan has safe and adequate flying qualities for its primary role as a medium bomber.

A close-up view of XA903's Olympus engine test bed installation. Note also the open brake chute housing which was re-located to the top of the tail ECM housing on Vulcan B.2s. (Rolls-Royce)

CHAPTER FIVE

The Victor

Handley Page's submission to Specification B.35/46 originated in 1945, when Sir Frederick Handley Page turned his attention to possible future requirements after learning that English Electric had been contracted to build a twin-engined jet bomber (which became the Canberra) to replace the Mosquito. He concluded that a similar requirement would be needed to replace the Avro Lincoln within the next five or six years. On 14 June he issued a confidential memorandum to his design team (Stafford, Radcliffe and Lee), requesting that they investigate the possibility of manufacturing two types of bomber. One would be of 100,000 lb all-up weight and powered by four Rolls-Royce AJ.65-size turbojet engines, and the other would be a 60,000 lb aircraft with two AJ.65 (Avon) engines. He indicated that both designs should have wings swept back 40°, based on the company's earlier experience with the H.P.75 Manx, a small tailless monoplane which first flew in 1943.

The Manx, so named because Manx cats do not have tails, was the result of research led by Dr Gustav Victor Lachmann, a former German air force pilot who had been chief designer of the Schneider and Albatros companies before joining Handley Page in 1929. Although Lachmann was a talented designer, his preoccupation with aviation probably led to his failure to seek naturalization, and when the Second World War began he was still a German national, and was therefore interned on the Isle of Man. However, his skills were still recognized, and in 1943 permission was given for communication with his deputy in Handley Page's Research Department, Godfrey Lee.

Their energies were initially devoted to the design of the H.P.75 Manx, to explore the properties of tailless aircraft and swept wings. The Manx flew just 18 hr before being grounded, owing to severe vibration which was literally shaking it apart. The design was a success though, encouraging the Handley Page team to look at more ambitious designs, and by 1943 they had already examined a 70-ton tailless bomber concept. When Sir Frederick issued his memorandum in 1945, Godfrey Lee, who was responsible for future projects, arranged to visit Germany as part of an Allied technical intelligence mission. While in Germany he spent a great deal of time talking to engineers and aerodynamicists at the Volkenröde experimental establishment near Brunswick. The German designers had gained a considerable amount of technical knowledge in the field of swept-wing design, and Lee learned a great deal during his visit.

When he returned to England, Lee

was taken ill with pneumonia and was forced to go into hospital. During a long period of convalescence he drew upon his new-found design knowledge to produce a preliminary design for a 50-seat, 50-ton transatlantic airliner, given the company designation H.P.72, which would have near-sonic-speed capability. Lee later commented that the airliner was a rather clumsy design which would not have been a practical proposition, but at the time there was little technical information on which to base any new design of this nature. The H.P.72 designation lived on as a convenient 'cover' for Lee's confidential investigations, based on Sir Frederick's memorandum, which led to a 90,000 lb bomber with an alternative transport role, powered by four Avon engines. The H.P.72A featured 45° swept wings with wingtip-mounted rudders, a small swept fin and rudder, and a swept tailplane.

During 1946 the bomber design was developed into a formal proposal, and a brochure was sent to Stuart Scott-Hall, the Principal Director of Technical Development. Designated H.P.80, the aircraft would carry a 10,000 lb bomb load at 520 kt over a still-air range of 5,000 miles. The Avon engines were expected to be too large for the aircraft, and smaller 5,600-lb thrust powerplants were suggested. The concept was proposed to the RAF's Director of Operational Requirements, Gp Capt Silyn-Roberts, who visited the company's Cricklewood headquarters on 19 July to discuss the matter further, in view of the Air Staff's emerging long-range bomber requirement.

Although there is little evidence to suggest that Handley Page's proposal influenced the Air Staff's thinking before Specification B.35/46 was issued, there is no doubt that Sir Frederick's foresight enabled the company to co-operate with the Air Staff in some detail during 1946.

During November a team of MoS research staff visited Cricklewood to discuss the new H2S Mk.9 radar being developed as the basis for a new NBS, with twice the accuracy at twice the speed and height of the rudimentary H2S radar used in the Second World War. The system's scanner would be 6 ft long and would rotate on a horizontal axis within a radome located under the new bomber's crew cabin. Like the 10,000 lb bomb which dictated the size of the bomb bay, the radar system would also influence the design of the aircraft quite significantly. Other early changes to the H.P.80 design included the addition of a visual bomb-aiming station, added as a precaution against any delay in the development of the NBS, and a jettisonable crew cabin.

The early design of the H.P.80 included a crew station for an ECM operator, situated within a pressurized cabin in the aircraft's tail section and accessible from the main cabin by means of a tunnel (in much the same way as Convair's B-36 incorporated a tail-gunner position). As the design progressed it became clear that this was not a practical proposition, chiefly because the atomic bomb proposed at that time would be up to 6 ft in diameter and 30 ft long, which meant that a crew access tunnel simply would not have fitted in the bomb bay. Additionally, a tunnel would also require complicated connections to the jettisonable main cabin, so the design was revised to incorporate remote operation of the 18 in ECM 'Red Steer' scanner from the main cabin. Like Vickers and Avro, Handley Page encountered many problems with the concept of a jettisonable cabin, and the original design was progressively modified by reducing the size of the cabin and removing armour plating.

In 1946 little information was available on the possible effects of ejecting from an aircraft at 50,000 ft. It therefore seemed logical that the best means of escape would be for the crew to remain attached to special seats, capable of withstanding an impact of up to 25g, inside their pressurised compartment. The nose section would be released from the main airframe, and fins would extend to give the capsule good descent stability. After deploying a brake parachute, the crew would be protected from impact by the absorption of energy by the collapsing nose and radome. Although Vickers and Avro quickly accepted that the idea was too advanced for the timescale and finances available, Handley Page pursued the concept for some time. A quarter-scale model of the nose was attached to a glider for flight trials, but it was destroyed during the first test because the electric cable which would deploy the parachute and fins had been mistakenly shortened, causing it to break and leave the nose without any means of opening the parachute. Further tests were to have been conducted with a Lincoln, but a combination of Ministry disillusionment and pressure from Avro effectively killed off the idea. Interestingly, the design progressed sufficiently to be partly incorporated into production Victors, which had their nose sections attached to the fuselage by four large bolts, where the explosive releases would have been fitted.

The basic design of the H.P.80 was thus largely established before Specification B.35/46 was issued. Handley Page had considered the delta-wing concept adopted by Avro, but the design team believed that the anticipated stability problems associated with it would make a delta layout unworkable. With hindsight it can be seen that the delta wing was a near-perfect solution to the Ministry's requirements, and that the gloomy instability predictions were unfounded, but, with relatively little data from which to work, Handley Page opted for a viable alternative. Godfrey Lee explained some of his thinking behind the H.P.80 design during 1954:

No layout or design formula is the best for all specifications. What is right in one case is not necessarily so in another. The Victor specification called for long range with an appreciable load, a high cruising Mach number and a high cruising altitude. It appeared from this that the required characteristics were: a moderate or fairly large aspect ratio in order to get long range and high cruising altitude; a high sweepback to permit a reasonable thickness/chord ratio on the wing and yet to enable the specified high critical Mach number to be obtained.

To combine these desiderata, however, is unfortunately inimical to good stalling behaviour because such a wing is liable to tip stall. 'Tip stall' means that when a wing is brought to a high incidence the stall begins at or near the tips. This is bad on a swept wing since loss of lift on the rearwardly-disposed tips leads to a nose-up pitching moment or a self-stalling tendency and the usual wing-dropping danger with a tip stall . . .

The crescent wing is a working compromise between the requirements for performance and for good tip stalling. Otherwise, the choice is between high sweep and low aspect ratio, or moderate aspect ratio with moderate or small sweep and correspondingly thin wings. In the crescent wing, the aspect ratio is as large as necessary for performance and high sweep is obtained over the centre wing, permitting a good thickness/chord ratio which is important structurally and for stowage reasons. By reducing the tip sweep, the tip stall problem is eased and the design penalty, a thin outer wing, is not too severe. It was for these reasons that we started work on a wing whose sweep varied with span . . .

Typical of early wind tunnel evidence in favour of the crescent wing were tests on an ordinary straight wing of 45° leading-edge sweepback, and a crescent wing with leading-edge sweeps of 50° at the root, 40° at the middle section and 30° at the tip. The tests showed the superiority of the crescent layout over the straight wing in that the stability near the stall was always better in the crescent case. Another point was that, as well as better tip stalling properties, the crescent wing actually had a higher root sweep than the straight wing.

Despite the reduced sweep at the tips, the highly swept root does not want to stall; so there remains, even for the crescent wing, a tip stall tendency. This can be brought within reasonable bounds by the careful choice of wing section, particularly camber. The wing-fuselage junction may in some cases be arranged so that it tends to promote a stall at the root. Aerodynamically, there is nothing very special about the stability and control of the crescent wing for flight cases where the flow is unseparated, i.e. not near the stall. It acts very much like a straight swept wing having about the same average sweep. It is important, however, that the tip sweep is not reduced too much as otherwise there may be a loss or even a reversal of aileron control at high Mach number. On the other hand, a loss of tip sweep is beneficial for aileron power at low Mach number and especially near the stall.

Sweepback has a profound effect on the dynamic stability of an aircraft; that is to say, the manoeuvre margin is largely influenced by sweep when, as is always the case in practice, the wing is flexible . . . Here again the crescent wing offers a useful compromise solution. Just as aerodynamically at the stall the crescent formula permits the use of a root with more sweep than would otherwise be possible, so it does the same aeroelastically. The reduced outer sweep is beneficial in itself and the crescent planform leads to a favourable twist over the centre wing . . .

The best way to review the performance characteristics of the crescent wing is to consider the possible solutions to the Victor specification described earlier. It calls for a long-range aircraft carrying a good load, having a high critical Mach number and a high cruising altitude. There are, currently, three different solutions to this problem: the high-aspect-ratio layout with engines usually installed in external pods, favoured by the Americans and especially by the Boeing Company; the delta layout and the crescent planform.

Assuming that the critical Mach number is equal in all cases considered, the value of the lift/drag ratio that can be obtained follows from the way in which the remaining problems are solved . . . With regard to tip stall, the engine nacelles help the podded layout because, apparently, they direct the air in a direction more or less parallel to the chord. They reduce the local angle of incidence near the tip at high angles of attack and the engine supports act partly as 'fences'. In a typical podded layout the outer nacelles are quite near the tip. The delta layout gets over its stall problems by using its lower aspect ratio. The stalling behaviour of the crescent wing has already been discussed.

. . . It may be concluded that, approximately, the total drag of the delta is some 10 per cent higher than for the other two layouts . . . No proper weight estimate can be made, but it is possible to consider weight trends. The podded wing has small thickness and torque box area but has very good weight relief due to the engine disposition, small wing area, and unbroken structure. The delta wing has large thickness and torque box area but small engine weight relief and much the largest gross area and a high rib weight; from this it would be expected that the delta wing weight would be highest. The crescent wing has moderate thickness, moderate torque box area and moderate wing surface area combined with small weight relief. The fuselage weight for the podded aircraft is probably largest because the undercarriage has to be stowed in it. The delta fuselage weight is probably the lightest because it is a small one. The weight of the delta tail should be the lightest since there is no tailplane.

Combining all the above tendencies, it may be concluded that none of the layouts appears to have a marked advantage. The crescent wing and the podded aeroplane have a fairly similar weight distribution; the delta weight distribution is different and what it loses on the wing it gains on the fuselage and the tail. A 10 per cent improvement in lift/drag ratio (as produced by the crescent wing) does not perhaps at first seem very much. But at long ranges where the useful load may be quite small — only 5 or 10 per cent of the all-up weight — and fuel is about half the all-up weight, then 10 per cent off the fuel weight adds 50 or 100 per cent more to the load that can be carried. Thus, for a long-range aeroplane, an extra 10 per cent on lift/drag ratio is undoubtedly well worth while.

Having thus briefly reviewed the whole matter, it is perhaps possible to attempt a short summing-up of the main points under consideration . . . The range/load performance of the crescent and the podded layouts seems to be about equal; that of both is better than the delta. The operational heights of the crescent and the delta are both better than that of the podded layout, which suffers from its high wing loading. This will reduce cruising altitude and will badly restrict manoeuvrability at altitude. The take-off and landing performance of the crescent and delta is satisfactory in both cases and is much better than the podded layout which suffers from high wing loading.

The manoeuvrability at height and at high equivalent airspeed is satisfactory for both the crescent and the delta. Both these aircraft are better than the podded aeroplane in this respect; it suffers from its high wing loading and the rather bad aeroelastic properties with regard to manoeuvre margin. The crescent wing layout thus provides an efficient and manoeuvrable aeroplane capable of satisfying an exacting specification. It is not the only way of meeting these requirements; but there are good grounds for believing it to be the best answer to the specification in question.

Although Lee's comments suggest that the crescent wing was a 'compromise', it was in fact a revolutionary concept in 1946, and Handley Page was no less certain about its design than Avro (which had opted for the delta wing), Vickers (which believed that both the Avro and Handley Page designs were too ambitious), or the ABPG at Farnborough, who would ultimately be unable (or unwilling) to choose between the Avro Type 698 and the Handley Page H.P.80.

The crescent wing was clearly a better proposition than a conventionally-swept wing with podded engines, as Lee pointed out. Boeing's B-47 and B-52 lacked manoeuvrability and relied on incredibly long runways which the RAF could not have provided. The delta wing contrasted sharply with Handley Page's design in having a low aspect ratio (i.e. the ratio of wing span to chord), which was offset by a very large wing area. A typical swept wing is likely to stall first at the tips, leading to an unstable pitching problem because the wingtips are well aft of the c.g., but the crescent wing's greater sweep towards the wing root meant that the inner wing was more likely to stall first, creating a more stable situation. Likewise, the wingtips of a swept wing with a straight leading edge are well aft of the wing root, so the outer wing's lift causes the wing to twist, leading to control or structural problems. The crescent design effectively brought the outer wing's lift further forward and dampened the twisting tendency.

The resulting wing design also required a thin outer wing section and a relatively thick inner wing section, which enabled Handley Page to bury the engines and undercarriage in the wing root. The engine air intakes in the leading edge of the highly-swept inboard part of the wing created a significant loss of standing thrust on take-off (air flow concentrates at the outer corner of the intake), which was not regained until the aircraft gained sufficient forward momentum, but in 1946 Handley Page had no way of knowing this, and, as Lee later said: 'Perhaps we were the only firm brave enough or daft enough to do it'.

As Lee described, the crescent wing appeared to be the best all-round solution at the time. The Avro design would not be able to achieve the same altitude, but with bigger engines the shortfall would be overcome, and the H.P.80's greater bomb load had to be matched against the Avro Type 698's much greater manoeuvrability. Lee was right in saying

that there was no perfect solution to Specification B.35/46. He was also keen to emphasize that the crescent wing design was not a direct result of his trip to Germany. Although Arado's chief aerodynamicist created a very similar design for the Arado Ar 234 bomber, Lee knew nothing of this. As he later commented: 'The one real concept we got out of the German visit was that sweep was a good thing'. The wing design was created entirely by Handley Page, and nobody is able to recall who originated the idea. Bearing in mind the company's 1912 H.P.5 'Yellow Peril' monoplane, which featured swept-back wings, the Handley Page design staff suggested that Sir Frederick might at least have guided them in the general direction.

The members of the ABPG at Farnborough were unable to decide between the Avro and Handley Page designs, stating: 'Because of the present uncertainty in basic information, we cannot put all our eggs into one basket. Several designs must be chosen to spread the risk.' Handley Page received an ITP on 1 January 1948, and design work intensified. Almost immediately the wingtip fins were abandoned, chiefly because Sir Frederick believed that asymmetric shock waves on the fins might cause the aircraft to yaw. While Godfrey Lee disagreed, his design staff of 20 was already consumed by other problems, and the substitution of a conventional tail avoided at least one potential problem. The addition of a tailplane was based on the RAE's advice, and its initial low position was later changed to a fin-top location to keep it clear of jet engine efflux and the wing's slipstream. The planned all-moving tailplane was modified to a fixed section with a pair of large elevators, eliminating the need for the ailerons to act in unison for pitch control. As many commentators have pointed out, the huge tailplane was just 11 in shorter than the wingspan of a Hawker Hunter.

To explore the characteristics of the design still further, Handley Page, like Avro, decided to construct flying scale models of the H.P.80. A one-third-scale radio-controlled glider was constructed (designated H.P.87), but on the first flight it dived into the ground and was written off. Subsequently, Specification E.6/48 was issued to cover the construction of a powered and piloted scale model, the H.P.88. As the aim of the exercise was to explore the properties of the crescent wing, and, to a lesser extent, the tail unit, there was little point in devoting resources to a totally new design, so Handley Page opted to attach the crescent wings to a Supermarine Attacker fuselage, with a scaled-down tail that was 0.4 full size. Because the drawing office at Cricklewood was already over-stretched, Handley Page subcontracted the design of the H.P.88 to General Aircraft Ltd at Feltham, which gave the aircraft its own company designation GAL.63. Further

design work led to the substitution of the Supermarine Type 510's fuselage, which had already been redesigned to mount a 45° swept wing, and Supermarine bestowed yet another designation, Type 521, on the aircraft. As if this was not confusing enough, General Aircraft was then taken over by Blackburn, which redesignated the aircraft Y.B.2.

Like the Avro 707s, the H.P.88 proved to be almost a pointless exercise, as the main H.P.80 programme maintained its own momentum and progressed independently of the smaller research vehicle. Essentially based on an Attacker fuselage with the wing roots, fuel system, and instrument layout of the Swift, the aircraft represented the company's 1949 crescent wing design. When the H.P.80's wing was later modified to increase the aircraft's critical Mach number, by moving the outer 'kink' further inboard and revising the shape of the wing root, the H.P.88 remained unmodified, and also retained an all-moving tailplane and elevons. Consequently, it bore little resemblance to the full-size bomber. The

Handley Page H.P.88 VX330 pictured at Carnaby during early flight trials. (British Aerospace)

large fuselage airbrakes were also completely unrepresentative of the H.P.80, and when they were extended the resulting airflow disturbance around the tail rendered any aerodynamic analysis useless.

After completion at Brough, the sole H.P.88, VX330, underwent a series of taxying trials before being partly dismantled for transportation to Carnaby airfield, where the huge wartime runway was still intact. With Blackburn chief test pilot G. R. I. Parker at the controls, VX330 flew a short five-minute circuit around Carnaby on 21 June 1951. It was then immediately grounded for a series of small adjustments to be made, and the second test flight took place on 7 July. After this flight, Parker reported that the aircraft was oversensitive in the pitching plane, and that even a small 'bump' would send it into a low-amplitude porpoising movement which had to be damped out by holding the control column in a fixed position. Two more flights confirmed that the problem became serious at 230 kt, and on the fifth sortie the H.P.88 was taken to 225 kt, at which speed it became difficult to control, and progressively worse as the speed increased.

To rectify this problem a strip of light alloy angle bracket was fixed to the upper surface of the tailplane leading edge, and this stabilized the aircraft up to 270 kt. By lengthening the strip and adding another to the undersurface the aircraft could comfortably fly at 450 kt, at which speed any disturbance would cause the aircraft to pitch for two cycles before being damped out by steady back pressure on the control column. With the handling difficulties resolved, Handley Page's Duggie Broomfield flew VX330 and confirmed the findings. He scheduled the aircraft for its 27th flight, which would be to Stansted, from where a series of airspeed calibration flights would be made before it made an appearance at the 1951 SBAC show.

On 26 August the first of these flights was begun, some 14 min being spent on the first tests. Broomfield then brought the H.P.88 back to Stansted and made a straight run-in over the airfield at 300 ft. Witnesses saw the aircraft enter a series of pitching oscillations, after which it

The Handley Page H.P.88, illustrating its Supermarine Attacker ancestry. (British Aerospace)

suddenly broke up over the centre of the airfield, disintegrating before Broomfield had time to eject. Subsequent investigation revealed that he had selected the airbrake emergency lever, and that the aircraft had started pitching at 475 kt, with peak accelerations at 7g and –5g. The problems had become worse as the aircraft continued to accelerate to 525 kt, at which stage the peaks reached 12g and –5g, although these were the recorder limits and the actual peaks could have been even higher. The H.P.88 programme lasted just 36 days and logged a total flight time of just 14 hr. The Handley Page team accepted that the H.P.88 had already given them some good information on how the crescent wing would handle, and that there was little point in manufacturing another test vehicle when the H.P.80 was already well advanced.

As mentioned previously, the H.P.80 slowly developed into a revised design which differed markedly from the H.P.88. Following wind tunnel tests at Farnborough, the wing configuration was revised when it was discovered that the aircraft's critical Mach number (the speed at which drag increases rapidly) was around Mach 0.8 instead of the predicted 0.875. The outer wing chord was increased by 20 per cent, and the outer 'kink' was moved inboard. Leading-edge 'nose flaps' were introduced to solve the tip-stalling problems, and the tailplane was given dihedral to provide an effective increase in fin area. On 28 April 1948 the MoS awarded Handley Page a contract to build two H.P.80 prototypes, each powered by four Metropolitan-Vickers F.9 engines (later to become the Armstrong Siddeley Sapphire). Construction began at Cricklewood and in the new experimental shop at Park Street early in 1951. The first prototype was to be a 'flying shell' aerodynamic test vehicle, and the second prototype a fully-equipped version.

In June 1952 production orders were placed for 25 Avro 698s and 25 H.P.80s. Like much of the design work, the construction of the aircraft required new techniques and new materials. For more than three years Handley Page examined the possibility of using honeycomb sandwich construction comprising two stress-bearing skins separated by a honeycomb material such as Dufaylite and held together by adhesive. American manufacturers were already experimenting with this technique, and Handley Page even went so far as to plan a honeycomb-winged Miles Messenger test airframe, under the designation H.P.93. However, further research revealed that the adhesive (Araldite) lost some of its strength under high humidity, and the structures team abandoned the idea.

The idea of sandwich construction survived, however, and Handley Page opted for the extensive use of alloy sheets spot-welded to a light alloy corrugated core. This saved a great deal of weight because no stringers were needed, and the sandwich could be easily riveted or bolted to wing ribs or fuselage frames. The process required more than 500,000 individual spot welds for each aircraft, and each one was X-rayed until stringent quality control had been assured. The fuselage was manufactured in three main sections; the front, centre and rear, and tail. The central wing spar box was well forward of the aircraft's c.g., which meant that the bomb bay only had to carry the weight of bombs or other loads attached to four girders anchored to heavy box frames. The two bomb doors retracted inwards, and the huge bomb bay was 5 ft longer than the Avro 698's.

More importantly, the H.P.80's bomb bay had almost twice the capacity of that in the Avro design. While the Boeing B-52, at twice the all-up weight of the H.P.80, could carry a 34,000 lb bomb load, the H.P.80 could carry no fewer than 48 1,000 lb bombs. Construction of the H.P.80 was broken down into a relatively large number of fairly small components, as opposed to Avro's approach of building a smaller quantity of larger pieces. This enabled construction to be divided between the Cricklewood factory and those at Radlett (Colney Street and Park Street), all components being easily transportable by road. Final assembly took place at Radlett, and it was from this airfield that Handley Page anticipated making the prototype's first flight.

Unfortunately for the company, the MoS decided that the bomber should be afforded the safety of a 10,000 ft runway, which meant that the H.P.80 had to be dismantled and conveyed by road to Boscombe Down. The Handley Page team were convinced that a decision between the Avro Type 698 and H.P.80 would soon be made, so every effort was made to beat Avro into the air. The aircraft had to be moved in secrecy, the most difficult aspect being the transporting of the main fuselage over 90 miles of busy roads. It was decided to carry the structure on a London bus axle, suitably reinforced, towed behind a tractor. Seven trips were made to survey the route, and the measurement of the widths of roundabouts on London's North Circular Road nearly caused several casualties. Scale drawings of critical points on the route were made, and a model of the fuselage and tractor assembly was used to determine the best lines of approach for each obstacle.

Two T-junctions proved impossible to negotiate, and local authorities were called in with bulldozers to clear suitable paths. At one point on the A30 a new track was cut through a corner, and at another junction a triangular section of field was flattened. An eighth journey was then made as a dress rehearsal, using a large wooden mock-up on a Queen Mary trailer. Finally came the ninth trip, the real thing. To disguise the true nature of the secret cargo, the H.P.80's fuselage was surrounded by a wooden structure and covered with white sheets, upon which the impressive pseudonym

The good ship Geleypandhy *en route to Boscombe Down (actually, the Victor prototype main fuselage, suitably disguised).* (Handley Page)

'Geleypandhy' was applied, together with the false destination 'Southampton'. The latter name, which was also given to an interwar Supermarine flying boat, was an amusing choice, but quite why the signwriter misspelled the anagram of 'Handley Page' remains a mystery. Nonetheless, the disguise worked, and most onlookers assumed that the cargo was nothing more than a new boat, rather than a top-secret nuclear bomber.

Steel plates and wooden ramps were used where the load had to cross pavements, and traffic was held up whenever necessary. The convoy made an overnight stop at the beginning of the Great West Road, and shortly after dawn the procession resumed. All went well until the temporary cutting near Andover was reached. The bulldozer used to clear the way had been left blocking the route, no amount of coaxing would start it, and the driver had disappeared. After a great deal of spadework the trailer eased through with inches to spare, just as the bulldozer driver turned up. At 10:30 on 25 May the convoy arrived at Boscombe Down, having completed a road journey lasting some 6 hr. Handley Page pointed out that the H.P.80 could complete the return journey by air in as many minutes.

Work quickly began on reassembly of the aircraft at Boscombe Down, but after completion it was found that the c.g. was well outside the aft limit owing to the absence of the nose-mounted radar assembly. Consequently, time was devoted to another problem which frustrated the pre-Farnborough effort still further. Half a ton of scrap iron plates were bolted under the flight deck pressure floor to provide suitable ballast. Interestingly, the second prototype also carried similar iron plate ballast because the aircraft was already well advanced in construction and it was too late to incorporate the long-term 'fix' of a 42 in fuselage stretch.

Having dealt with this annoying difficulty, the team then encountered another more serious delay which ended in tragedy. The hydraulic system in the rear fuselage was being tested when a fire broke out, covering three fitters with burning hydraulic fluid. One of them, Eddie Eyles, died in hospital 16 days later. As if this was not enough to discourage the team, further problems were

The second Victor prototype wearing a sinister black, silver and red colour scheme, at Radlett. (Handley Page)

encountered with the powered flying controls, requiring a further six weeks of work. By this time the Vulcan had made its first flight and the SBAC show was under way, so the incentive to get the first prototype into the air had gone.

Just a week before Christmas 1950, Handley Page chief test pilot Sqn Ldr Hedley George Hazelden taxied the prototype H.P.80, WB771, for the first time, making the short trip from the hangar to the compass-swinging base. Two days later he began a series of fast taxying runs along Boscombe's main runway, but no 'hops' were attempted because of heavy rain and poor visibility. Hazelden had already spent a considerable amount of time learning to handle the Sapphire engines in the outboard nacelles of a modified Hastings transport, as well as flying a Sapphire-engined Canberra. Having done as much preparation as possible, Hazelden and the H.P.80 waited for good weather.

On Christmas Eve the weather conditions had improved, and at long last the H.P.80 was prepared for its maiden flight. Lee and Joy had remained at Cricklewood, awaiting news of the H.P.80's progress, and when they heard that the first flight was imminent they sped off to Boscombe Down by car, fearing that they might arrive too late to see their creation take to the air. They arrived with a few minutes to spare, and after clearing security they quickly made their way to the control tower. Hazelden described the first flight as follows:

The Victor was on the apron and, in company with Mr I. K. Bennett my flight observer, I climbed aboard. This was it, the thing we had waited for! Cockpit checks were completed, engines were started and I taxied to the runway. Conditions were perfect with a light breeze straight down the runway, bright sunshine through a few woolly cumulus clouds and visibility up to 20 miles in the crisp December air.

I locked my radio on to transmit so that all we said could be heard on the ground. In a matter of seconds we would know if the Victor would fly. I opened the engines to fairly low power and released the brakes. The aircraft rolled up the runway, rapidly gaining speed. I pulled the control column back and the nosewheel left the ground. So far, so good. I held the Victor like that for a few seconds; the rumbling of the wheels ceased and I knew we were off. I kept close to the runway, still gaining speed, for a few more vital seconds, and then I knew it was all right. An imperceptible movement of the control column, and the ground started to fall away as we climbed.

Smoothly, effortlessly, the Victor had slid into its natural element. By doing so it had become an aeroplane instead of just the expression in metal of so many drawings and hieroglyphics on paper. Whatever happened now we all knew it could fly. After a few minutes in the air my thoughts turned to landing. I had got the Victor up there; now, could I get it back again? I tried reducing speed to see how it would behave at a suitable speed for the approach. Once more it was all right and, coming in on a long, straight approach, I headed for the runway. Lower and lower we came until the beginning of the runway was only a few feet below the wheels. I throttled right back, and in a few seconds the wheels started rumbling again and we were down. The Victor had come back to earth as smoothly as it had left. We had had a comfortable flight together with no anxieties.

Weighing less than 95,000 lb, WB771 was

smartly airborne in less than 1,500 ft, ironically just a quarter of the available runway at Radlett. The first flight lasted just 17 min, during which Hazelden flew a complete circuit and approach to check the aircraft's ground-effect handling (which was likely to be markedly different to that of other aircraft owing to its high tail and swept wings), followed by an overshoot. After landing he said: 'It was all so effortless . . . it is difficult to see why we were so apprehensive'. With typical understatement, he did not mention the very audible sigh of relief which was heard in the control tower when WB771 touched down.

Initial handling trials continued at Boscombe Down while Radlett's runway was extended northwards, ready to accommodate production aircraft. The name Victor was adopted for the H.P.80 on 2 January 1953, after the Air Council had discussed possible names during no fewer than 14 meetings. Although this was in keeping with the 'V-Bomber' policy, the name was greatly appreciated by Gustav Victor Lachmann for another reason.

Testing progressed smoothly, although on WB771's fourth flight an accident occurred when all 16 tyres on the main gears burst on landing because of a malfunctioning brake and gear retraction mechanism. One test flight included a flying visit to Radlett, where Hazelden put WB771 through its paces for the assembled Handley Page workers who had built her. On 25 February the prototype Victor returned to Radlett on a more permanent basis, landing on the extended 6,910 ft runway for the first time. More test flights followed, with only one notable difficulty when one of the main landing gear units skipped on touchdown, jamming in the vertical position. Hazelden carefully landed WB771 on the bogie's four rear tyres, and rotation dampers were subsequently

fitted to the undercarriage to cure the problem.

Although the Victor prototype was first glimpsed at the Royal Aeronautical Society's Garden Party in June, the aircraft made its first public debut at the 1953 Queen's Coronation Review at Odiham on 15 July, joining the huge flypast over the airfield. On 21 July Chief of the Air Staff (CAS) Air Chief Marshal Sir John Baker was treated to a flight in WB771, and although he was reportedly concerned by the poor visibility from the pilot's position, he was much impressed by the new bomber. He was particularly interested in Hazelden's demonstration of the Victor's self-landing capability, which enabled WB771 to be landed 'hands-off'. The high tail was not greatly influenced by ground effect, which would normally create a nose-down pitching moment just before touchdown, and provided the Victor was set up on a gentle approach path the swept wings would create a smooth nose-up lift just before touchdown, after which runway reaction brought the nose down on to the runway. Although Handley Page believed that this extraordinary ability might be of some significance, Boscombe Down's test pilots later commentated that it was 'of no particular advantage'. Later, when the Victor's tail was shortened and the wing leading-edge flaps removed, the self-landing qualities largely disappeared.

More VIP flights were included in WB771's busy flight schedule before the aircraft was temporarily grounded for its fuselage to be painted in eyecatching matt black with a red cheat line, while the wings were finished in silver-grey, a scheme devised by Sir Frederick. The Victor was then flown to Farnborough to appear at the 1953 SBAC show, where the prototype's futuristic shape and smart colours captured the public's imagination. Hazelden's first demonstration was made on three engines when an igniter plug failed shortly before take-off.

After Farnborough the flight trials progressed smoothly, and by 15 October Hazelden had flown WB771 to 50,000 ft without encountering any buffet. On the following day he reached Mach 0.83 at 47,000 ft (and was still accelerating), and just a few days later he reached Mach 0.91 at 47,500 ft, at which point he noticed only a slight nose-down trim change. Indeed, Hazelden's only concern was the Victor's tendency to roll to port on take-off. This was due to insufficient aileron movement, which was duly corrected. He also noted a rather annoying noise above Mach 0.75 and 38,000 ft which he described as varying between a flute-like note and the roar of an underground train. The cause was eventually traced to the air conditioning under the cabin floor, and the ramp intakes in the nose were first extended by adding 'nostril' scoops, then blanked off, and finally fitted with small vortex generators, which cured the problem.

During February 1954 the Victor almost broke the sound barrier when test pilot John Allam inadvertently reached Mach 0.98, which led to skin buckling on the tailplane. The aircraft was due for a thorough inspection, so the second prototype's tailplane was fitted to WB771 while the prototype's was stripped and rebuilt for attachment to WB775. It returned to the air on 14 June, a further 24 hr of flying being completed before airspeed calibration flights were begun at Cranfield, where the College of Aeronautics had better facilities for ground speed measurement.

Hazelden performed the first flights, but as he was scheduled to make a presentation at Woodley on 14 July he assigned that day's flight to his deputy, Ronald Ecclestone, a former RAE test pilot. The aircraft duly arrived over Cranfield, and the first calibration runs took place without incident. However, as the next run over Cranfield was started, the Victor's tailplane suddenly separated from the fin and, with no longitudinal control, WB771 nose-dived on to Cranfield's runway, instantly disintegrating and exploding in a huge ball of flame. Ecclestone and his crew were killed, onlookers watching in disbelief as

The prototype Victor sweeping over the airfield boundary at Radlett. (Handley Page)

the tailplane fluttered down ahead of the wreckage.

No direct evidence was available to identify the cause of the accident, but the calibration film and witness reports quickly turned attention to the tail unit. Testing and theoretical analysis led to the conclusion, on 3 August, that fatigue cracks around the bolt holes in the fin had allowed the three bolts securing the tailplane to loosen and shear. The 'cure' was relatively simple. The tailplane load was simply spread over four bolts, and corrugated sandwich construction, which was lighter and stronger, would be used on the fins of production aircraft. Despite the tragedy, the second prototype, WB775, was duly flown on 11 September, finished in the same colour scheme as its predecessor. The 57 min first flight (without main undercarriage doors, to save time) was completed to qualify the aircraft for appearance at the 1954 SBAC show that same afternoon. More company flight trials followed before WB775 was delivered to Boscombe Down for a preview assessment by A&AEE test pilots.

Although the aircraft was placed under a speed restriction following the Cranfield accident, the test pilots reported that there were no significant problems apart from a poor field of view for the pilot. Further work at Park Street established that the Victor's corrugated sandwich fin would be safe under all circumstances if it was reduced in height by 15 in, so production tails were suitably shortened and the dorsal fillet and equipment-cooling intake were removed. The second prototype was temporarily grounded in December for special one-piece metal skins to be added to the fin to prevent the 'flexural resonance' which had led to the demise of WB771. Handley Page had no one-piece sheets big enough for the job, so they were provided, ironically, by Vickers, from its Valiant production facilities.

The first 25 production Victors had been ordered during June 1952, and

Victor assembly lines at Radlett. Note Hastings production in the background. (Handley Page)

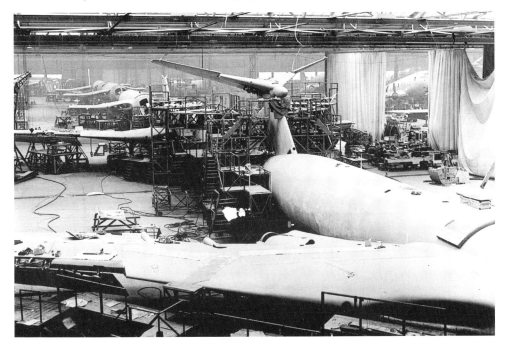

An in-flight view of the Victor prototype, resplendent in her Farnborough show paint scheme. (Handley Page)

a production specification was agreed at Cricklewood on 22 August. The production-standard Victor B.Mk.1 was essentially the same as the prototypes, although the fin was reduced in height, the fuselage was stretched by 42 in and additional windows were incorporated in the cockpit roof. The crew entry door was repositioned to avoid the danger of hitting the engine intake during an emergency bale-out. The tailplane centreline 'acorn' was redesigned, the fin leading-edge intake and fillet were removed, and vortex generators were added to the outer wings.

The first production Victor, XA917, took to the air on 1 February 1956, completing a 15 min test flight in the capable hands of Johnny Allam. Powered by Sapphire Sa7 Mk.202 engines rated at 11,000 lb, XA917 became the largest aircraft in the world to break the sound barrier when, on 1 June 1957, Allam 'inadvertently'

exceeded Mach 1.0 in a shallow dive at 40,000 ft during a test flight from Gaydon. The double sonic bang was heard over a wide area from Banbury to Watford, and flight test observer Paul Langston earned the distinction of becoming the first man to break the sound barrier backwards!

While XA917 was allocated to development trials at Radlett, WB775 performed a series of bombing trials over the Orfordness range with a representative Blue Danube dummy round. After its first flight on 21 March, XA918 began flutter tests, while XA919 was completed as a 'conference airframe' and did not fly until 13 March 1957. When the Colney Street assembly hall extension was opened on 26 March, a further two aircraft, XA920 and XA921, joined the first three for the opening ceremony performed by Minister of Supply Reginald Maudling. Unlike the first four aircraft, which were unpainted, XA921 was finished overall in anti-flash

A pre-production Victor crossing the runway threshold at Radlett, the extended nose flaps particularly evident. (Handley Page)

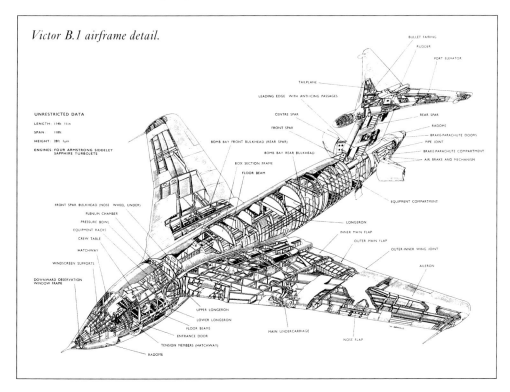

Victor B.1 airframe detail.

gloss white and, following its first flight on 20 June, it was deployed to RAF Marham a month later for static display at the Queen's Review of Bomber Command on 23 July. The flypast for the event included three Victors, three Vulcans, 18 Valiants and an incredible 72 Canberras.

CHAPTER SIX

Bigger Bombs

While the Vulcan and Victor B.1s were entering RAF service, the Valiant was already providing Britain with the means to deliver atomic bombs. Having commenced production of Blue Danube bombs, which were deployed to Wittering, and having test-dropped a live atomic weapon, the government turned its attention towards thermonuclear warfare. Britain was, essentially, a generation behind both the USA and the Soviet Union in terms of nuclear weapon development. Just six weeks after the first British atomic test at Monte Bello, the USA successfully detonated the first two thermonuclear (hydrogen bomb) devices at Eniwetok, the Soviets following with their own test on 12 August 1953. In 1954 Prime Minister Anthony Eden said that the hydrogen bomb had 'fundamentally altered the entire problem of defence', and in February 1955 the government produced a paper which included the following:

In the Statement on Defence 1954, HM Government set out their views on the effect of atomic weapons on UK policy and on the nature of war. Shortly afterwards the US Government released information on the experimental explosion at Eniwetok in November 1952, of a thermonuclear weapon many hundred times more powerful than the atomic bombs which were used at Nagasaki and Hiroshima in 1945. On 1 March 1954 an even more powerful thermonuclear weapon was exploded in the Marshall Islands. There are no technical or scientific limitations on the production of nuclear weapons still more devastating.

The US Government have announced that they are proceeding with full-scale production of thermonuclear weapons. The Soviet Government are clearly following the same policy; though we cannot tell when they will have thermonuclear weapons available for operational use. The United Kingdom has the ability to produce such weapons. After fully considering all the implications of this step the Government have thought it their duty to proceed with their development and production.

The power of these weapons is such that accuracy of aim assumes less importance; thus attacks can be delivered by aircraft flying at great speed and at great heights. This greatly increases the difficulty of defence. Moreover, other means of delivery can be foreseen which will, in time, present even greater problems.

The precise background to Britain's

thermonuclear weapon development remains unclear, but there is no doubt that British scientists returned from the Manhattan project with more than a little generalized knowledge of how such a weapon might be produced. Theoretical work on the hydrogen bomb appears to have begun in 1951, but early results were evidently disappointing, as during 1952 Lord Cherwell, the Prime Minister's chief technical advisor, told Churchill that hydrogen weapons were 'quite beyond our means'. Despite this pessimism, Britain's thermonuclear weapon programme was remarkably successful. The decision to manufacture hydrogen bombs was made by a Cabinet Defence Committee on 16 June 1954, and was discussed by the full Cabinet during the following month. The final Cabinet decision was taken on 26 July, when approval was given to 'the proposal that the current programme for the manufacture of atomic weapons . . . should be so adjusted as to allow for the production of thermonuclear bombs'.

Churchill stated: 'We could not expect to maintain our influence as a world power unless we possessed the most up-to-date nuclear weapons'. Likewise, the Cabinet agreed that thermonuclear bombs would be more economical than their atomic equivalents, and that in moral terms the decision to manufacture these new weapons would be no worse than accepting the protection of America's hydrogen bombs. Towards the end of 1955 the Defence Research Policy Committee (DRPC) commented: 'The earliest possible achievement of a megaton explosion is necessary to demonstrate our ability to make such weapons, as part of the strategic deterrent against war'. In fact, the main reason for the rapid development of hydrogen bombs was not directly due to any perceived deterrent policy; it was simply in response to growing pressure

for an international ban on atmospheric nuclear tests.

Britain maintained an even-handed diplomatic position by backing calls for a test ban while maintaining an active developmental programme. Aubrey Jones, the Minister responsible for the nuclear tests, said:

> In the absence of international agreement on methods of regulating and limiting nuclear test explosions — and Her Majesty's Government will not cease to pursue every opportunity of seeking such an agreement — the tests which are to take place shortly in the Pacific are, in the opinion of the government, essential to the defence of the country and the prevention of global war.

Britain was effectively caught up in a race to develop and detonate a hydrogen bomb before being forced to accept a ban on nuclear testing. The DRPC said: 'It is essential that this first series should be planned in such a way as to safeguard the future by obtaining the greatest possible amount of scientific knowledge and weapon design experience as the foundation of our megaton weapon development programme'. The committee identified four basic requirements; a megaton warhead for a free-falling bomb, a similar megaton warhead for a powered guided bomb (which was to become Blue Steel), a smaller and lighter warhead for a medium-range ballistic missile (which was to become Blue Streak), and a multi-megaton warhead intended to demonstrate that Britain could match the devices which had been tested by America and the Soviets.

Because Britain's scientific knowledge of thermonuclear weaponry was restricted to theoretical analysis, the DRPC report stated that the most certain way of achieving a megaton explosion in 1957 would be to use a large, pure-fission assembly in a Mk.1 case, surrounded by sufficient fissile material to ensure a megaton yield. The device would consequently be 'big, heavy and extravagant in fissile material', but it would work, although it could only be developed into a free-fall bomb. The Government agreed to proceed with a series of test explosions, and on 5 June 1956 the Cabinet agreed that the Prime Minister should make a Parliamentary statement about the tests. Two days later Eden announced to the House of Commons that Britain was to conduct 'a limited number of test explosions in the megaton range'.

Number 49 Squadron at Wittering began training for Operation Grapple (previously referred to as both 'Gazette' and 'Green Bamboo') on 1 September 1956, using standard Valiant B.1s until the first specially modified Grapple aircraft, XD818, arrived during mid-November. The Grapple Valiants featured a number of changes to equip them for their live weapon trials. Most notably they were sprayed with an anti-flash white paint capable of withstanding 72 calories of heat energy per square centimetre. The control surfaces were strengthened to withstand the bomb's pressure wave, the flight deck and bomb-aiming positions were fitted with metal anti-flash screens, and a number of sensors and cameras were installed.

Valiant XD818 departed for Christmas Island on 2 March 1957, via Aldergrove, Goose Bay, Namao, Travis, and Honolulu, as it had not been fitted with underwing fuel tanks at this stage. It was followed by XD822, XD823, and XD824 at one-day intervals. Flown by 49 Squadron's CO, Wg Cdr K. G. Hubbard, XD818 arrived over Christmas Island on 12 March, descending from a 1,500 ft

familiarization circuit to a rather more spectacular 50 ft for an ultra-low-level fly-by over the airfield dispersal area before landing. After a settling-in period the four Valiant crews began a series of training sorties, establishing a precise bomb-aiming capability and bomb-drop manoeuvres which would be used for each trial. The training was completed by 5 April, despite the unexpected torrential rain which made life in Christmas Island's 'tent city' rather unpleasant for some time.

Two aircraft, XD818 and XD823, were prepared for the first live drop, codenamed Short Granite, which was designed to test the Green Granite Small warhead. This was a two-stage device weighing 4,200 lb and contained in a lead bismuth casing with a total weight of 10,000 lb. It was a true thermonuclear 'fusion weapon', the spherical fission primary having a composite U–235 and Pu–239 core with a spherical secondary comprising of U–235 and a U–238 tamper, all packed in lithium deuteride. Valiant XD818, flown by Wg Cdr Hubbard, was to be the drop aircraft for the first test, with XD824 acting as 'grandstand aircraft', flying a second crew to give them 'experience of flash and blast from a thermonuclear weapon'. The historic 2 hr 20 min sortie took place on 15 May 1957, as reported by Hubbard:

> The aircraft became airborne at 09:00 'V' time and all anti-flash screens were in position prior to the aircraft commencing its first run over the target. After one initial run to check telemetry, the Task Force Commander gave clearance for the live run.
>
> The bombing run was made at 45,000 ft true, and as Green Satin drift was fluctuating badly, the set was put to Memory on average drift. The bombing run was steady on a course of

A Vulcan captain's view of a Handley Page Victor K2, with the centreline HDU basket trailed. Smaller, fighter-type aircraft normally refuelled from the wing HDUs which delivered fuel at a slower rate, but enabled two aircraft to hook-up simultaneously. (Mike Jenvey)

V-Bombers in colour

The receiver's view of the Victor K2 tanker, showing to advantage the positioning of the wing-mounted refuelling pods, the aerodynamic bodies and underwing fuel tanks. (Mike Jenvey)

Left: *Four Victors on No. 55 Squadron's dispersal at Marham, just a few days before the aircraft was finally withdrawn from RAF service. The same dispersal previously housed Valiants and B-29 Washingtons, and is now occupied by reconnaissance Canberras.* (Tim Laming)

Below: *No. 543 Squadron Victor SR2 pictured during a stopover at RAF Luqa, after completing a reconnaissance mission over the Mediterranean.* (Richard Caruana)

Below: *A dramatic farewell formation of three Victors, high over Norfolk. The aircraft still carry their Gulf War nose artwork and mission markings.* (Tim Laming)

Vickers Valiant BK.1 – XD816 – at Abingdon in 1968. The nose section of this aircraft is now preserved at the Brooklands Museum in Surrey. (M. J. Hooks)

Valiant XD857 makes an air display appearance at North Weald in 1964. (M. J. Hooks)

Valiant XD826 in silver colour scheme at Wethersfield in 1957. (M. J. Hooks)

All-white Valiant XD862 at North Weald in 1960. (M. J. Hooks)

XH558, the last flying example of the Avro Vulcan. This aircraft was the first Vulcan B2 to be delivered to the RAF and after conversion to B2(MRR) reconnaissance standard, and was later modified to K2 tanker configuration. Finally, it was re-converted to B2 standard for air show appearances around the UK. (Tim Laming)

Vulcan XH558 low over the Lincolnshire countryside on a farewell flypast just prior to retirement. (Tim Laming)

Vulcan XH561 pictured at Luqa during 1975 when assigned to the Scampton Wing. The aircraft was later converted to a single-point tanker and was eventually scrapped at Catterick, after serving as a fire training airframe for some time. (Richard Caruana)

The most famous aircraft from the V-bomber fleet, Vulcan XM607, is pictured at Waddington, just a couple of months after completing her historic 'Black Buck' bombing missions over the Falkland Islands. The markings of No. 44 Squadron have already been re-applied to the tail unit. (Mike Jenvey)

Vulcan K2 XH561 at Waddington during 1984. This picture compares with that of XH561, taken ten years previously, illustrating the dramatic change in colour scheme and the installation of the HDU box under the tail unit. (Tim Laming)

XM575 over 'Bomber Country' close to RAF Waddington. This in-flight view shows how the Vulcan's main undercarriage bogie was designed to pivot. (Mike Jenvey)

A close-up view of the air-sampling pod fitted to the Vulcan B2(MRR). The main body of the pod was manufactured from a Hunter drop tank, with the sampling filter attached to the nose section. Before Vulcans were introduced to the role, Victors were occasionally fitted with the same filter units, attached to the underwing fuel tanks. The 'sniffer' units are now assigned to VC10 tankers. (Mike Jenvey)

A nostalgic view of No. 617 Squadron's XL360 on final approach to RAF Luqa, during 1973. This aircraft was later assigned to No. 230 OCU before being retired to the Midland Air Museum, Coventry, where the aircraft was officially named City of Coventry. *(Richard Caruana)*

XM655, illustrating the harsh conditions in which the Vulcan often operated. Vulcan crews regularly deployed to Goose Bay in Canada to take advantage of the local low flying areas, where the mighty V-Bomber could be flown down to almost 'tree-top' level. (David Haller)

The detachment made by No. 44 Squadron to Darwin, Australia during May 1974 for Exercise Sunflower. (David Haller)

203° and the weapon was released at 10:36 'W' time. Immediately after release the aircraft was rolled into the escape manoeuvre which averages a turn of 60° bank, excess 'g' 1.8 to 1.9, airspeed Mach 0.76, rolling out on a heading of 073°. The time taken for this turn was 38 sec and at the time of air burst of the weapon, the slant range between aircraft and burst was 8.65 n/ms.

Neither crew nor aircraft felt any effect of flash, and the air blast reached the aircraft 2.5 min after release; the effect of the blast was to produce a period of 5 sec during which turbulence alike to slight clear air turbulence was experienced. Six minutes after release, all shutters in the aircraft were removed, and after one orbit to see the mushroom cloud effect, the aircraft returned to base and made a normal landing.

Hubbard's professionalism disguises the excitement of the event, although he later commented: 'It really was a sight of such majesty and grotesque beauty that it defies adequate description'. Nick Wilson, an able seaman on board HMS *Warrior*, witnessed the explosion from a distance of 30 miles:

I felt my back warming up and experienced the flash, though I had my hands over my face and dark goggles on. Five seconds after the flash we turned round and faced the flash, but it was still bright so I replaced them. There in the sky was a brightly glowing seething ball of fire. This rapidly increased and became more cloudy. Soon it was looking like a very dark ripe apple with a snow-white sauce being poured over it. On the horizon at sea level a cloud appeared that must have been dust and spray from the island. The whole sight was most beautiful and I was completely filled with emotions.

Impressive though the sight may have been, 'Green Granite Small' was not a perfect success. Yielding 0.3 Megatons from a predicted yield of up to 1.0 Mt, the lithium deuteride only partly ignited, but the test did at least demonstrate the bomb's potential (and an explosive force 100 times that of the Buffalo air drop), and it also provided the opportunity for another airborne test of a live Blue Danube casing. Despite the mixed results, Britain had entered the thermonuclear age.

The next drop, on 31 May, was Grapple 2, or 'Orange Herald', which tested Dr Penney's 'fallback' high-yield fission bomb, which was again contained in a Blue Danube casing. The warhead, which was developed into an operational physics package known as 'Green Grass', was, as in the first drop, detonated by barometric means at 8,000 ft, and yielded 0.72 Mt. Squadron Leader Roberts, captain of the release aircraft, XD822, was the most experienced Grapple pilot, but the 'Orange Herald' flight nearly ended in disaster, as his flight report calmly records:

My crew was detailed to take off at 09:00 'V' on 31 May in Valiant XD822 to drop Orange Herald on the target area south of Malden Island. The forecast weather for the target area was one- to two-eighths of cumulus, and wind velocity 090°/20 kt at 45,000 ft; conditions at base fine. In view of this fuel load was reduced to 5,000 gal in order to give an all-up weight of 99,000 lb immediately after release of the bomb.

The crew reached the aircraft at 07:40 and completed cockpit checks by 08:10. AWRE [Atomic Weapons Research Establishment] had connected the bomb batteries by the time the crew entered the aircraft at 08:40, but then the take-off time was delayed on orders from JOC [joint operations centre]. At 09:00 permission was given to start engines and we were airborne at 09:07. The flight to the RV [radar vector] took 50 min and was uneventful. Good contact on HF and VHF was established and maintained with the appropriate authorities throughout the flight. The first run over the target was navigation-type and the weather was found to be as forecast.

After the first run the remaining black-out shutters were fitted, and we went straight round on the initial run. Shortly after completing this, permission was given to carry on with the live run. The run-up was steady, and the bomb was released at 10:44, heading 202°, IAS [indicated airspeed] 216, IMN [indicated Mach number] 0.75. After a slight pause I initiated a steep turn to port at 60° bank. At this stage the second pilot should have started to call readings on the sensitive accelerometer, but on this occasion he was silent for a few seconds. I looked up and saw that the instrument indicated unity. Experience told me to believe the instrument, so disregarding my senses, I increased the backward pressure on the control column. At that instant the second pilot and I realized that the instrument had failed at the time of release; simultaneously, the aircraft stalled, and the bomb aimer, who was making for his seat, returned to the bomb-aimer's well with some force. After regaining control, the manoeuvre was completed in 43 sec, using the mechanical accelerometer. This instrument might have been referred to earlier had it not been so far from our normal instrument scan.

At 53 sec by the navigator's countdown a bright white flash was seen through chinks in the blackout screens, and the coloured glass in the first pilot's panel was lit up. At 2 min 55 sec after release the blast waves were felt, first a moderate thump, followed a second later by a smaller one. I waited a further two minutes before turning to port to allow the crew to see what had happened. The cloud top at this time appeared to be some 10,000 ft above our flight level, and it is a sight which will not easily be forgotten. The symmetry and the colours were most impressive, especially against the dark blue background provided by the sky at that height; as we watched, the upper stem and mushroom head started to glow with a deep peach colour. We then set course for base and landed at 12:47 'V'.

The third test, codenamed 'Purple Granite', took place on 19 June. This time the air drop involved the 'Green Granite Large' warhead, an enlarged version of the 'Green Granite Small' with a total weight of 6,000 lb, excluding the HE. Surprisingly, it was the least successful of the three drops, yielding just 0.2 Mt after being dropped from XD823. Clearly the tests had been useful, but they were rather disappointing in terms of results. Consequently, the situation was summed up at a Progress Meeting on 16 July, when the development of 'Yellow Sun', the standard megaton weapon for the V-Force, was discussed:

Whilst Grapple had been successful in providing data on the performance of two different types of megaton warhead, it had not provided sufficient data to enable a firm decision to be made regarding the warhead to be chosen for Yellow Sun. On the

XD823 was the first Valiant to be painted in the anti-flash white colour scheme, with most Valiants, Vulcans and Victors eventually receiving a similar finish. (via Richard Caruana)

evidence of the trials, a Green Bamboo type warhead had been chosen by the Air Staff for use in the interim megaton weapon.

Further trials, Grapple X, were scheduled for November 1957, and 49 Squadron was again tasked with the provision of aircraft and crews. This time the bomb–drop 'ground zero' would be just 20 miles from Christmas Island (instead of nearly 400), to avoid the expense and delays involved in setting up a naval task force to monitor the tests. Valiant XD825, captained by Sqn Ldr B. T. Millett, made the fourth drop on 8 November, the weapon being fitted with another 'Green Granite Small' warhead. This time however, the scientists were reportedly surprised at the result when the bomb delivered a yield of 1.8 Mt, the first 'true' megaton explosion. Sapper Arthur Thomas witnessed the test from Christmas Island:

Then it happened, the blast, a

lightning speed of wind and whistle of trees — a bang — it hit us all unexpectedly, lifting us off our feet and depositing us three to four yards away, landing on top of each other in a pile of bodies. We were not told to expect anything of this nature.

The apparent success of this drop explains why just one test was made when the Task Force Grapple Air Plan called for 'the air drop of two thermonuclear weapons with minimum risk to all concerned'. The records of 49 Squadron state: 'The results were entirely satisfactory, precluding the necessity for any further tests in this particular phase of Operation Grapple'. However, the test programme was far from complete, and 'Grapple Y' took place during April 1958. Valiant XD824, captained by Sqn Ldr R. M. Bates, made the next (fifth) drop on 28 April. Evidence suggests that the warhead was a 'Green Granite Large' device, and the resulting explosion delivered the biggest yield of any British

An interesting view of the Valiant's underside after application of anti-flash white paint, for Operation Grapple. Unlike most Vulcans and Victors, the Valiant's national insignia and serials largely remained in full colour, instead of the later 'washed-out' pink/lilac. (via Richard Caruana)

nuclear tests, a tremendous 3.0 Mt, which demonstrated that Dr Penney and his scientists could, if necessary, produce weapons which easily matched the destructive power of either the American or Soviet Union bombs.

Further tests, Grapple Z, took place during the summer of 1958, on a faster timescale, as Britain slowly moved towards an agreement to end nuclear testing. Number 49 Squadron's records state: 'Due to the decision to accelerate the entire dropping programme for political considerations, the intensity of the high-explosive drops in preparation for the nuclear drops has been increased'. These (final) nuclear detonations took place in September, as the squadron's records indicate:

The month of September brought to

fruition all the training for Operation Grapple Z with the dropping of two more nuclear weapons by the squadron. On the 2nd Sqn Ldr G. M. Bailey and crew in Valiant XD822 dropped the first device of the series. This weapon was the first to be dropped by ground-controlled radar. A 'Grandstand' aircraft on this occasion, Valiant XD818, was flown by Flt Lt S. O'Connor and crew. On 11 September Flt Lt S. O'Connor and crew, in Valiant XD827, dropped a second nuclear device. This weapon was released on a visual attack. Sqn Ldr H. A. Caillard and crew in Valiant XD824 flew as 'Grandstand'. Immediately after the second air drop the aircraft were prepared for the return trip to Wittering.

With the Grapple Valiants back at Wittering, 49 Squadron continued training for an anticipated further series of test drops, but by the end of November 1958 Britain had effectively decided to abandon nuclear testing, and the Government later stated that the United Kingdom would no longer carry out further nuclear tests, whether in or above the atmosphere, underwater or under ground. Christmas Island was gradually reduced to a 'minimum holding state', and HQ Task Force Grapple was disbanded on 3 June 1960. With effect from 1 December 1958, 49 Squadron reverted to a standard bomber role and the Grapple Valiants were de-modified and refitted with the standard radar navigational bombing system.

Although the Cabinet decision to manufacture thermonuclear bombs had been taken more than five months previously, Churchill made no reference to this historic date in British history when he said:

The advance of the hydrogen bomb has fundamentally altered the entire problem of defence, and considerations founded even upon the atom bomb have become obsolescent, almost old-fashioned. Immense changes are taking place in military facts and in military thoughts. We have for some time past adopted the principles that safety and even survival must be sought in deterrence rather than defence . . . and this, I believe, is the policy which also guides the United States.

Of course, Operation Grapple demonstrated quite clearly to the USA that Britain was more than capable of producing thermonuclear weapons which were, if anything, more efficient than its own counterparts. It is hardly surprising, therefore, that relations between America and Britain gradually improved after the first nuclear tests (Operation Buffalo) in 1956, and even survived through the days of the McCarthy period. The Atomic Energy Act, effectively a revision of the infamous McMahon Act, was signed in 1954, permitting the transfer of data concerning the external characteristics of nuclear weapons; size, shape, weight, yield, and effects. The USA and Britain agreed to co-operate within the terms of this Act in a bilateral agreement signed on 15 June 1955. However, the real breakthrough came, rather ironically, after the huge transatlantic rift which developed during the Suez Crisis.

Prime Minister Harold Macmillan and Eisenhower met twice in 1957. During their first meeting, in Bermuda during March, agreements were made for the deployment of Thor missiles to the UK which would be under 'dual key' control. Eisenhower commented that this was 'by far the most successful international conference' he had attended since the war. When they met for a second time, in Washington during October, revisions were made to the Atomic Energy Act to allow scientific co-operation among 'Great Britain, the United States and other friendly powers'. It can hardly be a coincidence that the President's enthusiasm for restoring the 'Special Relationship' came in the same year that Britain embarked upon the first Grapple tests, just months after the first operational hydrogen bombs had entered US service. Britain's thermonuclear advances had been remarkable, and the USA identified potential advantages for a new co-operative arrangement with Britain. Another important consideration was the launching of the Soviet Union's Sputnik satellite, which threw into question many assumptions of American technical superiority, and underlined the Soviet's ability to deliver nuclear weapons, to Europe and the United States, by missile. The Suez Crisis had also served to illustrate just how far apart Britain and America were, and possibly served as a catalyst in repairing the Special Relationship.

Finally, in 1958 the Agreement for Co-operation on the Uses of Atomic Energy for Mutual Defence Purposes was signed, enabling both countries to exchange virtually all types of nuclear information. Britain quickly learned a great deal from American expertise in engineering and weapons assembly techniques. Conversely, American officials were 'amazed' at the scientific and technical knowledge which Britain possessed, which in many respects was ahead of the Americans. The intimate and totally reciprocal collaboration continued into the 1960s and beyond, long after America could possibly have hoped to derive any further benefits from the co-operation. A British official illustrated the position in the 1970s when he stated:

The United States has two laboratories and we have one; they spend five times as much as we do on these establishments; they have conducted some 870 tests – how many of which were really necessary, I wouldn't say – and we have conducted 30. That gives, I think, a fair indication of the 'hardware balance', although in the idea end of the business, the relationship is rather more equal.

The first Air Staff Requirement for a thermonuclear bomb, ASR OR.1136, was issued on 6 June 1955. It called for a bomb which was not to exceed 50 inches in diameter (and would be made smaller if possible), was not to exceed 7,000 lb in weight, and would be capable of carriage internally by Valiants, Vulcans, and Victors, to be in service in 1959. When

the Cabinet made their historical decision to proceed with development of hydrogen bombs during June 1954, the meeting agreed that work on the programme should be performed 'as unobtrusively as possible', and that it was 'desirable' that costs be concealed as much as possible. Before them was a memorandum from the Chiefs of Staff which was based on a report by the Working Party on the Operational Use of Atomic Weapons (whose members included Sir William Penney, the Deputy Chiefs of Staff, and scientific advisors). The report concluded that hydrogen bombs would 'go a long way towards overcoming the difficult problems of terminal accuracy' simply by delivering a huge explosive force, and that only a relatively limited number of bombs would be required, beyond which any increase of stocks would not 'confer any corresponding military advantage'.

During a meeting on 6 April 1955 the Chiefs of Staff decided to develop, as a first priority, a thermonuclear bomb with a yield of approximately one megaton, and ASR OR.1136 was accepted by the Ministry of Supply on 28 July, leading to the start of development work on the weapon, called 'Yellow Sun'. During March 1956 members of the Operational Requirements staff visited Farnborough, where drawings and a wooden mock-up of Yellow Sun were prepared. Yellow Sun was 240 inches long, 48 inches in diameter, and had small cruciform stabilizing fins similar to the Second World War 'Grand Slam' design (larger ones would have had to fold out, to enable the weapon to fit into the Valiant's bomb bay). Unusually, however, the bomb had a flat nose which was intended to slow the bomb during free fall to increase the weapon's stability, and to simplify the requirements of the internal barometric detonation device. The warhead weighed approximately 3,500 lb, and the completed weapon had a weight of around 6,500 lb.

While Yellow Sun was being developed, a second weapon, Red Beard, was also produced, primarily as a tactical bomb but also as a replacement for the first-generation Blue Danube, which, as a relatively crude fission device, delivered a low explosive yield of around 20 kilotons despite weighing 10,250 lb. However it was quickly realized that, if the development of these two new weapons proceeded smoothly (and much depended on the outcome of Operation Grapple), the warheads would be ready before the bomb bodies being designed to carry them. Consequently it was suggested that an 'interim weapon' should be manufactured so that the RAF could acquire a thermonuclear capability as soon as possible. Three warheads, Green Granite, Green Bamboo, and Orange Herald, would be available which could be incorporated within a standard Blue Danube bomb casing.

A report prepared by the RAE in April 1957 described progress with the RAF's hydrogen bomb:

> The Yellow Sun weapon to meet Air Staff Requirement OR.1136 will provide the first British bomb having a yield in the megaton range; as such it is the keystone of the offensive deterrent policy. It is intended for carriage in the V-class bombers and will have a diameter of 48 in and a length of approximately 20 ft. The weight will be about 7,000 lb. The weapon is being designed around the Green Bamboo warhead under development at the Atomic Weapons Research Establishment. The means of making a warhead in this range wholly safe in storage and transport has not been finalized, but all schemes of providing in-flight insertion of some part of the fissile material have been abandoned.

Consideration has also been given to the alternative warheads Green Granite and Short Granite, which are being tested at Operation Grapple. Both are fission-fusion-fission types and differ only in that Short Granite is smaller and lighter. Neither warhead requires ENI [External Neutron Initiation]. Nuclear safety is ensured by some form of in-flight insertion.

After referring to other considerations, the report continued:

> Preliminary investigation indicates that if after Grapple Short Granite becomes the preferred warhead, no serious delay should occur, but the Green Granite would require a larger and heavier weapon, so that much of the ballistic and fuzing work already well advanced would have to be repeated, and the in-service date would have to be set back at least nine months.

A second Progress Statement, issued later in 1957, included the following:

> The Operational Requirement [OR.1136 Issue 2] calls for the development of a megaton bomb, the type of warhead to be carried not being specified except that it shall be capable of use in both Yellow Sun and Blue Steel. The original requirement was for incorporation of the Green Bamboo warhead and much of the work done has been on the assumption that this warhead will be used. It has however been evident for some time that as a result of the Grapple trials another warhead might be preferred, and preliminary investigations were made at an early stage into the problems which would arise if one of the Granite type of warheads were chosen. These have been followed by further work, especially in connection

with the possible use of Short Granite. The general position now is that an early decision as to the type of warhead, and information on associated matters such as nuclear safety systems, is essential if development of the weapon is not to be held up.

The revised Operational Requirement stated that Yellow Sun would be carried by the Vulcan and Victor, the earlier requirement for carriage by the Valiant having being cancelled. Despite this decision, however, many of the Yellow Sun trials were conducted by Valiants until Vulcans and Victors could be made available. The report continued:

Yellow Sun is being developed as a fully engineered weapon to meet the requirements of the OR. The provision of an interim megaton weapon only partially meeting these requirements is planned for introduction into service considerably earlier than Yellow Sun.

A paper issued by the MoS in August outlined the indecision which had surrounded the choice of warhead for Yellow Sun:

The object was to give the RAF a megaton capability at the earliest possible moment. It was proposed to base the interim weapon on one of the bombs to be dropped in Operation Grapple and it was stated that the date of introduction to the Service of Yellow Sun would not be affected by the interim missile. The results of Operation Grapple were such that none of the rounds dropped was immediately applicable to the interim weapon, but AWRE were satisfied that the principles had been cleared sufficiently for them to offer various alternative warheads to the Air Staff

for consideration. The Air Staff, largely on the basis of numbers which could be provided, chose a warhead similar in outside shape to Green Bamboo but having a yield of half a megaton . . . known as Green Grass.

The MoS also commented:

Throughout the discussions on this interim megaton weapon the general approach has been that, in the interests of providing a megaton capability to the RAF at the earliest possible moment, the Service is prepared to sacrifice rigorous testing, proofing, and clearance of the weapon and to introduce special maintenance procedures in association with AWRE. Furthermore, the Air Staff were willing for the same reason to discount many of the provisions of OR.1136.

With reference to Yellow Sun, the report said:

A reassessment of the Yellow Sun programme has recently been made primarily to examine the possibility of offering an earlier capability to the RAF in view of the successful progress of the development, but also taking into account the desirability of switching over to the Short Granite type of warhead if and when this is cleared by AWRE. This later type of warhead is very desirable because of the smaller amounts of fissile material needed.

After much deliberation it was agreed that an interim weapon, 'Violet Club', would be brought into service until the first deliveries of a limited-approval version of Yellow Sun could be made. The Deputy Chief of the Air Staff commented:

We are anxious to get megaton weapons into service as soon as we can. We most certainly think it worthwhile to have even as few as five by the time the Yellow Suns come along. At the same time we are anxious to get Yellow Sun as soon as we can because it does not have the serious operational limitations of Violet Club.

On 24 February 1958 the Assistant Chief of the Air Staff wrote to the AOC-in-C Bomber Command as follows:

I am directed to inform you that the first Violet Club which is now being assembled at Wittering is expected to be completed by the end of the month. A total of five of these weapons will be assembled on Bomber Command stations by July of this year, when deliveries of Yellow Sun should commence. Violet Club is still in some degree experimental and it will be subject to a number of serious handling restrictions. The extent of these and their effect on operational readiness are still under discussion with the Ministry of Supply. Until Violet Club has been formally cleared by the Ministry of Supply and it is possible to issue specific instructions on storage, handling, and transport, the weapon is to remain exclusively in the custody and under the control of the Atomic Weapons Research Establishment. It is possible that some such arrangement will continue throughout the life of these weapons as it is intended to replace them with Yellow Sun as early as possible. This will be done as soon as sufficient aircraft are modified to carry Yellow Sun. I am to say that the operational limitations of Violet Club, particularly those affecting readiness, are serious. Nevertheless, it provides a megaton deterrent capability several months

earlier than would otherwise have been possible.

Externally similar to its kiloton predecessor, Violet Club had the same ballistics as Blue Danube and could therefore be used with the same bombing equipment, suitably adjusted for the required burst height. The Bomber Command Armament School's (BCAS) Operations Records state that, on 28 February,

. . . a convoy from AWRE was stuck in a snow-drift at Wansford Hill at 15:00. An officer from this unit was sent to investigate. At 17:00 the vehicle was still unable to be moved. Rations and bedding were sent to the convoy and an officer and a team of airmen were detailed to stand by throughout the night to give help if required. It was not until the following day that vehicles began using the A1. The convoy arrived at the main Guard Room at 12:00. Personnel were sent immediately for a meal. Unloading was commenced at 14:00, when the convoy arrived at BCAS.

This wintry scene marked the arrival of the first Violet Club, and with it the very beginnings of the RAF's thermonuclear capability. By July a total of five bombs had been completed. Bombs 1 to 4 remained at Wittering, where personnel were trained by AWRE staff to install the Green Grass Warhead at the relevant site. Bombs 5, 6, 7, 8, and 11 were despatched to Finningley, and 9, 10, and 12 went to Scampton, production of all 12 weapons being completed by the end of 1958. Violet Club was, as DCAS commented, 'rather delicate', and could only be assembled at the base from where it would be used. Likewise, road transport was limited to relatively short trips from the assembly point to the storage building. Further details of Violet Club's use were contained in a document issued in July:

> In view of the very small number of Violet Clubs being made available to the Service, and the difficulties of clearing the Victor for the carriage of this weapon, it has now been decided to limit its carriage to the Vulcan. Vulcan aircraft modified to carry Yellow Sun are now being returned to service and it is desirable to transfer the warheads from all Violet Clubs to Yellow Suns as soon as possible, and at the same time to redeploy the weapons to Scampton and Finningley.

In November 1958 a further report stated:

Bomber Command wish to get rid of Violet Clubs as soon as possible, but they are anxious to have a number of Yellow Suns in store before they do this. As the obvious time to change over is at the six-monthly inspections, it is suggested that Violet Clubs should start to phase out at the rate of about one a month from April or May, providing the Yellow Suns are not late.

Consequently, by the end of 1958 the RAF possessed a force of 54 Valiants, 10 Victors, and 18 Vulcans, the last including suitably-modified aircraft capable of carrying the 12 megaton-range Violet Clubs. The remaining V-Force aircraft were, of course, equipped to carry kiloton-range Blue Danubes.

UK Nuclear Weapon Tests

Operation	Round	Location	Date	Yield	Height(m)	Type	Casing	Warhead	Aircraft
Hurricane		Monte Belle Islands	03/10/52	25 Kt	-3	Ocean surface burst			
Totem	T1	Emu Field	14/10/53	10 Kt	31	Ms tower mounted			
	T2	Emu Field	26/10/53	8 Kt	31	Ms tower mounted			
Mosiac	G1	Monte Belle Islands	16/05/56	15 Kt	31	A1 tower mounted			
	G2	Monte Belle Islands	19/06/56	60 Kt	31	A1 tower mounted			
Buffalo	One Tree	Maralinga Range	27/09/56	15 Kt	31	A1 tower mounted			
	Marco	Maralinga Range	04/10/56	1.5 Kt	0	Ground	Blue Danube		
	Kite	Maralinga Range	11/10/56	3 Kt	150	Air drop	Blue Danube		WZ366
	Breakaway	Maralinga Range	21/10/56	10 Kt	31	A1 tower mounted			
Grapple	Short Granite	Off Malden Island	15/05/57	0.3 Mt	2200	Air drop	Blue Danube	Green Granite Small	XD818
	Orange Herald	Off Malden Island	31/05/57	0.72 Mt	2400	Air drop	Blue Danube		XD822
	Purple Granite	Off Malden Island	19/06/57	0.2 Mt	2400	Air drop	Blue Danube	Green Granite Large	XD823
Antler	Tadje	Maralinga Range	15/09/57	1 Kt	31	A1 tower mounted		Pixie	
	Biak	Maralinga Range	25/09/57	6 Kt	31	A1 tower mounted		Indigo Hammer	
	Taranaki	Maralinga Range	09/10/57	25 Kt	300	Balloon suspended			
Grapple X	Short Granite	Off Christmas Island	08/11/57	1.8 Mt	2200	Air drop	Blue Danube	Green Granite Small	XD825
Grapple Y		Off Christmas Island	28/04/58	3.0 Mt	2500	Air drop	Blue Danube		XD825
Grapple Z	Pennant	Off Christmas Island	22/08/58	24 Kt	450	Balloon suspended			
	Flagpole	Off Christmas Island	02/09/58	1 Mt	2800	Air drop	Blue Danube		XD822
	Halliarda	Off Christmas Island	11/09/58	0.8 Mt	2600	Air drop	Blue Danube		XD827
	Burgee	Off Christmas Island	23/09/58	25 Kt	450	Balloon suspended	Blue Danube		

CHAPTER SEVEN

Into Service

The first Vulcan B.1 was delivered to the RAF on 20 July 1956, when XA897 touched down at RAF Waddington in Lincolnshire to join the newly-formed 230 OCU. The arrival was essentially symbolic, however, as XA897 quickly returned to Avro's factory at Woodford for a series of minor modifications before departing on a long-range 'flag-waving' flight to New Zealand. On 16 August another Vulcan, XA895, arrived at Waddington, but this, too, stayed only briefly before leaving for Boscombe Down, where the RAF had decided to base the Vulcan's Operational Reliability Trials. In fact, 230 OCU finally received its first 'proper' delivery in January 1957. The Vulcan was given a Service release on 31 May 1956, and on the same day authority was given (as outlined two months previously by the Air Ministry) for 'the formation of 230 OCU at RAF Waddington, equipped with 10 Unit Establishment Vulcan B.1'.

While the Operational Reliability Trials continued at Boscombe Down, involving roughly 200 hr of flying, Vulcan XA897 emerged from Woodford with a

Vulcan XA896 trailing a brake chute at Waddington, circa 1957. The early all-silver colour scheme was quickly replaced by anti-flash white. (British Aerospace)

Vulcan B.1A XH478 was used for in-flight refuelling trials, and the unusual dayglow panels on the tail, nose and wings are presumed to be associated with these flights. (ia John Morley).

complete internal fit comprising Green Satin, NBS, Blue Devil (T.4 bombsight), Gee Mk.III, Marconi radio compass, radio altimeter, air mileage unit, periscopic sextant Mk.II, and an instrument landing system (ILS). Departing Boscombe Down on 9 September 1956, the aircraft began a long flight to New Zealand on Operation Tasman Flight, captained by Sqn Ldr Donald Howard. The copilot's seat was occupied by the C-in-C of Bomber Command, Air Marshal Sir Harry Broadhurst, and the rear crew comprised Sqn Ldrs Albert Gamble, Edward Eames, and James Stroud (a Vulcan pilot who took turns on the flight deck with Sir Harry). Avro technical representative Frederick Bassett occupied a 'passenger seat'.

The outbound flight proceeded remarkably smoothly via Aden and Singapore, then on to Melbourne, Australia, in a flying time of 47 hr 26 min, including stopovers. (Vulcan XA895, held at Boscombe Down as a reserve, was consequently reassigned to trials work.) After visiting Adelaide and Sydney the crew flew XA897 to Christchurch, New Zealand, on 18 September, and the Vulcan literally 'stole the show' at a number of Battle of Britain celebrations during the tour. The return trip was made via Brisbane, Darwin, Singapore, and Ceylon, the final leg, from Aden, departing at 02:50 on 1 October. The seven-hour flight back to England was scheduled to end at Heathrow, where a party of VIP guests was assembled to celebrate the return of the aircraft and crew after completing a hugely successful trip. Unfortunately weather conditions at Heathrow were very poor, with heavy rain, little wind, and visibility no more than 1,100 yd, and the VIPs inside the warm Queen's Building could see nothing but gloom. As Howard approached the English Channel he called Bomber Command Operations at High Wycombe, only to receive the disappointing news that Heathrow's current weather status was eight-eighths cloud at 700 ft, and two-eighths cloud at 300 ft.

Although the weather was foul there was no reason why XA897 could not land at Heathrow, as normal airliner operations were continuing and the aircraft was equipped for an ILS approach. Howard was advised that

The ill-fated XA897 pictured at Darwin, 31 October 1957. (Denis O'Brien)

weather conditions at Waddington, the designated bad-weather diversion, were much better, so the choice of destination was left to him. Not surprisingly he opted for Heathrow, as XA897 had sufficient fuel to divert to Waddington if the approach to Heathrow was unsuccessful. With a party of VIPs waiting, and no good technical reason for diverting, Howard could hardly have been blamed for at least attempting an approach. Broadhurst rightly left the decision to Howard, and XA897 entered an instrument approach at 1,500 ft before starting a radar-monitored talkdown.

The ground controller's talkdown began, as usual, with a series of verbal glidepath and centreline corrections, and the approach continued uneventfully until the aircraft was less than a mile from touchdown. At three-quarters of a mile the ground controller announced that the aircraft was 80 ft above the glidepath. This was the last advisory comment from the controller before the aircraft suddenly struck the ground, 1,988 ft short of the runway. In and around the Queen's Building the assembled spectators saw nothing of the unfolding drama until their attention was drawn by the sound of the Vulcan's engines, spooling up to full power. Through the cloud and rain, XA897 suddenly emerged, climbing steeply with its landing gear extended until, at about 800 ft, the canopy was jettisoned and both Howard and Broadhurst ejected from the doomed aircraft. The bomber then eased over to starboard and entered a 30° dive towards the runway, where it exploded upon impact, killing the rear crew members. Those who had not witnessed the tragedy were informed that the Vulcan had crashed, while Heathrow's rescue services raced to the burning wreckage, which continued to burn for nearly an hour, despite the rain.

Avro chief aerodynamicist Roy Ewans, who was with the VIP party, quickly made his way to the crash site. Unusually, a large proportion of the Vulcan's sturdy undercarriage appeared to be missing, and after driving to the airfield boundary he could still find no trace of it. Ewans then drove out into the fields under the runway approach, where he found two deep holes which were rapidly filling with water. They had obviously been created by XA897's landing gear when the aircraft briefly struck the ground, just short of the runway and misaligned about 250 ft to the north. Ahead of the holes were two swathes cut into a field of Brussels sprouts where the Vulcan's exhausts had blasted the ground as the aircraft reared skywards. The undercarriage components were scattered around the field. Although the Vulcan's main gear was not designed for rough-field landings, a hard landing leading to loss of the gear assembly would not normally have resulted in catastrophe. However, XA897 had hit the ground with such force that the gear's drag struts had failed, allowing the main gear legs to swing back on their main hinges to hit the wing's lower surface, ahead of the trailing-edge control surfaces. The gear assembly had penetrated the wing at the point where the aileron control rods were located, damaging them to such an extent that all lateral control was lost.

A Court of Inquiry was set up to investigate the accident, and on 20 December the Secretary of State for Air, Nigel Birch, made a statement to the House of Commons in which he said:

The aircraft had ample fuel to divert, and Air Marshal Broadhurst emphasized to the captain that he should divert if he was dissatisfied with the weather conditions prevailing. The captain decided to make one attempt to land at London Airport. At about 10:00, at a height of 1,500 ft and at about 5 nm from touchdown, and

with both altimeters correctly set, the aircraft began its descent under the control of the Talkdown Controller at London Airport. The captain set his 'break-off height' at 300 ft. That is to say, he intended to come down under the talkdown control until his altimeter stood at 300 ft and, if he then found that it was not possible to make the landing, to overshoot at that height. The GCA [ground controlled approach] talkdown instructions were followed, with some undulation relative to the glidepath and some corrections in azimuth, up to a point about three-quarters of a mile from touchdown, when the pilot was informed that he was 80 ft above the glidepath. At this point the weather was at its worst. The pilot received no further information on elevation, and at a point about 1,000 yd from the touchdown point and 700 yd from the threshold of the runway, the aircraft struck the ground. Both main undercarriage units were removed, and the elevator [and aileron] controls were damaged. Subsequently the aircraft rose sharply to a height of 200–300 ft, when it was found to be out of control. The captain then gave the order to abandon the aircraft and himself used his ejector seat. The copilot repeated the order and after trying the controls also ejected. Within seconds of the order being given the nose and starboard wing of the aircraft dropped and the aircraft crashed to the ground. The remaining three members of the crew and the passenger were killed instantly on impact.

The Minister continued:

The Royal Air Force Court of Inquiry, which assembled the following day, found nothing to suggest any technical

Vulcan B.1 XA898 on the ramp at Pinecastle AFB, Florida during the 1957 Strategic Air Command Bombing Competition. (British Aerospace)

failure in the aircraft which could have contributed to the accident. They concluded that the captain of the aircraft was justified in deciding to make an attempt to land at London Airport but it was considered that, in the circumstances, he made an error of judgement in setting himself a break-off height of 300 ft and also in going below that height. The Court drew attention, however, to the facts that though the GCA controller informed the pilot that he was 80 ft above the glidepath, he did not subsequently advise him that he was below it, and that after the aircraft had hit the ground he continued his talkdown as if the approach had been normal. The Court concluded that, since the aircraft was under GCA control, the failure of the controller to warn the captain that he was going below the glidepath was the principal cause of the accident.

The Minister then turned his attention to the more specific examination of Heathrow's GCA approach, and said:

On receipt of the Report, I referred the passages relating to the GCA aspect to my right hon Friend the Minister of Transport and Civil Aviation, who immediately arranged for an inquiry into the operation of the GCA system to be undertaken by Dr A. G. Touch, the Director of Electronic Research and Development at the Ministry of Supply. In a report which he submitted last week, Dr Touch concluded that there was no evidence of technical failure or malfunctioning in the GCA equipment. His investigation confirmed that the pilot was not warned by the GCA unit of his closeness to the ground, but despite a detailed and exhaustive examination of various possibilities, Dr Touch was unable to establish the reason with certainty. He thought that the most likely explanation was that throughout the approach the controller concentrated too much on azimuth at the expense of elevation. He felt, however, that there were extenuating circumstances connected with the unusual speed of the aircraft and the number of corrections in azimuth. He also considered that even if a warning had been given in the final five or six seconds of the ten seconds which, in his opinion, elapsed after the captain was told that he was 80 ft above the glidepath, it would have been too late.

My right hon Friend the Minister of Transport and Civil Aviation and I have given most careful consideration to these findings. We are agreed that there was an error of judgement on the part of the pilot in selecting a break-off height of 300 ft and in going below it, and also that the GCA controller did not give adequate guidance on elevation during descent and, in particular, that he was at fault in the concluding stages in not warning the pilot that he was below the glidepath and therefore dangerously close to the ground. The apportionment of responsibility is difficult. I accept the conclusion of the Royal Air Force Court but neither I nor my right hon Friend feel able to define the degree of responsibility precisely. It would be unjust to the pilot and copilot were I not to make it clear in conclusion that it was their duty to eject from the aircraft when they did. The Court of Inquiry were satisfied on the evidence put before them that there could have been no hope of controlling the aircraft after the initial impact. In these circumstances, it was the duty of the captain to give the order to abandon the aircraft and of all those who were on board to obey if they were able to do so. Both the pilot and copilot realized when they gave their orders that, owing to the low altitude, the other occupants had no chance to escape and they considered that their own chances were negligible. The House will wish to join with me in expressing regret that so successful a flight should have ended so tragically

Martin Baker designed an ingenious ejection system for the V-Bomber rear crews. After firing the centre seat, the port and starboard seats would shift sideways before ejecting through the same upper fuselage hatch. Although the system worked, the expense of modifying the aircraft to carry it proved to be prohibitive (Martin Baker)

and in tendering sympathy to the bereaved.

Not surprisingly, the whole question of escape systems for the V–Bombers was raised once more, and on the day after the accident the Air Minister asked the Air Staff to outline their policy on ejection seats. The DCAS replied on 15 October, stating that when the Valiant, Vulcan, and Victor were first conceived they were to have been fitted with jettisonable cabins which would separate from the aircraft and make a parachute-retarded descent:

As design and development proceeded it became clear that this facility could not be provided, and agreement not to have a jettisonable cabin was reached in the case of the Valiant in June 1948, the Vulcan in May 1949 and the Victor in October 1952. In all three bombers the layout of the cabin, which was operationally very satisfactory, made it impossible, for structural reasons, to produce ejection facilities for aircrew other than the pilots. It was, however, agreed to provide ejector seats for the pilots so that they could remain with the aircraft for longer and help other crew members to escape. Facilities for the other crew members were provided by means of side doors in the Valiant and Victor and through an underneath hatch in the Vulcan, which has virtually no fuselage.

The result of this is that all three bombers and the developments of them will, according to present planning, have ejector seats for the pilots and escape by door or hatch for the three other crew members. A trained crew takes approximately 20 sec from the time the order to jump is given until the last man leaves the aircraft, but it is important to remember that it is unlikely that the three non-pilot crew members would

escape in conditions where high 'g' forces are being applied through battle damage or loss of control, when the aircraft is at low level. On the other hand, when the first Valiant had a fire in the air all five members got out of the aircraft successfully at high altitude — unfortunately the second pilot was killed by striking the fin.

I have discussed a possible modification plan for the V-bombers with Mr James Martin [managing director and chief designer of the Martin-Baker ejection seat company] and with the Ministry of Supply, and am of the opinion that it is certainly not impossible to incorporate ejection facilities for the three non–pilot members of the crew of the V-bombers . . . but the implementation of such a policy would naturally raise very grave issues. The first issue is whether or not we would be right to go in for such a policy, and the second is whether we could afford to do so, both in terms of money and effort as well as the delay of the V-Force build-up. A retrospective modification programme would naturally be an immense undertaking but it is not technically impossible, and if we do go in for it we must realize what may be involved. My own view is that we should not attempt to adopt such a policy.

Although the rear crew lost their lives in the Heathrow tragedy, it was something of a miracle that the pilot and copilot survived. When XA897 returned briefly to Woodford for modification before embarking on Operation Tasman Flight, Avro had just completed the design of a new system to interconnect the canopy release with the ejection seats' pull-down face blind handles which actuated the ejection sequence. Instead of requiring the pilot to perform two separate actions, first releasing the canopy and then pulling the ejection handle, the new system enabled either seat handle to blow off the canopy and fire the seat in one sequence. Although the Vulcan had been delivered without this system, it was incorporated in time for the New Zealand trip, and there is reason to assume that, without it, the few extra seconds required to escape would have led to the deaths of both Howard and Broadhurst as well.

In January 1957 Vulcans XA895 and XA898 were delivered to 230 OCU and, following a period of intensive flying trials, the task of training the first Vulcan crews began on 21 February. During March, April, and May three more aircraft, XA900, XA901, and XA902, were delivered, and it was on these Vulcans that the first OCU course qualified, graduating on 21 May 1957. No. 1 Course then re-formed as 'A' Flight of 83 Squadron, the first operational Vulcan squadron, which 'borrowed' aircraft from the OCU until the unit's first Vulcan, XA905, was handed over on 11 July, the day on which the squadron was commissioned. Although the OCU's Vulcans had been delivered with Olympus 101 engines, the aircraft destined for 83 Squadron had 12,000-lb thrust Olympus 102s. The Vulcan B.1 fleet eventually standardized on 13,500-lb thrust Olympus 104s.

The second OCU course also became a Flight of 83 Squadron, and upon graduation subsequent courses transferred to Finningley, where 101 Squadron was formed on 15 October 1957. By the end of that year four aircraft had been delivered to Finningley and the last aircraft from the 1952 order, XA913, had been handed over to the RAF. At the start of the new year the first of a new batch of Vulcan B.1s was completed, as part of a 37-aircraft order placed in September 1954.

The Vulcan's entry into RAF service proceeded surprisingly smoothly, encountering far fewer 'teething troubles' than anticipated. Only one major accident occurred during the Vulcan's early career; the loss of XA908 on 24 October 1958. The aircraft was flying on a 'Lone Ranger' exercise from Goose Bay, Canada, to Lincoln Air Force Base (AFB) in Nebraska, USA. When it was approximately 60 miles north-east of Detroit the main power supply failed, and although the engines continued to feed the electrical generators a short-circuit in the main busbar blocked the power supply. This should have presented few problems for the crew, as the aircraft had sufficient battery standby power for twenty minutes' flying, so the captain requested an emergency descent to Kellog Field. Tragically, the batteries lasted just three minutes, after which the powered flying controls failed, and without power the helpless Vulcan entered a steep descent and flew into the ground at an angle of 60°, killing all but one of the crew. The copilot ejected successfully but, as the only member of 83 Squadron who could not swim, his descent without a lifejacket into Lake St Clair on the US/Canadian border proved fatal.

Following this accident the Vulcan B.1 fleet was modified, the main busbar being divided into two to prevent the recurrence of such a disaster. However, before the update could be incorporated into XA891 this aircraft, too, suffered a power failure, but this time the batteries provided sufficient emergency power to enable the crew to bale out safely. Despite these accidents the Vulcan's safety record was outstanding, thanks to Avro's reliance upon simplicity and reliability. It was particularly sad, therefore, that the prototype Type 698 was destroyed on 20 September 1958 during a flying demonstration at the Battle of Britain celebrations at RAF Syerston,

Nottinghamshire. During a fast pass over the airfield the aircraft suddenly disintegrated, and post-accident investigation revealed that the wing had suffered a catastrophic structural failure. Further analysis, however, established that the aircraft had been flown beyond the design speed and 'g' limits, emphasizing that, even though it had the handling characteristics of a fighter, the Vulcan was a very large and heavy bomber which had to be treated with respect.

It is worth noting that, even though it was much less manoeuvrable, the Victor was by no means a slouch. It too had relatively light flying controls, thanks to the use of 'artificial feel' which effectively enabled the manufacturer to incorporate whatever response was felt appropriate, within the limits of the powered flying controls. Unlike the Vulcan with its fighter-style stick, the Victor had a traditional control column, reflecting Handley Page's and Hazelden's view that the aircraft's controls should reflect the size and manoeuvrability of the aircraft. Despite this the Victor prototypes required very gentle handling, and the RAF requested that the controls should be 'heavied-up' on production machines. The Victor's entry into RAF service was delayed by a number of modifications made to the aircraft, largely based on evaluations made by Boscombe Down. For example, the cockpit layout was redesigned in response to the following remarks in an A&AEE report:

The overall layout of the cockpit fell far short of the standard required in this class of aircraft. Generally, there appeared to be no logical grouping of associated controls and indicators and in certain aspects the layout was haphazard. The layout of the power

The Victor flight deck, illustrating the dual control 'spectacle' columns which contrast dramatically with the fighter-type stick installed in the Vulcan. (Handley Page)

The Radlett factory at the height of Victor production, with a B.1 partially painted on the ramp. (R. L. Ward)

control switch panel was illogical and dangerous. Some of the indicators and controls for primary services could only be operated by the first pilot, and several warning and monitoring devices were not visible to both pilots, making it impossible for either pilot to relax completely at any time. The extreme discomfort of the pilots' stations was severely criticized and will result in a lowering of efficiency and morale during only average-length sorties. In conditions of poor visibility the restricted view was inadequate for the circuit and landing, and concern was felt for possible external windscreen reflections during night flying. It is essential that these major criticisms be rectified before the aircraft can be considered acceptable for Service use.

These comments were particularly frustrating in view of the fact that the

A pre-production Victor illustrating the wing leading edge 'nose flaps' which were later abandoned. (Handley Page).

XA933 at Gaydon, shortly after delivery to the Victor OCU. Early Victors carried full-colour national insignia and serials. (R. L. Ward)

Victor B.1 XA926 about to touch down at Gaydon. (R. L. Ward)

cockpit layout had already been discussed with the RAF during a design conference in 1952. However, Handley Page managed to overcome a variety of minor problems and, even though the first deliveries were two years late, it is remarkable that the Victor survived at all when one considers the relatively small size of the company and the resources available to it, the Victor being by far the most technically sophisticated of the three V-Bombers. In retrospect, the Victor was probably more advanced than necessary, as the Vulcan's simpler systems proved to be just as effective. There is no doubt, however, that the Victor's range and ceiling performance figures were much better than those of the Vulcan,

RAF Cottesmore's flight line with Victor B.1s prepared for flight. The same concrete will be occupied by Harriers from the turn of the century. (RAF Cottesmore)

though the Vulcan could compensate for this deficit by using more powerful engines. While the Victor B.1 was powered by four Armstrong Siddeley Sapphire 7 engines, each rated at 11,000-lb thrust, the Vulcan B.1 had 13,500-lb thrust Bristol Olympus engines which, combined with the aircraft's superior manoeuvrability, gave it a performance which more than matched the Victor's. Consequently, the Air Staff's final choice between the two aircraft was never made, and the RAF was blessed with two outstanding jet bombers.

On 29 July 1957 the Victor was given an Air Ministry Initial Release to Service which stated:

> Subject to the observance of the limitations defined in subsequent paragraphs (such as a maximum take-off and emergency landing weight of 160,000 lb) the Victor B.Mk.1 is released for Service use by day and by night in temperate climates only.

Other limitations were imposed upon the aircraft until modifications could be made, and this delayed the arrival of XA930 at Boscombe Down for Operational Reliability Trials until 9 October. The first Victor to be delivered for RAF service was XA931, the 15th production aircraft, which arrived at Gaydon on 28 November 1957, touching down at 15:36 and joining 232 OCU. The arrival of the first Victor was not greeted with the enthusiasm and excitement that had surrounded the Vulcan's Service debut, possibly because the OCU had been active on Valiants for some time and the Victor was probably regarded simply as a successor, whereas it was, of course, the ultimate embodiment of Specification B.35/46.

More Victors arrived at Gaydon, XA924, XA925, XA932, XA933, and XA934 being followed by XA926 in March 1958. Two of these aircraft, XA924 and XA925, were fitted with 'Yellow Aster' radar at Radlett before being deployed to Wyton, where they were attached to 543 Squadron to participate in reconnaissance training before becoming the Radar Reconnaissance Flight. The first operational Victor squadron was No. 10, which received XA935 at Cottesmore on 9 April, followed by XA927 on 16 April

Right: *As part of the Victor's reconnaissance capability, trials were conducted with Red Neck sideways-looking radar pods, as illustrated by XA918. The system was not adopted for service use.* (Handley Page)

Below: *Victor B.1 XA930 climbing away from Radlett, with Red Neck radar pods attached to the wing hardpoints.* (Handley Page)

A dramatic view of XA930 roaring over Radlett at low level, with radar pods under her wings. (Handley Page)

XA930 was the only Victor B.1 to carry external fuel tanks, these being fitted as part of the Handley Page trials programme.
(Handley Page)

and XA928 on 5 May. The next unit to form was 15 Squadron, on 1 September, their first aircraft, XA941, arriving on the 16th.

By the end of 1958 the V-Force was well established, with seven operational Valiant bomber squadrons (138, 543, 214, 49, 207, 148, and 7), three operational Vulcan squadrons (83, 101, and 617), and two operational Victor squadrons (10 and 15), together with the respective OCUs. The Blue Danube atomic (fission) bomb was already in service, the 'interim' Violet Club was temporarily in service, and the first deliveries of the Yellow Sun Mk.1 hydrogen bomb were under way. The RAF now possessed more destructive power than at any time in its distinguished history, but improvements in Soviet defence technology meant that the V-Force could not stand still. Further improvements were needed to ensure that the RAF's bombers were capable — and seen to be capable — of delivering nuclear weapons to their targets.

Up to this point there had been little need for an advanced ECM fit in the Valiant, Vulcan, or Victor, thanks largely to the Soviet Air Force's rigid system of fighter control, which was well monitored by the West. Only a limited number of VHF channels were used by

the Soviets to control their interceptors, and just a single piece of equipment, Green Palm, was capable of jamming them all with a high-pitched wail. However, recent developments suggested that something rather more sophisticated would be required for the 1960s, so it was decided to install ECM equipment into both the Vulcan and Victor, rather than rely on the support of dedicated ECM aircraft such as those operated by 199 Squadron (and, later, 18 Squadron). Twenty-nine Vulcan B.1s, redesignated B.Mk.1As, were fitted with Red Steer tail-warning radar and other ECM equipment which included a flat-plate aerial (Red Shrimp) fixed between the starboard jet pipes. The first aircraft so converted was XH500, which entered service with 617 Squadron on 29 September 1960. Likewise, 24 Victor B.1s were suitably modified with Red Steer, jammers in the rear hatch and transmitters in the lower nose, and a passive radar warning receiver. The first conversion, XH613, arrived at Cottesmore to rejoin 15 Squadron on 22 July 1960. Thus the V-Bomber crews were not only capable of carrying a sizeable nuclear punch; they were confident of delivering it to the designated target, wherever it might be.

CHAPTER EIGHT

More Power

One direct result of Britain's possession of both fission and fusion weapons was, as indicated, a much greater level of nuclear co-operation between the USA and Britain. America's reluctance to share 'nuclear secrets' with Britain was largely due to pressure from politicians who either believed that America should endeavour to remain a 'nuclear monopoly' (even though the Soviet Union had begun manufacturing her own thermonuclear bombs) or that Britain simply could not be trusted to share nuclear knowledge, because of continual spy revelations or because Britain could even be invaded by the Soviets at some stage. Despite the fact that many American officials, including a succession of presidents, believed in the Special Relationship, it was not until the

An in-flight study of No. 15 Squadron's XH588, illustrating the uncluttered lines of the early Victor B.1 prior to the introduction of ECM equipment, fuel tanks and refuelling probes. (RAF Cottesmore)

Victor B.1s on the flight line at Tengah, Singapore, during the Malayan crisis. (Roger Brooks collection)

RAF received atomic weapons that the transatlantic friendship was restored. The strong working relationship between the RAF's Bomber Command and the USAF's SAC had survived the political ups and downs of the early post-war years and, as the climate improved, so the possibility of co-ordinating nuclear strike plans became a reality.

Moves towards co-operation in the field were first made by the British, and in September 1955 the CAS visited the USA with a briefing paper which set out Britain's objectives. It began by stating: 'The primary aim of the defence policy of the United Kingdom is to prevent war', and went on to say:

The main instrument for achieving this aim lies in the nuclear capability together with the means of delivery, which is possessed by the United Kingdom and the United States alone.

We should achieve a closer association with the United States world-wide in the field of defence strategy. This is particularly important in strategic air operations, where Bomber Command and the Strategic Air Command will be attacking components of the same vast target complex. It follows that unless there is a full exchange of information and a co-ordinated plan of attack, wasteful overlapping and dangerous omissions will result.

The Chiefs of Staff had tried unsuccessfully to persuade the Americans to begin joint planning for some years, but little progress was made until the USA realized that the V-Force was to become a reality. Finally, agreement was achieved in August 1956 and a team of senior USAF officers was sent to London to discuss the co-ordination of strike plans with Bomber

Command. Additionally, in a remarkable volte-face, the USA had also agreed to supply the RAF with atomic weapons as a stop-gap measure, until sufficient British-made bombs could be completed. Because the McMahon Act was still in force, the bombs would be kept in USAF custody on RAF bases, from where they would be released to the RAF in a wartime emergency.

The detailed agreements made in London included references to the general concept of Allied atomic air operations, stating that, in a general war, atomic weapons would be used right from the outset. It was established that if an atomic war began, it would probably begin with an initial phase 'characterized by an intensive exchange of atomic blows', followed by a subsequent exchange of indeterminate duration at a reduced atomic intensity. The 'Brief Plan of Action' stated that the Allied counter air offensive would begin with 'heavy co-ordinated attacks against airfields, logistic facilities, control centres and command headquarters', creating a contraction of forces which would concentrate the surviving enemy aircraft on remaining airfields, enabling SAC and Bomber

Command to 'exploit the vulnerability of such concentrations'. In January 1956 the British defence minister, Duncan Sandys, wrote to Charles Wilson, his American counterpart, with a detailed set of proposals. The reply from Wilson was positive, and agreed that arrangements should be made to 'furnish the Royal Air Force with United States atomic bombs in the event of general war, and to co-ordinate the atomic strike plans of the United States Air Force with the Royal Air Force'. However, Wilson also added:

. . . the provisions of United States legislation must govern and that the United States cannot engage in a commitment to transfer custody of such weapons to the Royal Air Force other than by Presidential decision in strict accordance with his constitutional and legislative authority.

The supply of American atomic bombs (Project 'E') was discussed by President Eisenhower and Prime Minister Macmillan when they met at the Bermuda Conference in March 1957. The 1956 Suez Crisis had been a turning point for Anglo-American relations, and

Victor B.1s from the Cottesmore Wing. (RAF Cottesmore)

the Bermuda meeting marked a significant improvement in mutual confidence between the two countries. After the conference, Eisenhower outlined his views, stating:

> The United States Government welcome the agreement to co-ordinate the strike plans of the United States and United Kingdom bomber forces, and to store United States nuclear weapons on RAF airfields under United States custody for release subject to decision by the President in an emergency. We understand that for the present at least these weapons will be in the kiloton range. The United Kingdom forces could obviously play a much more effective part in joint strikes if the United States weapons made available to them in emergency were in the megaton range, and it is suggested that this possibility might be examined at the appropriate time.

Interestingly, America's willingness not only to co-operate with Britain but actually to supply weapons, was a fairly well-kept secret at the time, as the President indicated by saying in his communication to Macmillan:

> With respect to the item 'Nuclear bomb release gear for RAF bombers', I agree of course that you shall probably have to make some statement in order to prevent speculation in the press that might prove not only inaccurate but damaging. However, as I explained to you verbally, the United States would prefer not to be a party to a public statement which might give rise to demands upon us by other Governments where we should not be in a position to meet the requests. Consequently, I suggest the possible adequacy of a unilateral statement by yourself or by the British Defence Minister to the effect that Canberras

A full load of 35 1,000 lb free fall bombs pictured on release from Victor B.1 XH648. The photograph has probably been 'massaged' as a complete stick of bombs would almost certainly occupy much more airspace. (Handley Page)

*The   Vulcan   B.2's
capacious bomb bay.*
(R. L. Ward)

are now being equipped to carry atomic bombs.

In fact, Project 'E' covered the supply of atomic bombs not only to the RAF's Canberra tactical bomber force, but also to the V-Force. An Air Ministry meeting in August 1956 reported that the US Government had not given any indication of the numbers of 'E' weapons to be supplied, nor were they likely to, but it was believed to be 'almost certain' that the numbers would exceed any delivery capacity that the UK was capable of developing. Records do not indicate when the first 'E' weapons arrived in the UK, but US transport flights began towards the end of 1958, and both Honington and Waddington received the first suitably modified V-Bombers in October of that year. Approval was given for modifications to be made to 72 aircraft at Honington, Waddington, and Marham to carry American Mk.5 (6,000 lb) bombs (and subsequently the Mk.7, Mk.15/39 and Mk.28), and 90 and 57 Squadrons at Honington, with Valiants and Victors respectively, were the first

units to be assigned to Project 'E' during the spring of 1959, followed by 148, 207, and 214 Squadrons (Valiants) at Marham, and 83 Squadron (Vulcans) at Waddington. In 1960 7 Squadron (Valiants) and 55 Squadron (Victors) at Honington, together with 44 Squadron (Vulcans) at Waddington joined Project 'E', and finally 101 and 50 Squadrons (Vulcan) at Waddington were assigned in 1961.

The supply of American bombs enabled Bomber Command to equip the V-Force with atomic weapons at an earlier date than would have been

A unique illustration of a Victor B.1 demonstrating the dramatic recovery from a toss-bombing manoeuvre. (Handley Page)

possible with British weapons, and before 1961 there would otherwise have been more bombers than bombs. However, Project 'E' was a less-than-perfect solution to Britain's early problems, chiefly because of American restrictions on the deployment of the weapons. The 'E' weapons could not be distributed throughout Bomber Command, nor could they be dispersed to remote sites from which 'clutches' of V-Bombers would operate during wartime, in order to evade enemy attack. Consequently, Project 'E' was relatively short-lived, and the decision to begin a phase-out was taken on 7 July 1960. Although America was reluctant to disclose how many nuclear bombs were stored at RAF bases, they were equally ambiguous when revealing the nominal yield of each weapon. Eventually it was established that the bombs were largely of a type which would deliver only half the yield which they had previously been thought to possess, which meant that once British equivalents were available, the greater

flexibility they afforded (not least in being 'dispersable') enabled the American weapons to be withdrawn, although the Valiants assigned to Supreme Allied Commander Europe (Saceur) and RAF Germany's Canberras would continue to carry 'E' weapons.

While Project 'E' progressed, the co-operation between SAC and Bomber Command became much more intimate, as the CAS's comments relating to a November 1957 meeting indicate:

Examination of the separate Bomber Command and SAC plans has shown that every Bomber Command target was, understandably, also on SAC's list for attack and that both Commands had doubled-up strikes on their selected targets to ensure success. A fully integrated plan has now been produced, taking into account Bomber Command's ability to be on target in the first wave several hours in advance of the main SAC forces from bases in the US. Under the combined plan, the total strategic air forces disposed by the Allies are sufficient to cover all Soviet targets, including airfields and air defence. Bomber Command's contribution has been given as 92 aircraft by October 1958, increasing to 108 aircraft by June 1959. 106 targets have been allocated to Bomber Command as follows:

a) 69 cities which are centres of government or of other military significance.
b) 17 long-range air force airfields which constitute part of the nuclear threat.
c) 20 elements of the Soviet air defence system.

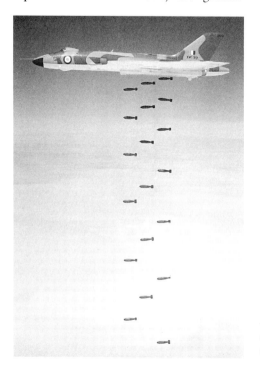

An impressive image of a Vulcan B.2 releasing a conventional bomb load over a weapons range during the 1960s. (British Aerospace)

Vulcan B.1A XH499 illustrating the B1's high nose angle. XH499 was scrapped at Bitteswell in 1966. (R. L. Ward)

Although SAC had 380 B-52s and 1,367 B-47s by the end of 1958, compared with Britain's 73 V-Bombers, it is worth noting that Bomber Command's contribution to the Allied counter air offensive plans was out of all proportion to the relative size of the SAC and RAF forces. The V-Bombers possessed superior speed and altitude performance, and the RAF's training and technical expertise was 'at least as good'. More importantly, although the RAF forces were obviously more vulnerable to air attack, Bomber Command had introduced a dispersal plan which would enable the V-Force to deploy in groups of four or two aircraft to a total of 36 airfields scattered around the UK, from where the combined force would be capable of getting airborne in less than ten minutes. The performance of the V-Bombers, together with Britain's geographical location, meant that Bomber Command's aircraft would reach their targets long before SAC's aircraft would arrive, so the V-Force was very much at the forefront of the West's nuclear strike capability.

As previously mentioned, the 1957 Bermuda Conference was an historical turning point in Anglo-American relations. After the political embarrassment of the Suez Crisis, which had highlighted Britain's impotence in the face of American economic and political pressure, Macmillan was eager to restore the Special Relationship. Fortunately Eisenhower shared the same sentiments, as highlighted in a letter to Churchill, in which he wrote: 'I shall never be happy until our old-time closeness has been restored'. Consequently America agreed, as described, to joint strike plans, the supply of nuclear weapons and, as first mentioned in July 1956, the supply of the Thor intermediate-range ballistic missile (IRBM) system to the UK. In essence, these nuclear-armed rockets would be all-American, but they would be jointly operated by RAF personnel and located on RAF bases. Thor would ease American worries of a growing 'missile gap' between the USA and the Soviet Union by placing missiles within striking distance of key Soviet targets, and at the same time it would give Britain 'a megaton rocket deterrent at least five years before we could provide it ourselves', as Macmillan commented. He also added:

United States would provide weapons and specialized equipment, including anything costing dollars. Nuclear warheads would be held under same conditions as nuclear bombs for British bombers. We would undertake site works and would provide general supporting equipment. United States estimate of the cost to us for the four sites (eventually there were in fact, five sites) is £10 million, apart from the costs of personnel and their training and housing.

Britain had already addressed the possibility of manufacturing a ballistic missile, based on Air Staff Requirement OR.1139 of 8 August 1955. The Blue Streak missile was to be housed in a series of underground silos scattered around the UK, whereas Thor would be a surface-housed weapon, stored horizontally in shelters before being erected for fuelling and launch. It was considered that Thor might provide some useful experience in advance of Blue Streak, which was expected to enter service in 1964, whereas Thor would be operational by 1958. In January of that year agreements were made for the establishment of SM-75 Thors in the UK, with the first missiles arriving by July. Each squadron would be deployed on five sites, and each site would house three missiles. The initial list of bases (which was subsequently changed) was: Feltwell, Honington, Witchford, Marham, Watton, Hemswell, Caistor, Ludford Magna, Waddington, Bardney, Driffield, Full Sutton, Holme-on-Spalding Moor, Riccall, Leconfield, Dishforth, Scorton, Leeming, Marston Moor, and Sherburn-in-Elmet.

A White Paper issued on 25 February 1958 stated that the missiles would be 'manned and operated by United Kingdom personnel', and that any decision to launch the Thors would be a joint one between the two governments, that the one-megaton warheads would remain 'in full United States custody', and that the Thor agreement would remain in force 'for not less than five years'.

The first missile was delivered to 77 Squadron at Feltwell on 19 September 1958, and the first live firing of a Thor by an RAF crew took place at Vandenberg AFB on 18 April 1959. Deployment was completed by March 1960 on the following airfields, many of which had long since been abandoned, only to be repurchased by the Air Ministry: Feltwell, Mepal, North Pickenham, Shepherd's Grove, Tuddenham, Hemswell, Caistor, Bardney, Ludford Magna, Coleby Grange, Driffield, Carnaby, Catfoss, Breighton, Full Sutton, North Luffenham, Folkingham, Polebrook, Harrington, and Melton Mowbray.

Sixty Thors were deployed to the UK, all arriving on board transport aircraft from the USA. Although the Thor missile could be accommodated easily inside Military Airlift Command's huge Douglas Globemaster and Cargomaster aircraft, the task of delivering the missiles, and transporting some back to the USA for RAF live firings at Vandenberg, was far from easy. The transport aircraft had to operate within strict rate of ascent and descent figures to avoid pressure damage to the Thor's fuel tanks. Even more exacting was the need to transport the hugely expensive guidance unit gyroscopes, which were suspended in a lubricant which had to be maintained at a constant temperature. Control of the temperature required direct power from the transport aircraft's engines, so the crews had to keep the outboard engines throttled up to high power, even while taxying, brake power being applied against the thrust. Once the missile was installed, however, it was regarded as being a very effective and reliable weapon. Its downfall was the fact that it was not mobile and could not be housed underground, rendering the entire Thor force vulnerable to a Soviet attack. Much consideration was given to the possibility of extending Thor's service life beyond the planned five-year period, but like Britain's Blue Streak it was accepted that a fixed IRBM system could not remain viable as a credible nuclear deterrent.

The last RAF Thor complex to close was at North Luffenham, and on 23

August 1963 the component squadrons, 144, 130, 218, 223, and 254, disbanded, marking the end of Bomber Command's IRBM era. The CAS commented:

When Thor came into service we knew that we would be faced with many new and complex technical and administrative problems and we fully expected that one of the greatest of these problems would be the task of maintaining the morale of the officers and men allocated to the missile sites. In the event, the problems were met and solved with a degree of enthusiasm, skill and resourcefulness which was in the finest traditions of Bomber Command and the Royal Air Force. The high morale which was a feature of the Force from its inception has never flagged, and Thor's fine record of serviceability and state of readiness over the years is a remarkable tribute to the loyalty and sense of duty of all the personnel who played a part. They will be able to look back with pride on a most valuable contribution to our deterrent force.

As the Thor era ended in 1963, the Blue Streak programme had ended in 1960, less than five years after the Air Staff Requirement for it had been issued. A Commons statement in April 1960 said:

The Government have been considering the future of the project for developing the long-range ballistic missile Blue Streak and have been in touch with the Australian Government about it, in view of their interest in the joint project and the operation of the Woomera range. The technique of controlling ballistic missiles has rapidly advanced. The vulnerability of missiles launched from static sites, and the practicability of launching missiles of considerable range from mobile

platforms, has now been established. In the light of our military advice to this effect, and of the importance of reinforcing the effectiveness of the deterrent, we have concluded and the Australian Government have fully accepted that we ought not to continue to develop, as a military weapon, a missile that can be launched only from a fixed site.

Today, our strategic nuclear force is an effective and significant contribution to the deterrent power of the free world. The Government do not intend to give up this independent contribution and, therefore, some other vehicle will in due course be needed in place of Blue Streak to carry British-manufactured warheads. The need for this is not immediately urgent, since the effectiveness of the V-Bomber force as the vehicle for these warheads will remain unimpaired for several years to come, nor is it possible at the moment to say with certainty which of several possibilities or combinations of them would be technically the most suitable. On present information, there appears to be much to be said for prolonging the effectiveness of the V-Bombers by buying supplies of the airborne ballistic missile Skybolt which is being developed in the United States. Her Majesty's Government understand that the United States Government will be favourably disposed to the purchase by the United Kingdom at the appropriate time of supplies of this vehicle. The Government will now consider with the firms and other interests concerned as a matter of urgency, whether the Blue Streak programme could be adapted for the development of a launcher for space satellites.

In fact, Blue Streak did eventually

become part of the European Space Agency's rocket design process, but as a military weapon the fixed-site IRBM was obsolete. Britain was already looking towards American developments, most notably the aforementioned Skybolt and the sea-launched Polaris missiles, as possible future means of delivering British warheads to their targets. But even as the V-Force was being created, the concept of guided nuclear missiles had already been established, and by 1954 the Air Staff had issued OR.1132, calling for a propelled air-to-surface missile for the V-class bombers. Capable of being launched at up to 100 nm from its target, the missile would rely on the parent aircraft's NBS system for aiming, and would use Green Satin Doppler equipment to determine ground speed and drift, and to provide an accurate heading reference. Responsibility for the weapon, named Blue Steel, was divided between the MoS and Avro's Weapons Research Division, which had completed a design study for a stand-off bomb which resulted in a development contract being awarded in March 1956.

Tests of a two-fifths-scale model of the guided bomb were conducted in 1957–8, a series of drops being made from Valiant WP204 over the Aberporth range off the Welsh coast. Development of Blue Steel was far from easy, not least because virtually the entire programme represented a move into completely unknown territory as far as technical knowledge was concerned. In essence, Blue Steel was an aeroplane, and Avro treated the missile as such. Some 35 ft long, with small delta foreplanes, rear-mounted 13 ft-span wings, and vertical fins, it was powered by a hydrogen peroxide and kerosine Armstrong Siddeley Stentor rocket motor. Guided by inertial navigation, and with automatic flight control and trajectory decision-making, the missile manoeuvred at

supersonic speeds before delivering a 1 Mt 'Red Snow' warhead to its target. The all-up weight of the bomb was about 17,000 lb, which included 400 gal of high-test peroxide (HTP) fuel and 80 gal of kerosine. After release at 40,000 ft the bomb would free-fall to 32,000 ft, at which stage the motor would ignite and the missile would climb to 59,000 ft, where the speed would increase to Mach 2.3. The missile would then cruise-climb to 70,500 ft, where the engine would burn out and a steady dive towards the target would begin.

Bearing this very complicated system in mind, and the fact that Avro had no previous experience of designing and manufacturing guided missiles, it is hardly surprising that the development programme timescale began to slip, especially when the MoS were unable even to supply a Valiant test bed aircraft on time. The Air Staff's hope that Blue Steel would be operational by 1960 was quickly discounted, despite the fact that they were already looking for a missile which could fly up to ten times further. In May 1958 Air Staff Requirement OR.1159 called for an extended-range air-to-surface guided missile, stating:

By 1963 it is expected that the Russian SAGW [surface-to-air guided weapon] and the fighter defences will be so improved and expanded that the V-bombers, even with Blue Steel and RCM, will find it increasingly difficult to penetrate to many of their objectives. In order to maintain an effective deterrent during the period commencing with the decline in effectiveness of Blue Steel and continuing during the build-up of the RAF ballistic missile force, it will be necessary to introduce a replacement for Blue Steel having a range for attacking targets from launching points outside the enemy defence perimeter. It is envisaged that V-bombers equipped with this missile should be able to supplement the

An Avro Blue Steel test round being attached to a modified Valiant trials aircraft at Woodford. Two Valiants were equipped to carry Blue Steel, although the weapon was only carried operationally on the Vulcan and Victor. (British Aerospace)

ballistic missile deterrent for several years.

The statement continued: 'A missile range of 600 nautical miles will be acceptable as an initial operational capability but a range of 1,000 nm is desirable'. Duncan Sandys, the Minister of Aviation, recognized that it would be foolish to distract Avro's efforts to get Blue Steel into service by adding the complication of a long-range Blue Steel development, so the subsequent cancellation of both Blue Streak and Blue Steel Mk.2 enabled Avro, the RAE, and the Royal Radar Establishment to concentrate on getting Blue Steel Mk.1 into service at the earliest opportunity. On 28 April 1961, Minister of Aviation Peter Thorneycroft reported:

Blue Steel was accepted as a requirement in January 1956. It was then thought that the first delivery of missiles would be made to the RAF in 1961/2. By the end of 1960, however, it had become apparent (owing to delays in the development programme) that the number of trial firings that could be expected to have been made by early 1962 would not be sufficient to enable the first deliveries of missiles to the RAF to be approved for normal operational use. It is, however, expected that by mid-1962 the functioning and safety of the weapon (including its warhead) will have been sufficiently proved to enable the missile to be used in an emergency, if required, thus providing a deterrent capability. Further trials will continue during the succeeding months to enable approval to be given for normal operational carriage and use of the missile.

The Minister added that the delays in the programme were due to detailed engineering faults and problems which 'are a normal part of the development

A Blue Steel test round attached to a Vulcan at Woodford. Unusually, the missile is painted all-black, presumably for photo calibration purposes. (British Aerospace)

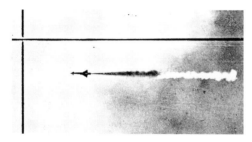

Footage clip of a Blue Steel round firing into action over the Woomera range. (British Aerospace)

process and may be expected to continue'. An order was placed for 57 missiles, made up of a Unit Establishment of 48 operational rounds, plus four backing rounds and four proof rounds. Additionally, there would be 16 training rounds, ten of which would be manufactured from light alloy, and six with steel carcasses. During 1959 Vulcan B.1 XA903 joined the Blue Steel programme, and a variety of full-sized missile test bodies, mostly powered by de Havilland Double Spectre engines, were dropped from both the Valiant and Vulcan. Most of the later test flights were made over the Woomera range in Australia, where two Vulcan B.2s, XH538 and XH539, were employed.

The development programme was dogged by a series of relatively minor problems which led to increasing frustration on behalf of the Air Staff. Avro was accused of poor management, and of wasting time on projected plans for a long-range Blue Steel when it should have devoted all of its efforts to completion of Blue Steel Mk.1. In reality, Avro simply suffered from a combination of initial over-optimism (shared by the Air Staff) and a whole range of new technical problems which, as an aircraft manufacturer, the company had never before encountered. Considering that the typical development period for a conventional military aircraft could be anything up to ten years, it was perhaps unrealistic to expect a system as complicated as Blue Steel to be completed in a significantly shorter timescale.

The Minister of Aviation also said in 1961:

Blue Steel was a fully navigated cruise-type missile with a range of 100 nm designed for launching from Mk.2 Victors and Vulcans. It was intended to provide the main deterrent weapon between the time when

A Blue Steel training round at Scampton with a Vulcan B.2 in the background. (British Aerospace)

Vulcan B.1 XA903 over the Woomera range, carrying a Blue Steel test round. The weapon carries red/white calibration colours. (British Aerospace)

bombers equipped with free-falling bombs were likely to become less effective against enemy defences, and the introduction of Skybolt. Its cost was currently estimated at £60 million for R&D and £21 million for production; of this total, some £44 million had been spent or committed. Trial firings had proved disappointing in some respects, but it appeared that the difficulties were caused by teething troubles rather than by any basic fault which might invalidate the concept of the weapon. Further trials were proceeding at Woomera and it should be possible to make a comprehensive review towards the end of the year.

When progress was reviewed at the beginning of 1962, the Cabinet Defence Committee learned that the firing of W.100A rounds, closely representative of the final production version, was about to start, and that by August or September enough preliminary information would be available from launchings to enable the Air Ministry to assume an emergency capability.

Finally, in July 1962, a production-model Blue Steel was successfully fired after being air-launched from a Vulcan over Woomera, and on 25 July the Minister of Aviation, now Julian Amery, wrote to the Air Minister, stating:

I am glad to be able to inform you that Sir George Gardner [Controller of Aircraft, Ministry of Aviation] has today forwarded to DCAS a CA Release for Blue Steel to be carried on Vulcan Aircraft, complete with its operational warhead, in a national emergency. The clearance does not specifically authorize the launching of the missile because the required trials to prove the safety of the systems are not yet complete. However, no difficulties have been experienced up to date which affect the safety after launch and we are confident that further trials will provide the necessary proof. We expect to issue the operational launch clearance in December 1962. We have issued the present clearance on the under-standing that, should a national crisis occur which warrants the carriage of the operational Blue Steel with its warhead, limitations as to its use could

Blue Steel No. 753568 being fuelled with High Test Peroxide, an extremely volatile liquid, hence the protective suits. (via J. Marshall)

Squadron at Scampton. A great deal of time was spent discussing when the RAF should officially declare that the squadron had an 'operational capability', as Bomber Command wanted to arrange a press facility to show the Blue Steel system to the public. It was feared that a premature display of Blue Steel might lead to embarrassing questions as to the true extent of the RAF's capability at that time, and so the date of the press day was continually delayed until 14 February 1963, by which time the squadron was fully operational with at least six missiles available. Unfortunately, by this time the Skybolt programme had been cancelled, and the press were more concerned with plans for the V-Force's future than with the event being celebrated at Scampton

be overridden. In effect this means that you could declare an operational capability with Blue Steel as soon as you consider that you are in a position to do so.

The first unit to be declared operational on Blue Steel was 617

Blue Steel missiles inside their storage and servicing hangar at Scampton. (via J. Marshall)

Blue Steel No. 408680 undergoing servicing at Scampton. (via J. Marshall)

that day. However, 27 and 83 Squadrons subsequently re-equipped with Blue Steels at Scampton, followed by 139 Squadron on Victors at Wittering, their conversion beginning in October 1963, followed by 100 Squadron. On 21 August an Air Ministry Nuclear Weapon Clearance for the use of Blue Steel on Quick Reaction Alert (QRA) standby was issued, although the weapons were to be unarmed and unfuelled except in an emergency. Clearance for a fully armed and fuelled Blue Steel on QRA was finally issued on 16 April 1964.

Victor B.2R from No. 139 Squadron, carrying a Blue Steel missile on a training sortie from Wittering. (Roger Brooks collection)

Vulcan XL321 from No. 617 Squadron on the Operational Readiness Platform at Finningley. (via John Morley)

CHAPTER NINE

Second Generation

The continuing advances in Soviet defence technology dictated that the V-Bomber programme had to develop continually to remain viable as a credible nuclear deterrent. On 1 May 1960 USAF pilot Francis Gary Powers was shot down while flying his Lockheed U–2 reconnaissance aircraft over the Soviet Union at more than 65,000 ft. The fact that a surface-to-air missile could reach an altitude higher than the ceiling achievable by the V-Bombers underlined the fact that the RAF's nuclear bombers could no longer enter Soviet airspace and expect to emerge unscathed. Clearly, the bomber force had to be improved.

Blue Steel went some way to improving the effectiveness of the V-Force by enabling both the Vulcan and Victor to release their megaton–range bombs some 100 miles from the intended target. However, the 'second-generation' V-Bombers which were to carry Blue Steel represented a leap in performance capability over the Mk.1 bombers which had entered RAF service in the 1950s. A decision to proceed with the development of Mk.2 V-Bombers was first taken at a meeting of Ministers on 31 May 1956, when all of Britain's military aircraft programmes were evaluated. The meeting concluded that Vulcan development should be limited to a '2C' variant, together with a Victor 'A', both of which would be powered by Rolls-Royce Conway engines. However, the Bristol Aeroplane Company was devastated to learn that its Olympus engine was to be dropped, and by December the Minister of Supply reported:

> Bristols, faced with the cancellation of the Olympus 6, have themselves offered to carry all the development costs over and above that to which HMG were committed by the time their offer was made and to supply engines to us at the same price as Conways, if we place an order for 200 engines.

Consequently, it was agreed that the Vulcan Mk.2 should proceed with Olympus engines, and the Victor Mk.2 with Conways.

During the first half of 1955 it had been established that the Bristol B.01.6 engine would be capable of delivering 16,000-lb thrust, and promised even more power at a later stage. Design analysis indicated that, without suitable modifications, a Vulcan fitted with these more powerful engines would suffer from the high-altitude/high-speed buffet problems which the Phase 2 wing on the Vulcan B.1 had been designed to overcome. The Vulcan's delta wing would have to be redesigned again, and in

Vulcan B.2 XL385 met its fiery fate on 6 April 1967, when an engine fire broke out as the aircraft prepared for take-off at Scampton. (via Robert Jackson)

September 1955 Avro submitted a brochure to the MoS, outlining what would become the Vulcan B.Mk.2. Avro had been discussing this programme in general terms with the MoS for some time, and funds had been made available to the company to enable it to carry out R&D on the concept. Although the revised wing layout was the most obvious external difference between the Vulcan B.1 and B.2, many other changes were made to the aircraft. It was restressed to a gross weight of over 200,000 lb, more than double the weight specified in B.35/46, and the landing gear was strengthened to withstand greater take-off and landing weights. The electrical system was changed to 200V AC, and instead of direct-drive 112V generators, each engine would have a constant-speed drive and alternator. A gas turbine auxiliary air starter was installed, driven by a Rover 2S/150 engine, and the flying controls were revised, the ailerons and elevators being replaced by inner and outer elevons (combined elevators and ailerons), each with independent power control units.

The new Phase 2C wing extended the span by 12 ft to 111 ft, and increased the

Vulcan XA894 was used as a development aircraft for the Bristol Olympus engine which was to have been fitted in the TSR-2. The test engine was slung under the bomb bay. (Rolls-Royce).

thickness/chord ratio from 7.92 to 4.25 per cent and the wing area from 3,446 sq ft to 3,965 sq ft. The compound taper of the leading edge was increased over that of the B.1, and the trailing edge was also now swept. A contract for a B.2 prototype was issued to Avro in March 1956, followed by a further contract in April for the conversion of the final 17 B.1s into B.2s. The second Vulcan prototype, VX777, was selected to serve as the B.2 prototype, and on 31 August 1957 it made its first flight in the revised configuration. Unlike production B.2s, however, it was not fitted with ECM modifications (similar to those retrofitted to B.1As), and retained the tapered B.1 tailcone.

With VX777 back in the air, the new Vulcan B.2 with 12,000-lb thrust Olympus 102 engines was displayed for the first time at the 1957 SBAC show. After the Farnborough event, VX777 began a series of flight trials, and a further seven Vulcan B.1s were brought into the development programme to explore every aspect of the redesigned airframe. Early in 1958 XA891 was fitted with Olympus 200 engines rated at 16,000 lb, while XA890 was employed on avionics work and XA892 was devoted to weapons research. Vulcan XA893 was fitted with the B.2's electrical system, XA894 was used to prove the B.2/B.1A ECM fit, XA899 was also devoted to avionics work, and XA903 was used for Blue Steel trials.

Flight trials with the B.2 prototype revealed a 25–30 per cent increase in range over the B.1, effectively extending Bomber Command's target range by the same amount. Certainly the high-speed/high-altitude buffet problem did not arise, and on 4 March 1959 the first production B.2, XH533, reached 61,500 ft during a test flight. This aircraft had made maiden flight on 19 August 1958, powered by Olympus 200s rated at

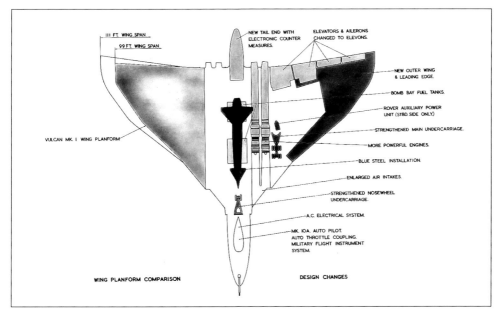

Vulcan B.2 design features.

Vulcan B.2s nearing completion on the Woodford production line. (British Aerospace)

16,000 lb, and it is interesting to note that it took to the air before the final Vulcan B.1s had rolled off the Woodford production line, the last B.1 to be completed making its first flight in February of the following year. Likewise, the second production B.2, XH534, flew in January, ahead of the last B.1, and was the first aircraft to fly with production-standard Olympus 201s rated at 17,000 lb, together with a full ECM fit. Conversely, the following three B.2's first flew without ECM modifications, though these were fitted later.

As production of the Vulcan B.2 got under way, the first seven aircraft, including the prototype, were assigned to trials work, XH534 being deployed to Boscombe Down for CA Release trials. The CA Release was granted in May 1960, and on 1 July 1960 Vulcan B.2 XH558 was delivered to RAF Waddington, joining 230 OCU as the first B.2 to enter RAF service. In August XH559 was delivered, followed by XH560, XH561, and XH562 before the end of the year. Bristol Siddeley was loaned XH557 for engine trials, and it was re-equipped with what was to become the ultimate development of the Vulcan's powerplant, the Olympus 301, rated at 20,000 lb. Two 301 engines were fitted in XH557's outer engine nacelles, the bomber flying for the first time in this configuration on 19 May 1961. Although these immensely powerful engines required a greatly increased amount of intake airflow compared with the engines of the Vulcan B.1, the first production B.2s retained the same intakes as their predecessors, XH557 being the first B.2 to be modified with a slightly deepened lower intake lip designed to accommodate an increased airflow mass.

After completing trials with Bristol Siddeley, XH557 received a further two

Vulcan B.2 trials aircraft XH533 prior to installation of tail ECM modifications. Hawker Siddeley and Avro emblems are painted on the fuselage and tail, together with 'Bristol Olympus Engines' on the engine intakes. (British Aerospace)

A line-up of Vulcans at Scampton. The smaller B.1-sized intake fitted to early B.2s is clearly evident on XH554. (Tim Laming collection)

Olympus 301s and entered regular RAF service. Approximately half of the B.2 fleet was fitted with Olympus 301s, the remaining aircraft retaining 17,000 lb Olympus 201s. Contrary to statements in many historical accounts, the Vulcans fitted with 20,000-lb thrust engines were not given a new designation; the Vulcan 'B.2A' never actually existed.

Although the continued production of Vulcans enabled the RAF to form more squadrons, official policy dictated that the B.2s should first be delivered to an established unit, which would pass their B.1s to newly-converted squadrons. Consequently the first crews to leave 'B' Flight of 230 OCU went to 83 Squadron at Scampton, where conversion on to the B.2 began in November 1960. On 1 April 1961, 27 Squadron formed on B.2s at Scampton, and the Scampton Wing was completed in September 1961 when 617

Squadron began the transition to B.2s. Waddington, however, standardized on the B.1A, 44 Squadron forming on 10 August 1960 with former 83 Squadron aircraft (the first B.1A arriving in January 1961). In June 1960 101 Squadron relocated from Finningley, and 50 Squadron formed on 1 August with former 617 Squadron Vulcans. The Vulcan OCU then moved to Finningley, where it was divided into 'A' Flight with B.1s and B.1As, and 'B' Flight with B.2s. Finningley also became the home of the Bomber Command Development Unit (BCDU), which operated a mixed fleet of Valiants, Vulcans, and Victors for various trials.

The second Vulcan B.2 Wing was formed at Coningsby, where 9 Squadron was established on 1 March 1962, followed by 12 Squadron on 1 July and 35 Squadron on 1 December. The Wing

Vulcan XM600 on final approach to Coningsby. The aircraft crashed near Spilsby during January 1977 after developing an engine fire. (Denis O'Brien)

relocated to Cottesmore in November 1964, and the final production Vulcan, XM657, was delivered to that station on 15 January 1965, joining 35 Squadron. Following an initial order for 25 Vulcan B.2s, a further contract for 24 aircraft was followed by a final one for 40 aircraft. The final B.1A conversion was XH503, which was delivered to Waddington during March 1963, after which the remaining unmodified B.1s were withdrawn from use or reassigned to the BCDU or OCU at Finningley. Starting in 1966 the Waddington Wing converted on to B.2s, completing the transition at the end of 1967. The OCU then relinquished its remaining B.1s and the RAF effectively standardized on the Vulcan B.2 from 1968 onwards.

The relatively small firm of Handley Page was keen to continue the production run of Victor B.1s to maximize returns on the R&D costs which had gone into the Victor programme. The Air Staff, however, wanted more powerful Victor B.2s, initially to be powered by 14,000 lb Sapphire 9s and having an increased wingspan of 115 ft, progressing to 137 ft wingspan to accommodate Conway or Olympus engines. The Air Staff were unconvinced that the Rolls-Royce

Conway would reach its promised potential, whereas the Government was keen to pursue development of the same engine. Therefore, while the Air Staff looked at the possibility of acquiring a Victor Phase 3 with four Olympus or even six Sapphire engines, Handley Page proposed a Victor Phase 2A powered by four Conways within a minimally modified 120ft-span wing. If the Phase 3 development failed to live up to expectations, it could be refitted with Olympus engines at a later stage. The Air Staff liked this proposal, and ordered that the first eight Victor B.1s of the second production batch should be completed with Sapphire 7s, while the next 25 would be fitted with Sapphire 9s. A further contract placed in January 1956 covered a further 18 Victors to the as yet undefined Phase 2A standard.

On 9 February 1956 work on the Sapphire 9, designed for the abandoned 'thin-wing' Gloster Javelin, was terminated, leaving Handley Page with a Victor Phase 2 but no suitable engine to power it. In November the Air Staff decided that the Victor Phase 2 would be cancelled, and that production of the standard Victor B.1 (i.e. Phase 1) would be continued up to the 25th aircraft of

Vulcan B.2 XL425 pictured at Scampton whilst serving with No. 617 Squadron. (via British Aerospace)

the second contract, which finished with XH667. The remaining eight aircraft would then be completed as Victor Phase 2A (B.Mk.2) aircraft with 17,250 lb Conway Co.11 engines. The new Conway engine was physically larger than the Sapphire, although Handley Page retained the existing B.1 engine-bay ribs to avoid the costs and delays of producing new centre-section assembly jigs. Deeper intake ducts were required to cater for the increased airflow mass, and this imposed a greater load on the wing spar, which would already be carrying greater aerodynamic loads. As a consequence the Conways were surrounded by reinforced 'spectacles' forged from 6ft square slabs of alloy, which strengthened the whole structure. Initial trials of the Conway engine were dogged by technical troubles, not least the engine's susceptibility to surging, which created many dramatic scenes of flaming jetpipes during numerous ground runs. The engine problems took nearly two years to solve completely, partly by making modifications to the engine itself, but also by adding vertical plates inside the Victor's huge engine intakes to smooth the swirling intake air before it entered the engines' compressors.

As with the Vulcan, the more powerful engines in the Victor B.2 required greater wing area, and this was increased to 2,600 sq ft to maintain a good manoeuvre margin above stalling speed at the higher altitudes achievable with the Conways. The increase in span to 120 ft could not be achieved simply by adding extra surface to the wingtips, as this would

A majestic in-flight view of Victor XA930, the prototype's clean lines having already been lost, thanks to the development of underwing fuel tanks and a refuelling probe. (Handley Page)

Victor salutes Victor in a classic Vauxhall publicity photograph from the 1960s. (Handley Page)

have moved the wing's c.g. too far aft, so the 'stretch' was achieved by adding 3 ft 6 in to each wingtip and 18 in to each wing root. The electrical system was changed to constant-frequency AC, and a Blackburn-Turbomeca Artouste auxiliary power unit was installed in the starboard wing stub, giving the aircraft (like the Vulcan B.2) a self-start capability. As with the Vulcan B.2, the Victor B.2's all-up weight rose dramatically beyond the figure specified in B.35/46. Its maximum take-off weight with a bomb bay fuel tank was 204,000 lb, and this increased to 223,000 lb with underwing drop tanks (which were also designed by Avro for the Vulcan, but were never manufactured). The new B.2 could reach an altitude of 60,000 ft, but its maximum speed was, conversely, less than that attainable by the B.1, as beyond Mach 0.92 the aircraft began to suffer from buffeting in much the same way that early Vulcan B.1s had before the introduction of the Phase 2 wing.

The January 1956 contract included the construction of one prototype Mk.2

Victor, and B.1 XH668 was suitably modified to undertake this role, making its first flight on 20 February 1959. The aircraft departed for Boscombe Down early in June to begin 'preview handling', and on 20 August it took off from Boscombe Down to explore the wing buffet boundary at 52,000 ft, during a series of high-speed turns up to Mach 0.94. The flight's progress was monitored on the ground by radar, and at 11:37 the Victor disappeared from the radar screen, reappearing briefly as multiple traces before vanishing again somewhere over the Irish Sea. Radio contact was lost, though much of the flight had been conducted in radio silence in any case. Fears that the Victor's tail unit might have separated again were only compounded by reports from the crew of a small boat, who had heard two loud bangs followed by a splash south of St Bride's Bay.

Farnborough's Accident Investigation Branch ordered a search for the aircraft wreckage, and a salvage vessel located the remains of XH668 at a depth of 400 ft.

Victor B.2 XL164 at Radlett, illustrating the wing aerodynamic fairings fitted to the B.2 fleet.
(Handley Page)

Some 16 trawlers were then brought in to gather nearly 600,000 pieces of wreckage, representing about 70 per cent of the airframe. These components were transported to Farnborough, where they were compared with parts of the second B.1 prototype, WB775, which was dismantled for the investigation.

The copilot's wristwatch, which had stopped at 11:30, confirmed the radar evidence of the disaster, while a voltmeter registering 200V indicated that the electrical system was still functioning when the aircraft crashed. Finally, investigators turned their attention to the

Victor's wingtips. The port pitot head was found in a severely damaged condition, while the starboard pitot head was completely missing from its mounting socket. It was concluded, therefore, that it must have come adrift before the wingtip hit the sea, and vibration tests confirmed that the pitot head's retaining collet could work loose if it was subjected to the kind of buffeting which would have been experienced in the high-speed turns which the Victor was making at the time of the accident. It therefore seemed certain that the pitot head must have disconnected at about

A Wittering-based Victor B.2 in clean configuration, minus refuelling probe and under-wing fuel tanks.
(Handley Page)

A Victor B.2 XL232 from No. 139 Squadron, Wethersfield, May 1962. (R. L. Ward)

Mach 0.4, effectively disabling both the Mach trimmer and stall detector systems. This would have caused the former to depress the aircraft's elevators in order to push the nose down, while the stall detector would have lowered the wing-leading-edge nose flaps. In the midst of some very severe test flight manoeuvring this sudden forceful nose-down attitude would probably have been beyond the control of the pilots, and, as the wrecked throttles had been found in the closed position, it appeared that one of the pilots had attempted to reduce speed in what must have rapidly become a supersonic dive. Tragically, the Victor B.2 prototype had been destroyed because of a simple collet, which was subsequently locked positively so that it could not vibrate loose.

Production of the first Victor B.2s began long before the final B.1s were completed. For example, the 40th B.1, XH619, was rolled out in May 1959, while the second B.2, XH669, was completed just three months later. Following the loss of the prototype and the tragic deaths of Sqn Ldrs R. J.

Morgan and G.B. Stockman, Flt Lts L.N. Williams and R.J. Hanniford, and Handley Page's Bob Williams, XH669 took up the B.2 development programme, XH670 joining it in November. Victor XH671 was completed in March 1960, and XH672 completed test work on the Conway engines before beginning autopilot trials. For the 1960 SBAC show XH669 made the first public display by a B.2, complete with the new ECM fit which had also been incorporated into the Vulcans. The first B.2 to be delivered to Bomber Command was XL188, which joined the B.2 Trials Unit at Cottesmore on 2 November 1961. Two more Victors, XL165 and XL189, arrived on 8 November and 16 December, after which the unit was renamed as 'C' Flight of 232 OCU in preparation for the arrival of the first B.2 students. The rest of 232 OCU remained at Gaydon, where space was limited, which led to the decision to relocate the B.2 element to Cottesmore.

On 1 February 1962 139 Squadron formed at Wittering as the first Victor B.2 squadron, with XL231 as its first aircraft, further deliveries being made at monthly intervals. The next unit to form was 100 Squadron on 1 May 1962, after which the two squadrons, both assigned Blue Steel missiles, were joined by the OCU B.2 element, which had been renamed the Victor Training Flight. Changes to the Victor B.1 fleet involved the establishment of 10 and 15 Squadrons (with Victor B.1s) at Cottesmore, while 57 Squadron was formed at Honington on 1 January 1959, receiving XH614 in March and the last Victor B.1, XH667, as its tenth aircraft. Twenty-five aircraft from the 1955 B.1 order were designated for conversion to B.1A standard, with the B.2's ECM fit, although XH617 was written-off after an accident, leading to the conversion of just 24 airframes. On 1 September 1960 55 Squadron formed at Honington and, unlike the Vulcan, both Victor B.1s and B.1As remained in service together, distributed among the Gaydon, Cottesmore, and Honington units.

The delivery of the last Victor B.2s represented the culmination of Britain's long-established plans to equip the RAF with an effective nuclear deterrent. By 1961, with a combined force of 144 Valiants, Victor B.1s and B.2s, and Vulcan B.1s and B.2s, Bomber Command possessed awesome striking power beyond anything imaginable during the Second World War. The first-generation 20-kiloton Blue Danube fission weapon was gradually withdrawn during 1960, Red Beard replacing it as the RAF's main fission weapon. Red Beard was essentially a tactical bomb, however, developed into Mk.1 (15-kiloton) and Mk.2 (25-kiloton) versions to be carried by RAF and Fleet Air Arm tactical strike aircraft (the Canberra, Scimitar, Sea Vixen, and Buccaneer), although Valiants, Vulcans and Victors were capable of carrying the weapon. The Yellow Sun Mk.1, with a yield of 500 kilotons, was superseded by

Yellow Sun Mk.2 beginning in February 1962, initial stocks going to Waddington. The Red Snow warhead, which was also fitted to Blue Steel, was manufactured to deliver one of three different yields, and it is likely that both the Blue Steel and Yellow Sun warheads were largely of the one-megaton variety, the remainder being 500-kiloton.

The government's unease at the prospect of relying on fixed-site ballistic missiles, which could take at least 15 min to prepare for launching, prompted a search for a more suitable nuclear delivery system to replace Blue Steel towards the end of the 1960s. The difficulties and costs associated with the production of Blue Steel Mk.1 effectively killed off the Mk.2 project and, with the Thor missile system as a 'stop-gap', Britain seemed destined to rely upon the developing Blue Streak missile as the main nuclear deterrent for the late 1960s, though the system, which differed very little from Thor, was likely to be obsolete even before it entered service.

It was at this stage that Britain again looked towards America, where the Douglas GAM-87A Skybolt missile was being developed. This air-launched nuclear-tipped guided bomb was to be capable of delivering a sizeable warhead from a range in excess of 1,000 miles, far beyond the capabilities of Blue Steel. Talks with the US President at Camp David suggested that there would be no American objection to the British purchase of Skybolts if necessary, and it was also indicated that the sea-launched Polaris might also be made available, should Britain be interested. The ever-increasing cost of the Blue Streak programme, and the pressing fears that the weapon would be very vulnerable to Soviet attack, led to the conclusion that an updated V-Force, equipped with Skybolts, would be a much cheaper and much more credible option than relying on another non-mobile IRBM which would be an easy target for Soviet attack. Consequently, Blue Streak was abandoned.

Skybolt was originally designed in response to a USAF requirement for an air-launched strategic-range nuclear missile to be carried by SAC Boeing B-52s and Convair B-58s. It was quickly established that development of the weapon would be completed to enable the first Skybolts to enter RAF service in 1966, although a new carrier for the weapons would probably be required by 1970 because the Vulcans and Victors would reach the end of their useful life at that time. Macmillan was keen to place a provisional order for 100 Skybolts, but the Chancellor was rather more cautious, not least because the missile was only just beginning development. However, following the meeting between Macmillan and Eisenhower in March 1960, a minute was issued by the US Government which stated:

In a desire to be of assistance in improving and extending the effective life of the V-bomber force, the United States, subject only to United States

priorities, is prepared to provide Skybolt missiles — minus warheads — to the United Kingdom on a reimbursable basis in 1965 or thereafter. Since Skybolt is still in the early stages of development, this offer is necessarily dependent on the successful and timely completion of its development programme.

The minute also made mention of Polaris, stating:

As the United Kingdom is aware, the United States is offering at the current Nato Defence Ministers' meeting to make mobile Polaris missiles — minus warheads — available from US production to Nato countries in order to meet Saceur's requirements for MRBMs [medium-range ballistic missiles]. The United States is also offering to assist joint European production of Polaris if our preference for United States production proves unacceptable.

Given that Britain and France were the only Nato countries outside the USA with a nuclear capability (and therefore,

Two Vulcan B.2 Skybolt trials aircraft at Woodford, destined to be the only V-Bombers to carry this weapon. (British Aerospace).

the only countries able to operate the missiles), this offer was of particular significance to Britain, who effectively had the luxury of a choice between two weapons systems.

However, Britain continued to pursue the Skybolt programme, even though American concerns over the possible success of the development programme were being expressed as early as 1961. With more than 150,000 component parts, 60,000 of which had to function perfectly in order to launch the missile, Skybolt was a very complex piece of hardware. The first five launches in 1962 ended in failure, and the US Secretary of Defense notified his British counterparts that, although they did not believe Skybolt was a technical failure, they did believe that continuing the programme would be a waste of money in view of the emergence of other delivery systems at that time, such as Hound Dog and Minuteman. It was pointed out that the Skybolt missile was essentially a research programme at the time when Britain first requested it, rather than being a production weapon. Consequently, the path would be open for Britain to continue development of Skybolt in association with a scaled-down American effort, or to develop Skybolt in isolation, albeit by using American technology. Another option would be to adopt the Hound Dog missile, or to participate in a multilateral force of sea-launched (Polaris) missiles, under the terms being offered in March 1960. The Hound Dog option was quickly discounted because the weapon could not be carried by V–Bombers, and the Ministry of Defence (MoD) concluded that the real options for Britain were to acquire Polaris, complete Skybolt in America, complete Skybolt in the UK, or produce a ballistic weapon in co-operation with France.

It had already been agreed that the V-Force dispersal concept, whereby the bombers would leave their home bases in a wartime emergency and relocate in groups of four or two to 36 dispersal airfields scattered around the UK, would not be a credible option for very long without improvement, as the increasing sophistication of Soviet attack forces meant that bombers on the ground in any location would be at risk from attack. The best alternative to a dispersal policy would be to mount a continuous airborne alert, with Skybolt-equipped bombers maintaining a round-the-clock airborne presence, immune from attack. It was an expensive and technically difficult concept, but one which America was pursuing at the time. If Skybolt was abandoned, Britain would have to choose one of two expensive alternatives; either adopt an Anglo-French ballistic missile system, which would mean accepting all the disadvantages of Blue Streak again, or buy the Polaris missiles, and a submarine fleet from which to launch them. When Prime Minister Macmillan met President Kennedy at Nassau in the Bahamas during December 1962, Macmillan pressed Kennedy to continue with the Skybolt programme, but as a post-talk report stated, Kennedy, who was fairly ambivalent towards British interests, wanted to abandon the project:

The President and the Prime Minister reviewed the development programme for the Skybolt missile. The President explained that it was no longer expected that this very complex weapon system would be completed within the cost estimate or the timescale which were projected when the programme was begun. The President informed the Prime Minister that for this reason, and because of the availability to the United States of alternative weapon systems, he had decided to cancel plans for the production of Skybolt by the United States. Nevertheless, recognizing the importance of the Skybolt programme for the United Kingdom, and recalling that the purpose of the offer of Skybolt in 1960 had been to assist in improving and extending the effective life of the British V-bombers, the President expressed his readiness to continue with the development of the missile as a joint enterprise between the United States and the United Kingdom, with each country bearing equal shares of the future cost of completing development, after which the United Kingdom would be able to place a production order to meet its requirements.

This was a very generous offer to Britain, bearing in mind that Kennedy had little practical reason to provide any further funds for the Skybolt programme, and was not a great believer in the Special Relationship. Macmillan recognized the value of Kennedy's offer, but the continuing doubts over technical difficulties, rising costs, and delays in the delivery timescale prompted him to decline the opportunity to divert more financial responsibility on to Britain. Likewise, Macmillan could not accept Hound Dog because of the time and expense which would be involved in modifying the Vulcan and/or Victor to carry it. Instead he 'held out' for Polaris, and Kennedy agreed that America would provide Polaris missiles, minus warheads, for British submarines. Consequently, Skybolt was officially cancelled by America on 31 December 1962, just a few days after a test round had made a perfect launch from a B-52 over the Eglin weapons range. As far as the RAF was concerned the programme officially ended on 3 January 1963, and, having abandoned Skybolt in favour of Polaris,

the British airborne nuclear deterrent was to be transformed into a seaborne system. However, until Polaris could be brought into service the V-Force would have to remain viable, and the Air Staff turned their attention to ways in which Bomber Command could maintain a credible nuclear deterrent until the end of the 1960s.

The Air Staff concluded that, beyond the mid-1960s, improvements in Russian air defences would mean that it would be practically impossible to penetrate Soviet airspace at high level. The V-Force would have to attack at low level if it was to survive. Soviet radar systems had been geared towards the detection of high-flying bombers, and although the range and sensitivity of their equipment was continuing to improve, radar detection was not effective at heights of around 3,000 ft or lower, where aircraft radar returns began to merge with other forms of ground-generated 'clutter'. Clearly, if the V-Force was trained to attack at low altitude (500 ft or less), the Soviet radar systems would probably be unable to detect them at all. Fears were expressed that the V-Bombers would not be capable of performing a low-level penetration role, bearing in mind that they were designed for high-altitude operations. The BCDU at Finningley pioneered a series of test flights to prove that low-level sorties could be conducted safely, and a Vulcan and Victor were sent to Libya to perform a series of ultra-low flights over the desert to demonstrate the capability still further. In any case, the Valiants which had been assigned to Saceur had already begun low-level operations without experiencing any significant problems. The Vulcan B.1A squadrons at Waddington (44, 50, and 101), and the Victor B.1A squadrons at Honington (55 and 57) and Cottesmore (10 and 15), were assigned to low-level operations in March 1963. Training

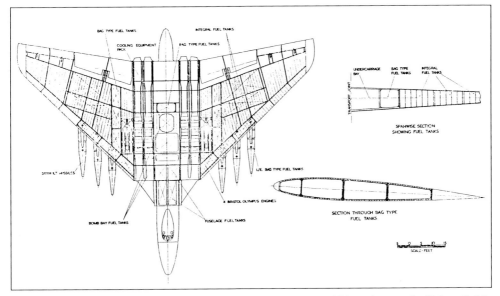

Arrangement drawings for the Vulcan Phase Six design which would have become the Vulcan B.3 in RAF service. With six Skybolts the aircraft would have given the RAF a round-the-clock airborne deterrent capability.

flights were normally made at 1,000 ft (a conservative figure aimed at preserving aircraft fatigue life), but every third sortie was flown at 500 ft. The Mk.2 Victors and Vulcans assumed a low-level role as of 1 May 1964.

Blue Steel also had to be 're-roled', as outlined in a revised version of the original Operational Requirement: 'The Air Staff requires the further development of the Blue Steel missile to enable it to be launched from Mk.2 V-bombers flying at the lowest possible level in the height band 250 ft–1,000 ft'. After a further series of trials in the UK and at Woomera, the Blue Steel missile was found to be readily capable of being launched at low level, and after release its motor was ignited and Blue Steel zoom-climbed to 17,000 ft before beginning a terminal descent to its target. Having been designed for high-altitude launch, and then having had operational profiles developed around it, Blue Steel entered RAF service primarily as a low-level weapon, requiring a completely different

training programme.

The V-Force's main nuclear weapon, Yellow Sun Mk.2, was incapable of low-level delivery, however, and bombers assigned to Yellow Sun delivery were trained to make low-level penetrations followed by brief 'pop-up' ascents to medium altitude, from where the bomb could be released. This was a far-from-ideal situation, and the Air Staff accepted that a new weapon would be required for low-level delivery. Joint Naval/Air Staff Requirement NASR.1177 gave the appropriate details:

Because of envisaged enemy counter-measures and the need to change aircraft approach and delivery tactics, the existing British nuclear bombs Yellow Sun, Blue Steel, and Red Beard will be unsuitable as primary weapons beyond 1975. Moreover, with the cancellation of Skybolt as the planned replacement for Yellow Sun and the introduction of Polaris unlikely to become effective before 1970, and

A dramatic shot of a Vulcan B.2 over the North Sea, clearly illustrating a slightly rippled wing skinning, revealing the internal structural layout. (RAF Cottesmore).

urgent need exists for a new bomb to maintain the United Kingdom independent deterrent during the interim period and as a supplementary capability thereafter.

By 1966, the manned bomber aircraft may survive enemy defences in the European theatre and deliver a successful strike only by flying at high speed at very low level. Yellow Sun and Blue Steel are designed for release at medium/high altitude where the

delivery aircraft and/or bomb is vulnerable to interception, whilst Red Beard cannot withstand the low-level flight environment, is limited in method of fuzing and delivery, and possesses some undesirable safety restrictions when held at readiness in an operational state. Early replacement is essential. The replacement bomb must be multi-purpose by design. It must satisfy joint Naval and Air Staff requirements for carriage and

Vulcan B.2s on detachment to New Zealand, with personnel looking on as a Vulcan begins a traditional ear-splitting demonstration. (RAF Cottesmore)

Vulcan XM646 illustrating the standard V-Bomber camouflage scheme for the 1960s. The national insignia markings were confined to the nose, tail and port upper wing. (RAF Cottesmore)

delivery in current medium-bomber aircraft and planned high-performance aircraft, to exploit fully their low-level strike capability against strategic and tactical, hard and soft targets, with corresponding different warhead yields. Research and development studies show clearly that such a bomb can be produced fully within the timescale. However, to maintain an effective United Kingdom nuclear deterrent during development of the Polaris weapon system, priority is given to

Victor B.2R XL513, the first Victor to receive grey/green disruptive camouflage. Unusually, the lower surface colour demarcation line is high on the fuselage side, and 'washed-out' national insignia have been retained, together with white serials. (Handley Page)

production of the high-yield version for the RAF medium bomber force.

The bomb, WE177, was to be used as a 'laydown' weapon, either by ballistic/loft mode or by retarded (parachute) delivery. It was also to be as small and light as possible, the type 'B' version not to exceed 1,000 lb (in fact it weighed 950 lb, while WE177A weighed 600 lb). Both 'A' and 'B', the designations referring to different yields of 200 kilotons and 400 kilotons, were 144 in long and had a carcass diameter of 16.5 in and a tail-fin span of 24 in. Deliveries of the WE177A began in September 1966, and trials were conducted with a Vulcan B.2 at Cottesmore. The WE177C was a 10-kiloton naval derivative of the same weapon, carried by Buccaneers and Sea Harriers until the weapon was withdrawn in 1992.

The aircraft in the low-level Vulcan and Victor force were modified with an updated ECM fit, sidescan radar, roller maps, ground position indicator equipment, and terrain-following radar. The all-white anti-flash paint was replaced on their upper surfaces by a disruptive grey/green camouflage, the first aircraft so finished being Vulcan XH505, which emerged from Hawker Siddeley Aviation's Bitteswell plant on 24 March 1964.

Thus the V-Force was assigned to 'high-low-high' delivery profiles, with 'a low-level phase of up to 1,000 nm in the extreme case' (for training sorties this would normally be 350–500 nm). All-weather operations were practised, and the practice height of the low-level phase of an operational sortie would be left to the discretion of the aircraft captain. In poor visibility conditions this might be 1,000 ft, but in good weather it could be as low as an incredible 50 ft. For delivery of Yellow Sun, and possibly of Red Beard if required for a 'second strike', the captain would fly a 'pop-up' manoeuvre to 12,000 ft. Consequently, the unmistakable shape and sound of Valiants, Vulcans, and Victors became a more regular part of country life in the UK as the V-Force crews thundered around at 500 ft, or even lower in specific low-flying areas.

Vulcans and Victors at Tengah, Singapore. (Roger Brooks collection)

CHAPTER TEN

The Final Years

As Britain prepared to accept deliveries of Polaris missiles, the V-Force's Blue Steel operations began to wind down. The two Victor B.2 squadrons at Wittering, 100 and 139, were disbanded on 1 October and 31 December 1968, while the Scampton Wing continued operations until 1969, when 83 Squadron disbanded on 31 August, followed by 27 Squadron's transfer to free-fall operations on 31 December. The unit's records note:

> On 1 July at 00:01 Quick Reaction Alert ended without fuss at midnight.

A congratulatory signal was received from the C-in-C, thus marking the end of one of the most important chapters in the squadron's history. It seemed a pity that there was no greater recognition for a job well done.

The final Blue Steel unit, 617 Squadron, made its last Blue Steel training flight on 31 December 1970, marking the end of the RAF's operational experience with the stand-off weapon.

As 27 Squadron's records indicated, the QRA posture also ended in 1969,

617 Squadron Vulcan XL360 taxying onto RAF Luqa's flight line. Vulcans were regular visitors to Malta on long-range training exercises. (Richard Caruana)

having first begun in 1962, when the AOC-in-C Bomber Command first suggested that one aircraft in each V-Bomber squadron (two aircraft in some cases from the end of 1962 onwards) should be maintained at 15 min readiness as a deterrent against a 'bolt from the blue' attack. No-notice exercises had also begun in 1962, requiring the V-Bomber crews to scramble their aircraft quickly to the chain of dispersal airfields around the country. As the Thor system was gradually withdrawn the number of aircraft held at 15 min readiness increased to 20, and in 1963 many of the dispersal airfields were modified to incorporate Operational Readiness Platforms (ORPs) close to the runway threshold, from where either two or four bombers could start engines and roll directly on to the runway for immediate take-off.

From 1966 onwards the number of dispersal airfields was reduced, reflecting the gradual run-down of the QRA commitment. Waddington's Vulcans were assigned Finningley and Marham as 'near dispersals', and Wattisham, Filton, Machrihanish, Manston, Valley, and Brawdy as 'distant dispersals'. Scampton's Blue Steel Vulcans deployed to Coningsby and Bedford for near dispersal, and Kinloss, Lossiemouth, and Boscombe Down for distant ones, while Cottesmore's Vulcans used Honington and Leconfield for near dispersals and Pershore, Leuchars, Lyneham, Yeovilton, Ballykelly, and Leeming as distant ones. Wittering's Blue Steel Victors were assigned to near dispersals at Gaydon, Wyton, and Coltishall, with distant dispersal at St Mawgan. Dispersals

Four Vulcan B.2s on Finningley's Operational Readiness Platform. Both the aircraft and the RAF station are now long gone.
(British Aerospace)

A line-up of Vulcans pictured during a detachment to Cyprus. XH560 in the foreground was later converted to B.2(MRR) standard, and then to K.2 tanker configuration. This aircraft was finally scrapped at Marham. (RAF Cottesmore)

abandoned in 1966 were Middleton St George, Cranwell, Prestwick, Llanbedr, Burtonwood, Bruntingthorpe, and Elvington.

Following the merger of Bomber Command into Strike Command at the end of April 1968, Strike Command's records state:

At midnight on 30 June 1969 the Medium Bomber Force of Strike Command handed over to the Royal Navy the responsibility for providing the UK permanent peacetime QRA force. Over the past seven years a proportion of the V-force has been held at a high state of readiness to counter surprise attacks whilst, at all times, the remainder of the force has maintained the capability to generate all weapon systems to meet their commitments to Nato. The peacekeeping value of this contribution to Nato and the Western cause has been inestimable; the burden has been a very heavy one and has demanded dedicated service from air and ground crews alike. The handover of the QRA responsibilities will entail only minor changes in the state of readiness of the V-force and in all other respects it will continue to function and have the same operational commitments as before. The V-force will maintain its unique contribution to the long-range Western deterrent and will continue assigned as part of the Nato deterrent force.

Many previous accounts of the RAF's V-Force have regarded the handover of the QRA commitment to the Royal Navy as being the official ending of the V-Force itself. This was not the case, as both the Vulcan and Victor continued to form a vital part of the RAF's (and therefore Britain's) nuclear strike plans for many more years.

The Valiant, however, followed an operational career which was markedly different to that of the Vulcan and Victor. Designed primarily as an 'insurance' aircraft against the possibility of the Vulcan and Victor being unsuitable for the bomber role, the Valiant's raison d'être was essentially removed when the Vulcan and Victor entered RAF service. Of course, the aircraft had become much more than a 'stop-gap' and had proved to be an excellent bomber, as well as a strategic reconnaissance platform and aerial refuelling tanker. During

Wittering Wing Victor B.2 XL231 pictured during a visit to RAF Luqa. The Wittering wing badge is visible on the tail. (Richard Caruana)

December 1957 the Air Staff suggested that Valiants could replace Canberras which had been assigned to Saceur as part of the Nato alliance, 'to make the best use of the Valiants that will become surplus to the front line in 1961'. During the previous August it had been established that the front-line strength of the V-Force should be 144 aircraft, which would mean that many of the Mk.1 bombers (especially Valiants) would no longer be required once the final deliveries of Mk.2 Vulcans and Victors had been made. Saceur's Canberras did not have a blind-bombing capability, and their low-level role was using up airframe fatigue life at a fairly rapid rate; therefore the Valiant would be a useful replacement. In view of the Valiant's higher running expenses it was proposed that the fleet of 64 Canberras be replaced by 24 Valiants each capable of carrying two tactical nuclear bombs, effectively balancing the shortfall in delivery capability.

Valiant B.1 WZ362 ended her operational career with the Bomber Command Development Unit at Finningley, before being scrapped in 1964. (R. L. Ward)

WP206, a Valiant B.1, served with Nos 138 and 49 Squadrons before joining Marshalls at Cambridge, where the aircraft was engaged on a variety of equipment trials. (R. L. Ward)

The Air Staff decided that two squadrons of Valiants (16 aircraft) would remain assigned to aerial refuelling duties, which were becoming increasingly important to both Bomber Command and Fighter Command, while three squadrons of bombers (24 aircraft) would be assigned to Saceur. Consequently 207 Squadron at Marham was transferred to Saceur (albeit with Bomber Command still retaining national control) on 1 January 1960. The Mk.5 American nuclear bombs with which the Valiant was armed were returned to the USA after agreement was given to supply Mk.28 bombs (with a varying yield of up to 100 kilotons) to the Valiant Tactical Bomber Force (TBF). These weapons were assigned to the Valiants under the same terms as the Project 'E' bombs supplied to the rest of the V-Force, although when Project 'E' was terminated the TBF weapons were retained. The remaining two Valiant squadrons at Marham, 49 and 148, were transferred to Saceur on 13 July 1961, and the Valiant's dual-carriage weapon capability came into effect on the same day.

Like the rest of the V-Force, the Valiant

Valiant B(PR).1 WZ394 served exclusively with No. 543 Squadron at Wyton throughout its operational career, ending her days on that station's scrap heap in the summer of 1965. (R. L. Ward)

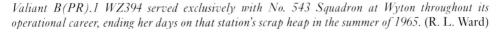

An interesting meeting of two Valiants from Bomber Command and a Strategic Air Command B-36. Although the Valiant was essentially a medium-range bomber, it contrasts dramatically with the piston-engined (but ultra long-ranged) Peacemaker.(B.Hulme)

TBF also maintained a QRA commitment, although arrangements were slightly different because of the American ownership of the aircraft's weapons. This is indicated in a Bomber Command report, which states that Saceur aircraft would be:

. . . held in readiness in an alert parking area which, with the exception of a removable barrier across the access taxiway, will be entirely closed by a 6 ft chain-link fence. Permanent security lighting to the same standard as at present in use at supplementary storage areas [where the RAF housed the V-Force's nuclear bombs] will be provided to illuminate the area during the hours of darkness. This parking area will be able to accommodate up to four aircraft. Aircrew and groundcrew at readiness will be accommodated in buildings within 250 yd of the alert parking area.

Bomber Command also stated that a US Custodial Attachment would:

. . . retain custody of special weapons being transported to the alert site from the storage area, retain custody of all special weapons on QRA and those additional weapons brought to a QRA

status and provide a minimum of one US custodial with each weapon on alert status. When two weapons are loaded on an aircraft, an additional US custodial will not be required.

While the main bomber force of Valiant B.1s gradually withdrew to make way for Vulcans and Victors, the main bomber force at Marham remained active as Saceur's main strike force. The remaining Valiants were assigned to the increasingly important tanker role and to strategic reconnaissance, the latter role being the responsibility of 543 Squadron at Wyton. During July 1954 three of the squadron's aircraft set out on a long-range exercise which terminated at Salisbury in Rhodesia. One of the unit's Valiants, WZ394, was found to have developed a crack in the wing rear spar, necessitating the return of the aircraft to Wyton for repairs. On 6 August WP217 was in the middle of a training sortie with 232 OCU when the aircrew heard a loud bang and then felt a severe shudder. The aircraft was quickly flown back to Gaydon, and on final approach to the airfield it was found that the starboard flap would not extend. Following a flapless landing, engineers found that the aircraft's rear spar had cracked and the starboard flap drive had sheared. As a

A magnificent illustration of Valiant XD819 climbing away from Marham during the early 1960s. (B. Hulme)

precautionary measure most of the Valiant fleet was inspected, and it was discovered that all of the Valiants were suffering from rear-wing-spar cracks. This meant that most of the fleet would have to be grounded, or at least restricted to minimal flying, until repairs could be effected.

Early in December 1964 further inspections revealed that the Valiant's front spars were suffering from even bigger cracks, and a signal was sent to Bomber Command on 9 December ordering a complete cessation of flying expect in a national emergency. With the exception of just one aircraft the entire Valiant fleet was affected, and none could be cleared to a normal flight safety standard. Clearly it was not financially practical to repair the wing spars of a 61-strong bomber force which was due for retirement in 4–5 years, and the only alternative was to withdraw all of the Valiants from RAF service. The MoD formally ordered their withdrawal on 26 January. In the meantime 12 Valiants had been returned to flying condition, and a handful were also cleared for limited operations until 11 December, when all flying stopped, pending a decision on the Valiant's future. The Saceur

commitment had been maintained throughout this period, although no flying took place after 11 December, the date which effectively marked the end of all RAF Valiant operations.

In the case of 543 Squadron the Valiant's untimely withdrawal was not a major problem, as plans had been made to re-equip with reconnaissance-configured Victors towards the end of 1965. Victor B.1s were first attached to 543 Squadron (for radar reconnaissance duties) in March 1958, and following the grounding of the Valiant fleet the Victor B.2(SR) conversion programme was simply brought forward, XL230 arriving at Wyton on 18 May 1965. Nine aircraft were converted, and when the last (XL193) arrived on 21 June 1966, 543 Squadron was back to full strength.

Reconnaissance was a vital part of RAF operations, and a very important aspect of V-Force planning. From the outset, Bomber Command not only had to acquire nuclear bombs and high-performance aircraft to carry them, but also had to identify routes and targets to which the bombs would be delivered. As with many aspects of the V-Force, America provided invaluable assistance to the RAF by setting up a joint

RAF/USAF unit at Sculthorpe, operating a fleet of four North American RB-45C Tornado reconnaissance aircraft during 1951–52. Flown by RAF crews, the RB-45s obtained radar photographs of vital Soviet targets which were not only of great use to SAC (who were unable to fly regular Soviet overflights because of Presidential sensitivity), but also of vital importance to Bomber Command, establishing the location and predicted radar picture of many potential targets.

Records suggest that a small number of overflights were also made by the RAF using a Canberra PR.3 fitted with an American long-range reconnaissance camera, but most of the RAF's security-sensitive information came directly from the USA, which continually afforded access to images gathered by U-2 high-altitude 'spyplanes'. (Perhaps this was not surprising, given the history of the V-Force.) Indeed, the CIA provided U-2 reconnaissance facilities for the RAF during the Suez crisis, even though it was American pressure which forced Britain to end the confrontation. Eisenhower believed that U-2 overflights of the Soviet Union were not worth the obvious risks which were attached to them, not least the political protests which accompanied each mission. Consequently the CIA found it increasingly difficult to obtain Presidential approval for flights, and eventually approached Macmillan to approve a series of U-2 overflights (as Churchill had done with the RB-45), which would be manned by RAF pilots. Permission was granted, and even when these missions were ended, when Soviet defences improved, the CIA and USAF continued to supply potential target information to the RAF, and this appeared to continue even in the 1990s. Certainly, during the 1982 Falklands conflict, a Lockheed SR-71 overflew the

The Victor SR.2 reconnaissance fleet at Wyton. (Roger Brooks collection).

islands to gather intelligence on Britain's behalf.

Aerial refuelling was the other main task assigned to Valiants at the time of their premature withdrawal. In-flight refuelling had been introduced into the RAF primarily in support of fighter operations, but in January 1954 the Air Staff decided that V-Bombers should also be capable of refuelling in flight, initially to provide the bombers with a means of attacking Soviet targets via more circuitous (and therefore safer) routes, but also to enable the V-Force rapidly to reinforce overseas bases in Aden, Gan, Singapore, and beyond.

Provisional plans to convert Victor B.1s into tankers were first made in 1962, when the Air Staff first looked at ways to use the surplus Victor B.1s which would not be required when the last B.2s had been delivered. During 1964 the second production B.1, XA918, was fitted with a Flight Refuelling FR17 hose-and-drogue unit in the bomb bay and an FR20B pod

Victor B.1 XA918 was the trials aircraft for the refuelling tanker fit. Note also the nose ram air intake fairings which caused unusual airframe noise and were later reshaped. (Handley Page)

under each wing. Originally the underwing pods were to have been fitted on a common strongpoint which would have been used for external fuel tanks, the hose-and-drogue pods, and Red Neck sideways-looking radar which was considered for adoption by Wyton's reconnaissance unit but later abandoned. However, the pods would have brought the trailing drogues fairly close to the Victor's tail, which would have presented a collision danger to the receiver aircraft, so they were fixed under the outboard wing section. The conversion of XA918 proceeded smoothly, and plans were made to convert Victor B.1s as they were relinquished by 10 and 15 Squadrons. However, when the Valiant tankers were suddenly grounded, frantic plans had to be made to bring Victor tankers quickly into service.

Six B.1As were rapidly fitted with wing-mounted refuelling pods, and the first B(K).1A, XH620, was completed in April 1965. The A&AEE at Boscombe Down quickly evaluated the revised configuration and found that the Victor handled perfectly with pods attached. The six conversions were delivered to

Marham, where 55 Squadron re-formed after moving from Honington in May 1965. The unit was still assigned to bomber duties, and the Victor tankers retained their bombing capability. The first of ten three-point Victor K.1 tanker conversions, XA397, first flew on 2 November. Externally similar to the two-point conversions, these did not retain a bombing capability owing to the permanent installation of two 15,300 lb fuel tanks and a Mk.17 Hose Drum Unit (HDU) in the bomb bay. The K.1 entered service on 14 February 1966 with 57 Squadron, which also re-formed at Marham at the end of the previous year. As Victor B.1As were withdrawn from the bomber squadrons, a batch of 14 were converted into three-point tankers at Radlett. These K.1A Victors were delivered from January 1967 onwards, causing a 'shuffle' of aircraft between the two Marham squadrons, which now included the former Valiant unit 214 Squadron, which re-formed on 1 October 1966. With the arrival of the Victor K.1A, the tanker training responsibilities assumed by 55 Squadron were taken over by the Tanker Training

Just one Victor B.1 survives, (XH648) courtesy of the Imperial War Museum at Duxford. (Heather Brooks)

Flight, which acquired three of the two-point tankers, the other three being distributed among the tanker squadrons for continuation training. To clarify the Victor nomenclature system (or confuse it, depending on one's viewpoint), these two-point tankers were redesignated Victor B.1A(K.2P). The Tanker Training Flight was eventually enlarged to become 232 OCU from May 1970.

As the V-Force's QRA commitment came to an end, the Blue Steel-equipped Victor B.2s were placed into temporary storage. Although the Vulcan B.2 continued operating as a nuclear bomber for many years, the low-level flight regime had taken its toll on the Victors, which had been designed for high-altitude flight. The extremely robust Vulcan airframe withstood low-level flight without any significant problems, but the long and flexible Victor wing would have required complete reconstruction if the aircraft were to continue flying at low level. When the aircraft were withdrawn in 1968 they were all suffering from fatigue cracks in the lower boom forgings to which the mainplanes were attached. However, the airframe could be repaired and converted to the tanker role, and the Victor B.2, with more power and additional fuel

A tanker Training Flight Victor K.1 at Marham. (Roger Brooks collection)

capacity, would be an ideal successor to the Victor K.1s, which were reaching the end of their useful lives.

Handley Page prepared a conversion proposal for the Victor B.2 fleet, and although the company's design expertise was employed, the conversion contract was awarded to Hawker Siddeley. In an act of extreme irony, the conversion programme was to be completed in the former Avro factory at Woodford, where the Vulcan had been built. Handley Page was in extreme financial difficulty by 1969, largely because of soaring development costs associated with its Jetstream twin-turboprop passenger transport. Its only hope of survival lay in the Victor K.2 contract, but the MoD no longer had any confidence in the company's future, and after the contract had been awarded to Hawker Siddeley the company went into voluntary liquidation on 8 August 1969. The Ministry having already contributed to the company's downfall by cancelling the final 25 aircraft in the batch of 57 Victor B.2s, when it was decided to concentrate Skybolt modifications on the Vulcan airframe, the placing of the Victor tanker contract with Hawker Siddeley took away

Left: *Victor K.1 XA937 comes into land after the last operational K.1 tanker sortie on 27th January, 1977.* (Roger Brooks collection)

Below: *Vulcan B.1 XA903 during engine trials for the Olympus 593 engine destined for the Concorde. Note the engine icing rig attached to the lower forward fuselage.* (Rolls-Royce)

Handley Page's last hope of survival.

The prototype Victor K.2, XL231, first flew from Woodford on 1 March 1972, and was immediately transferred to Boscombe Down for investigation of the behaviour of the refuelling pods before completion to full tanker standard. The same three-point installation as used in the K.1 was fitted to the K.2, and virtually all of the equipment associated with the Victor's bomber role was removed. Additionally, the wingspan was reduced by 1.5 ft at each wingtip to minimize fatigue, and the whole wing structure was strengthened to give the tanker a further 14 years of fatigue life. The first production Victor K.2 to enter service was XL233, which joined 232 OCU at Marham on 8 May 1974. Twenty-eight Victor B.2s were to be converted to the tanker configuration, and 543 Squadron's Victor B.2(SR) reconnaissance aircraft were withdrawn to provide sufficient airframes from which to make up this figure. The unit disbanded on 31 May 1974, the radar reconnaissance role being taken over by 27 Squadron with a fleet of Vulcan B.2(MRR) and B.2 aircraft (although a Flight of four Victors was retained until 30 May 1975 to monitor French nuclear tests in the Pacific).

However, financial constraints eventually reduced the Victor K.2 order to 24 airframes. As this quantity was deemed sufficient to equip just two squadrons plus the OCU, 214 Squadron disbanded on 28 January 1977, taking with it the last of the Mk.1 Victors. The tanker fleet, standardized on the K.2, settled into a long period of routine operations which continued into the 1990s, while the Vulcan squadrons continued to operate in the bomber role. A great deal of consideration was given to the possible replacement of the Saceur-assigned Valiant MBF with Vulcan B.1As, but severe financial constraints prompted

Victor K.2 conversions at Woodford. Nimrod and Andover assembly lines are visible in the background. Sir Frederick Handley Page must have been turning in his grave! (British Aerospace)

In addition to underwing air sampling pods, the Vulcan B.2(MRR) also carried a small 'localizer' sensor under the port wing. (British Aerospace)

the government to propose that the Valiant's premature withdrawal was a good enough opportunity to end the Saceur undertaking completely. on 1 April 1965 the Defence Secretary said:

> After most careful consideration of all the operational and other factors involved, the government have formed the view that replacement of the Valiants for the few remaining years of their planned service with Nato cannot be justified by military or other considerations sufficient to override the countervailing need to deal with the pressures upon our defence programme. Saceur and the North Atlantic Council have been so informed.

The Air Staff then waited to establish whether there would be a strong adverse reaction from Britain's Nato allies. In fact, there was no objection to the MBF's withdrawal, so the Saceur assignment — and the possibility of re-equipping with Vulcans — was dropped.

The Vulcan's post-QRA career was far from mundane, however. Beginning in January 1959, Vulcans from 9 and 35 Squadrons, based at Cottesmore, deployed to Akrotiri in Cyprus to replace the Canberra force assigned to the Central Treaty Organization. A total of 16 Vulcans was assigned to the Akrotiri Strike Wing, and as such they were the only V-Bombers to be permanently stationed outside the UK. They remained in Cyprus until January 1975, when 9 Squadron re-formed at Waddington and 35 at Scampton, a four-Vulcan Strike Command detachment taking their place. Having returned to the UK, the remaining V-Bomber squadrons were divided between Scampton (35 and 617

A Vulcan B.2(MRR) air sampling pod. The main pod body was manufactured from a Hunter fuel tank. (British Aerospace)

Right: *Victor XL231 was used as trials aircraft for the K.2 tanker modification. Apart from the application of dayglow orange panels on the wings and tail, the aircraft also had a sensor unit attached to the tail cone.*
(Roger Brooks collection)

Below: *XM597 captured during an interesting transition between 1960s-vintage high-visibility national insignia, and 1980s-era tail-mounted radar warning receiver fit.* (British Aerospace)

Squadrons, plus 27 Squadron assigned to maritime radar reconnaissance, and 230 OCU) and Waddington (9, 44, 50, and 101 Squadrons), with the Victor tankers (55 and 57 Squadrons, together with 232 OCU) at Marham. The Vulcan B.2s were assigned to low-level 'lay-down' nuclear strike operations, armed with WE.177B bombs, Yellow Sun and Red Beard having been withdrawn shortly after the QRA commitment ended. It was with some surprise, therefore, that the Vulcan finally went to war 'for real', as a conventional bomber, in 1982.

CHAPTER ELEVEN

Conclusions

Early in April 1982, when the prospect of war with Argentina suddenly seemed likely following that country's invasion of the Falkland Islands, nobody seriously believed that the V-Force would play a key part in Britain's recapture of the islands. By this stage only three squadrons remained operational on the Vulcan, and they were scheduled to be withdrawn by June 1982, at which stage the Vulcan would be retired from RAF service. The planned demise of the Vulcan changed drastically on 5 April, when personnel at Waddington were instructed to restore the Vulcan's flight-refuelling system in ten aircraft. The system had long since been abandoned because the Vulcan's post-1969 tactical role did not require refuelling support. Although the refuelling probes and associated fuel transfer systems were still fitted to most aircraft, seals and valves had been allowed to deteriorate to such an extent that the refuelling capability no longer existed. To make matters worse, some aircraft had recently had their refuelling probes removed after nearly 20 years and installed on Hercules transports and Nimrod reconnaissance aircraft for long-range missions to the South Atlantic.

Five of the fleet of ten 'restored' Vulcans, XL391, XM597, XM598, XM607, and XM612, were selected for conversion back to the conventional bombing role. They were the only Vulcans remaining in service which had complete Skybolt attachment points and the associated refrigeration ducting which would be required to route cables to underwing hardpoints. Under the codename Black Buck, the Vulcans were prepared to carry a full load of 21 1,000 lb HE bombs over a staggering distance of 3,900 miles from the nearest available operating base; Wideawake airfield on Ascension Island. The aircraft were also fitted with an inertial navigation system, and hastily-constructed underwing pylons enabled them to carry Westinghouse AN/ALQ-101 ECM pods, normally carried by Buccaneers.

Five crews were selected for Black Buck, although only four were subsequently trained, and aerial refuelling sorties began on 14 April, 'Catching up on thirteen years of inexperience in thirteen days,' as one Vulcan captain later commented. Unfortunately the Vulcan's refuelling probe no longer operated as efficiently as during the 1960s, and each 'prod' resulted in spilled fuel washing over the Vulcan's windscreen, almost completely obscuring the pilot's forward view. A 'quick fix' was introduced by attaching two rows of flat plates to the Vulcan's nose, directly ahead of the flight deck, which directed the fuel away from the windscreen. On 16/17

A No. 230 OCU Vulcan B.2 in company with a Strike Command Bombing School Hastings T.5. (Tim Laming collection)

April the crews began night refuelling practice, a task with which even the Victor crews had to familiarize themselves, as their had been no previous requirement for Victors to refuel from Victors at night.

The five Vulcans were all powered by Olympus 301 engines, and to preserve engine life the throttles had been modified with a restriction device which reduced maximum thrust to 18,000 lb, more than adequate for normal operations. For Black Buck the limiting mechanism was removed, restoring the engines to full 20,000-lb thrust. Squadron markings were overpainted, and the light grey undersides were painted dark sea grey.

With no sign of a political solution to the growing Falklands crisis, night training missions were continued, operating down to just 200 ft. On 29 April, while preparations were being made to celebrate the conversion of 9 Squadron on to Tornado GR.1s (one example of which was deployed to Waddington), XM607 and XM598 departed for Ascension Island, XM597 taking off as reserve before returning to Waddington. Supported by Victor tankers, the two Vulcans flew their 4,100-mile trip to

No. 9 Squadron Vulcan B.2 XM648 at Waddington. The aircraft was scrapped at Waddington during December 1982. (John Hale)

The last flying Vulcan B.1 returns to Farnborough after completing its last test sortie on 1 March 1979. Sadly, the authorities failed to preserve the aircraft and this historic machine was broken-up on the airfield during the 1980s. (Tim Laming collection)

Wideawake with no technical problems.

The political decision having been made to begin military action to recapture the Falklands, the first Black Buck mission was scheduled for the morning of 1 May. The aim of the sortie was to perform a surprise attack on Port Stanley's airfield, where Argentine Dassault Mirage, Douglas Skyhawk, and Dassault Super Etendard jet fighter-bombers had been deployed. Destruction of the single runway was not the priority; the aim was to disable the runway to such an extent that Argentina's high-performance aircraft could no longer use it (but to avoid causing so much damage that British forces could not repair it).

Shortly before midnight on 30 April the two Vulcans, XM598 with XM607 as reserve, taxied to the Wideawake runway threshold, accompanied by four Victor tankers. At one-minute intervals and in total radio silence with all navigation lights switched off, the combined force roared into the night sky, followed by a second wave of seven Victors. Each Vulcan carried a full bomb and fuel load, taking its all-up weight to 210,000 lb (normal maximum being 204,000 lb), while the Victors were carrying full fuel loads. Once airborne the 13 V-Bombers climbed to 27,000 ft, and when the crew of

XM598 reported problems with cabin pressurization, XM607 took over as the primary aircraft.

Climbing to 33,000 ft at 260 kt, the formation settled at a compromise altitude and speed to suit the performance of both aircraft types. The plan was for the Vulcan to make five 'prods', but six refuellings were needed at heights between 27,000 ft and 32,000 ft as the formation headed south, around severe turbulence and thunderstorms. Eventually just two Victors remained with the Vulcan. The others, having delivered their fuel, headed north. Although the mission had already encountered problems in the form of the Vulcan's pressurization and severe turbulence, things got even worse. After refuelling XM607 for the last time before the attack, Sqn Ldr Bob Tuxford in Victor XL189 was tasked to refuel the second Victor, XH669, captained by Flt Lt Steve Biglands, over a huge thundercloud. At times XL189's refuelling basket was waving up and down by 20 ft, and even some superb flying was not sufficient to avoid disaster, XH669's refuelling probe breaking before fuel transfer was complete. The only option was for the Victors to reverse positions and re-transfer XH669's fuel to XL189, enabling

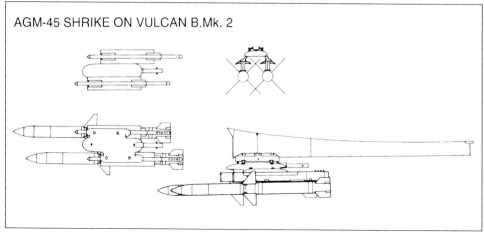

AGM-45 SHRIKE ON VULCAN B.Mk. 2

AGM-45 Shrike installation. (Drawing: Bob Downey)

the latter aircraft to support Vulcan XM607. Because the broken probe would not allow any further refuellings, Steve Biglands had to retain sufficient fuel to reach Ascension, and after refuelling XM607 Bob Tuxford was left with insufficient fuel to reach Wideawake

without a further in-flight refuelling.

Back at Ascension, the returning Victors had to land in stream, making short parachute-retarded landings, before one of the Victors was rapidly refuelled and launched to refuel Tuxford's XL189.

Meanwhile, XM607, captained by Flt

Refuelling plan for the first Operation Black Buck mission. (via RAF Waddington)

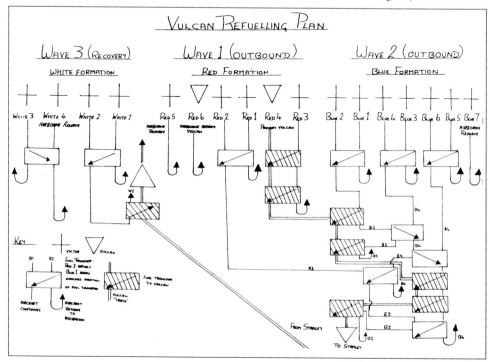

Lt Martin Withers, descended to 300 ft at a distance of 250 nm from Stanley. At 40 miles a classic V-Bomber 'pop-up' manoeuvre was executed, and XM607 levelled out at 10,000 ft, turning on to 235°. After some initial difficulty a good radar picture of the airfield was established, and, although at least one Argentine radar picked up the Vulcan, the AN/ALQ-101 was switched on and the radar lost contact. As the bomber crossed the runway diagonally to ensure that at least one bomb would strike the concrete, all 21 bombs were dropped in just five seconds, although the crew later reported that it seemed like an eternity. A few seconds later the airfield erupted into a blaze of light and Britain had dramatically announced that the occupation of the Falklands was about to end. At 07:46Z the code word 'Superfuze' was signalled to confirm to Strike Command and the Task Force that the attack had been successful. Turning northwards, and with 8,000 lb less fuel than planned, XM607 successfully refuelled off the coast of Brazil and touched down at Ascension at 14:52Z, completing the longest bombing mission in the history of aerial warfare (until Gulf War B-52 missions flew even further).

Post-attack reconnaissance revealed that, precisely as planned, one bomb had struck Stanley's runway, effectively cutting the runway in half and rendering it useless for fast-jet operations. Additionally, the Vulcan's attack also served to show that the RAF still retained a truly strategic bomber capability, and if a Vulcan could reach the Falklands, it could just as easily reach the Argentine mainland. Not surprisingly, Argentina's defence forces were quickly reconfigured to protect the mainland from possible attack, diverting resources from their Falklands forces and making the British recapture somewhat easier. A second mission, Black Buck Two, was flown on 3 May, XM607 making a repeat performance with an attack from 16,000 ft. This time the crew were slightly off course and the stick of bombs fell wide of the runway, but extensive damage was caused to Argentine forces on other parts of the airfield. A third mission was scheduled for 16 May, but forecast winds would have reduced fuel reserves beyond acceptable limits and the mission was cancelled.

Vulcan XM607 returned to Waddington, where the port weapons pylon was removed because the air and ground crews thought, wrongly, that it was causing unnecessary drag, and XM598 also returned to the UK after being replaced by XM612. Martin Withers, XM607's captain, later said:

Thanks to the massive team effort involving 20 aircraft and about 200,000 gal of fuel, we managed to put a bomb on the runway, which was the aim of the exercise. We thus denied its use to high-performance aircraft and showed the Argentineans that we had the capability to attack their mainland — a threat which they certainly took seriously, because many of their Mirages which had been deployed south were recalled to defend their own bases. This must have considerably helped the Harriers to attain air superiority.

Attention then turned to the Argentine radar units scattered around the Falklands. The Black Buck Vulcans could carry the AS.37 Martel anti-radar missile on their wing pylons, and as a good supply was still available for the Buccaneer force, Waddington's ground crews worked furiously to equip the Vulcans to fire the weapon. On 4 May XM597 made a test flight with a Martel on the port wing hardpoint and an ECM pod under the other wing, and a live firing was made the next day over the Aberporth range after a cold soak at high altitude. The test firing was successful, but there were doubts as to the missile's reliability after a long, cold flight south at altitude. Once again the US Government stepped in, offering to supply AGM-45 Shrike anti-radar missiles, two of which could be carried on each of the Vulcan's hardpoints. Throughout the conflict Argentina protested that the USA was pretending to be 'even-handed' in its search for a diplomatic solution to the crisis, whereas in private it was firmly behind Britain. With hindsight it seems that they were right, but after the Secretary of State's diplomatic mission failed, the US Government openly offered support to the British Government, supplying weapons and logistic support and, most importantly, by providing refuelling tanker support for UK training operations while the Victor tankers were heavily involved in Operation Corporate, the Falklands mission.

On 26 May XM596 flew to Wideawake, followed a day later by XM597. The first anti-radar mission was launched on 28 May but, after a supporting Victor's hose units failed, the mission was called off and rescheduled for the following evening. This sortie proceeded smoothly, and after descending to 300 ft at 200 nm from the Falklands, XM597 popped up to 16,000ft. After acquiring a signal from an Argentine radar, two Shrikes were fired, causing substantial damage to the radar. On 2 June another successful attack was mounted, a radar unit being completely destroyed. The return flight was not so smooth, however, for while XM597 was refuelling en route to Wideawake its probe broke off, forcing the crew to divert to Rio de Janeiro. To enable the bomber to reach Brazil, the pilot climbed to 40,000 ft to conserve fuel. Sensitive documents were dumped in a hold-all which was dropped out of the Vulcan's crew door (after de-pressurizing the cabin), and the two remaining Shrikes were fired off, but one refused to drop.

After a 'Mayday' had been called at a range of 200 nm, clearance was eventually given for a descent to 20,000 ft, and at a distance of just six

A Sea Harrier reconnaissance photograph of Port Stanley's runway, following the first Black Buck mission. (Royal Navy)

XM607 returns to Wideawake airfield after completing the first Black Buck mission. (Tim Laming collection)

Black Buck Vulcans (XM607, XM597, XM612 and XL391) making a farewell flypast tour on 21 December 1982. (Tim Laming collection)

Twin Strike installation as carried by Vulcan XM597 for a series of Black Buck missions. (Mike Jenvey)

miles final approach was authorized, requiring captain Sqn Ldr Neil McDougal to heave the XM597 into a steep spiral descent with airbrakes extended, levelling out at 800 ft one and a half miles from touchdown. The Vulcan arrived at Rio with just 2,000 lb of fuel remaining; less than that required for one airfield circuit. After landing, the hung-up Shrike was made safe before it was impounded by Brazilian authorities. The crew were well treated by their surprised hosts, and elected to stay with XM597 until it was cleared to leave for Ascension on 10 May.

The final Black Buck mission was flown by XM607 on 11 June, when anti-personnel air-burst bombs were dropped on Stanley's airfield. Argentina surrendered four days later, and Operation Black Buck ended. The Vulcans returned to Waddington, but conventional bombing and anti-radar training missions were still flown until 21 December 1982, when 44 Squadron disbanded, marking the end of all Vulcan bomber operations.

Even the ending of all V-Force bomber operations did not mark the end of either the Vulcan's or the Victor's RAF service. The Falklands crisis had led to a sudden requirement for a huge increase in aerial refuelling capability which clearly could not be handled in isolation by the Victor squadrons. Plans were made to covert former VC10 and TriStar airliners, but as a short-term 'stop-gap' the Lockheed Hercules transport and Vulcan bomber were earmarked for conversion into single-point tankers. British Aerospace (BAe) quickly began work on a rapid conversion programme for six Vulcans, which were to be dual-role bomber/tanker aircraft designated Vulcan B(K).2. However, preliminary investigations revealed that the Mk.17 HDU hose-and-drogue equipment could not simply be fitted in the Vulcan's bomb bay, as this would position the extended

Vulcan B.2 XM597 back in the UK after completing her Black Buck missions. The aircraft is now displayed in the Museum of Flight, at East Fortune. (British Aerospace)

Vulcan B.2 XM607 running-up to full power on Waddington's runway during July 1982. Note the Shrike training rounds under the wing.
(Tim Laming)

refuelling basket, and therefore the receiver aircraft, too close to the Vulcan's tail. The obvious alternative was to fit the HDU inside the bomber's ECM tailcone, which would otherwise be redundant. Vulcan XM603, recently retired from RAF service, had been presented to BAe by the RAF, and it was used as a suitable test airframe into which the HDU could be installed. J. J. Sherratt, BAe's assistant chief designer for Victor tanker systems, recalls:

Sunday morning saw a group of us standing around a crated HDU, thinking that if it was anything like the size of the crate, we wouldn't stand much of a chance of fitting it. Even with the crate removed it looked big, but by this time we had resolved to get it into the Vulcan even if it meant restyling the back of the aircraft. There was no way of straight-lifting the 5 ft-wide HDU through the existing ECM opening of 4 ft, but we noticed that the top part of the HDU could be separated from the bottom, and that we might be able to get the top half through the opening, leaving the bottom half to be straight-lifted in. A piece of wood the same size as the top section was called for to investigate the possibility. The verdict was that there was plenty of room if we had a good shoehorn, and if necessary we could put the odd blister here and there to cover any awkward bits. After a design team meeting in the afternoon, we

agreed to tell the MoD that we could do the job, and in the general euphoria, a target of three weeks to first flight was set.

On Monday, two representatives from Flight Refuelling arrived to advise us on splitting the HDU, and at around midday we received authority from MoD to proceed with the conversion of six aircraft. The first aircraft, XH561, arrived on Tuesday, by which time a whole army of workers had been mobilized to work all the hours needed to do the job. Seven weeks to the day, on Friday 18 June, the first converted aircraft made its first flight at 12:32. An interim CA release was granted on 23 June, and the first aircraft was delivered to the RAF on the same day.

The Vulcan K.2 was an excellent tanker aircraft, although its single-point system obviously imposed limitations on how the six-aircraft fleet (belonging to 50 Squadron, who also retained XM652, XM597, and XL426 as standard B.2s for continuation training) could be used. Bombers old and new met regularly as Tornado GR.1s came into service and called upon their Vulcan predecessors to refuel them. In one case, Vulcan tankers were assigned to the support of Tornado GR.1s returning to the UK from Canada, and to avoid bad weather en route the Vulcans effortlessly climbed to higher altitudes, the low-level Tornados struggling to keep formation and often resorting to reheat simply to stay plugged in to the Vulcans' HDU baskets. Naturally the net fuel gain to the Tornados was almost nil, so the 'trail' was called off and rescheduled. The Vulcan K.2's career was relatively short, simply because their HDU equipment had previously been assigned to VC10s which were being converted for long-term RAF service. As the VC10s were made ready the Vulcans were withdrawn, starting with XJ825 on 4 May 1983. Finally, in March 1984, 50 Squadron disbanded and RAF Vulcan operations officially ended.

The remaining Vulcan tankers were ferried to their final resting places. While B.2 XM597 departed for the Museum of Flight at East Fortune in Scotland, XM652 was dismantled and moved to Sheffield, where it was to be reassembled as an attraction at a recreational facility, but the plan failed and it was cut up for scrap. Of the tankers, XM571 flew to Gibraltar and stood guard at the road crossing in the centre of the airfield there before being scrapped in 1989; XL445 was flown to Lyneham, where it was used for rescue training before being scrapped; XJ825 remained at Waddington until 1992, when it, too, was cut up; XH561

met a similar fate at Catterick after being used for rescue training; and XH558 flew to Marham, destined to end its days at the mercy of the fire crews. However, B.2 XL426 and K.2 XH560 remained at Waddington, where the former was retained for air show appearances as the RAF's last flying Vulcan, with XH560 as a future replacement. As XL426 approached the end of its fatigue life, XH560 was brought into use, but as the display flight ground crews began to remove usable equipment from XH558 at Marham it was discovered that this aircraft had 600 hr of usable fatigue life left, while XH560 had only 160. Consequently XH558, in a rather sorry state, was ferried back to Waddington and exchanged for XH560, which eventually expired at Marham in 1992.

Vulcan B.2 XL426 was purchased by businessman Roy Jacobsen, who planned to keep the aircraft flying in private hands. Unfortunately the Civil Aviation Authority (CAA) did not relish the idea of a four-engined strategic bomber flying around the UK with a civilian crew and technical backup team, and permission to operate the aircraft was never granted.

Vulcan-to-Vulcan refuelling rendezvous over the North Sea during 1982. No. 50 Squadron retained a couple of non-modified Vulcan B.2s for continuation training, whilst operating a six-aircraft tanker fleet. (Mike Jenvey)

An interesting view of Vulcan K.2 XM571, displaying her white undersides and dayglow refuelling alignment stripes. Having just been converted, the aircraft still retains No. 101 Squadron's tail markings, indicative of her previous owner. (British Aerospace)

Jacobsen eventually abandoned his plans, and XL426 was handed over to the Vulcan Restoration Trust, based at Southend Airport in Essex. A team of dedicated volunteers gradually restored the aircraft to near-flyable condition, and plans are still being made to fly the aircraft if a sponsor can be found and the CAA can be persuaded to give their permission. In the meantime, XL426 makes occasional high-speed taxying runs at Southend.

Restored to B.2 configuration, XH558 continued to thrill air show crowds around the UK until 1993, when display flying finally ended. The aircraft was approaching the end of its fatigue life, and to give it a further lease of life a major servicing programme would have to be undertaken, costing nearly £1 million. Although this expense was minute when compared with other display commitments such as the Red Arrows, the MoD decided that it was not practical to continue operating the Vulcan, and it was

Vulcan K.2 Hose Drum Unit housing. (Drawing: Bob Downey)

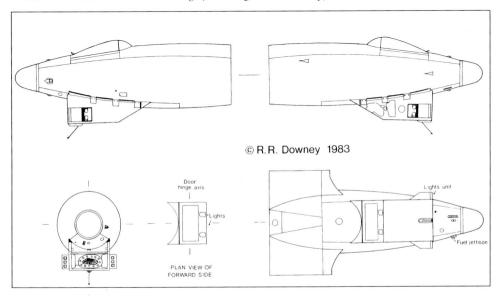

© R.R. Downey 1983

Door hinge axis

Lights

PLAN VIEW OF FORWARD SIDE

Lights unit

Fuel jettison

Vulcan K.2 XH560 trailing her single-point hose over the North Sea. The aircraft retained an air sampling capability, as evidenced by the small localiser pod under the port wing. (British Aerospace)

offered for sale. Businessman David Walton purchased the aircraft, and on 23 March 1994 the RAF's last Vulcan taxied on to Waddington's runway for the last time. Watched by hundreds of spectators who had gathered on nearby roads, XH558 became airborne shortly after 11:00 to fly a short tour of sites which had been associated with the Vulcan. After visiting Finningley, Scampton, Coningsby, Cottesmore, Woodford, and Marham, XH558 made a final salute to Lincoln Cathedral before turning back towards Waddington. With bomb doors open to reveal 'Farewell' painted on the inside, one last pass over the airfield was made, the huge 111 ft span wings waving

for the final time as the spectators clicked their cameras, waved, and (in many cases) cried. The Vulcan might have been one of Britain's ultimate weapons of destruction, but hundreds of thousands of people just loved it.

Vulcan XH558 finally landed at Bruntingthorpe in Leicestershire, where plans were made to prepare it for more air display flying, in civilian hands. But once again the CAA would not give permission for the aircraft to fly, even though the same aircrew would be at the controls and the same ground crew would be providing technical support. With all their efforts devoted to just one aircraft, XH558 was likely to be kept in even better condition

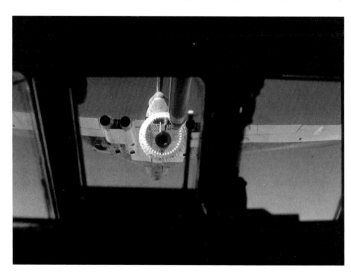

A VC10 captain's view of a refuelling rendezvous with a Vulcan K.2 tanker (Mike Jenvey)

than during its RAF career, but the CAA refused to budge, insisting that BAe should provide full technical support for the aircraft. Sadly, BAe would not give such an undertaking, and at the time of writing the situation remains unresolved. Although XH558 makes occasional fast taxying runs along Bruntingthorpe's runway, years of relative inactivity and long periods of external storage make the prospect of flight seem increasingly remote.

As for the Victor tankers, their outstanding contribution to the RAF's operations continued into the 1990s, and included heavy participation in Operation Desert Storm during the Gulf War. Victors were deployed to Muharraq on 14 December 1990, the four-aircraft detachment increasing to eight by 19 January. They provided refuelling support for RAF Tornados, Buccaneers, and Jaguars, as well as for carrier-based US Navy aircraft, Canadian Hornets, French Mirage 2000s and Saudi Tornados on combat missions. Six Victors returned to Marham on 17/18 March 1991 after completing 299 combat support sorties totalling 870 hr. Victors were also deployed to Akrotiri to participate in Operation Warden, the protection of Kurdish communities living in northern Iraq, flying 177 sorties in support of RAF Jaguars based in Turkey. Victors returned to Muharraq in December 1992 to support Tornado GR.1s assigned to Operation Jural, flying allied patrols over Iraq. The Victors, from 55 Squadron, the sole remaining unit, flew 202 sorties before returning to Marham in September 1993.

The deployment to Bahrain also marked the end of the Victor's operational career, as the remaining Victors had

A sad sight at Scampton as the Vulcan B.2 fleet is broken-up for scrap. (Tim Laming collection)

finally reached the end of their fatigue lives. Disbandment of 55 Squadron took place on 15 October 1993 (57 Squadron had disbanded on 30 June 1986), Victors XH672, XL231, and XL161 making a low flypast over Marham to mark both the end of the last Victor squadron and the end of the V-Force. On 19 October XL190 flew to St Mawgan for rescue training, although the aircraft was eventually saved from destruction and is currently preserved at the base. On 20 October XL161 was ferried to Lyneham for rescue training after making a 4 hr sortie to enable the captain, Flt Lt Attwood, to complete 2,000 hr on the Victor. On 11 November XL134 flew to Brize Norton for crash training; XM715 joined David Walton's Vulcan at Bruntingthorpe on 19 November; XL231 was delivered to the Yorkshire Air Museum at Elvington on 25 November; and, finally, on 30 November, XH672 made the final Victor (and final V-Bomber) flight to Shawbury, with Johnny Allam, the pilot of the first production Victor B.1, on board. After landing, XH672 was dismantled for trans-portation to Cosford, where it joined the Aerospace Museum. The Victors remaining at Marham (XM717, XH671, XH675, XL158,

and XL512) were scrapped on site.

Thus the story of the V-Force ended in 1993, nearly half a century after it began. The very fact that the RAF never engaged in nuclear warfare emphasizes the fact that the V-Force was a success. The deterrent worked. But at what price? Even in the 1950s both Avro and Handley Page never seriously believed that both the Vulcan and Victor would be brought into RAF service, yet the MoS and the Air Staff were incapable, or unwilling, to decide between the two. With hindsight, the RAF was fortunate to have been provided with two outstanding aircraft.

The Victor was by far the most sophisticated, with better altitude and weapon-carrying capabilities than the Vulcan. Although it became a successful carrier of the Blue Steel stand-off bomb, the Victor was far from compatible with the proposed Skybolt system, having insufficient ground clearance to carry it safely, and this led to its withdrawal from the bomber force, even though the Government pulled out of the Skybolt programme. However, the Victor proved to be even more useful as a three-point refuelling tanker, and had it not been for the high workload associated with Operation Corporate and Operation Desert Storm, the Victors might still have

For a short period, the RAF retained two Vulcans for air display appearances, these being XL426 and XH560. Both aircraft were later replaced by XH558. (Ray Ball)

Vulcan XL426 is currently preserved at Southend Airport, and efforts are being made to restore the aircraft to flying condition. If successful, funds will be required to operate the aircraft as a civilian 'warbird'. (Vulcan Restoration Trust)

been flying, stretching out their precious hours of remaining fatigue life.

The Vulcan was a much simpler design, but with its outstanding manoeuvrability and huge power reserves it eventually proved to be the better of the two V-Bomber designs in terms of overall flexibility. As for the Valiant, it was designed primarily as an 'interim' aircraft, and in this respect it was a great success. It went on to provide the RAF with a first-class reconnaissance and refuelling tanker platform, but the sudden appearance of wing fatigue ended what could have been a very long and useful career. The fact that the Valiants 'wore out' so quickly was not indicative of a design fault; it was simply a manifestation of the RAF's switch to low-level operations, something for which all three V–Bombers were not designed or built.

Although all three V–Bombers can be judged to have been outstanding aircraft, the Valiant emerges as the most impressive because of the speed at which it was designed and built, and the performance of the finished product. The Valiant pioneered many new constructional techniques and systems, and it also pioneered many important steps in the RAF's operational history. With hindsight, there is no doubt that the

Air Staff could have obtained an aircraft to meet Specification B.35/46 with just one design, the Valiant, albeit in two distinct versions.

While the Valiant B.1 was the 'stop-gap' bomber to bridge the period between the Lincoln/B-29 and the Vulcan, the Air Staff were also offered the Valiant B.2, designed in response to Specification B.104D for a medium-range target-marker aircraft. During the early post-war years the RAF still maintained a Second World War mentality, and plans were made to produce a new target-marker aircraft to penetrate enemy airspace at low level, dropping flares to designate targets for high-flying Vulcans and Victors. The absurdity of this proposal seems clear some 40 years later, but at the time the Air Staff regarded this as a serious proposition, even though the V-Bombers were destined to deliver nuclear weapons which clearly would not need to hit their targets with pinpoint accuracy.

The Valiant B.2 was designed to carry 6,000 lb of target indicators over the same 3,350 nm range as the Valiant B.1, with a maximum cruising speed of not less than 450 kt and at an altitude of 45,000 ft. The aircraft was to descend to tree-top height (around 50 ft) near the target area, and to

An early shot of XH558, the first Vulcan B.2 to enter RAF service. Coincidentally it was also the last Vulcan to leave RAF service after completing an extended period of display flying. (British Aerospace)

spend up to 30 min manoeuvring at low level at maximum continuous engine thrust, before climbing back to cruising altitude. No structural limit on top speed at sea level was imposed, the design diving speed initially being set at 580 kt. The resulting high structural strength enabled the B.2 to carry the same 41,000 lb bomb load as the B.1 over 4,000 nm at high altitude, albeit with a considerable penalty in structural weight.

The B.1 had been stressed for cruising in smooth air at high altitude, and was not intended to withstand the rigours of low-level and high-speed operations. A major structural redesign was therefore required for the B.2, particularly with regard to the wing, where the higher loads required the elimination of the cutouts for the undercarriage that were a feature

of the B.1's wing. The main landing gear was therefore mounted behind the wing torsion box, retracting rearwards into fairings behind the wing trailing edge. This left the wing torsion box intact and allowed a four-wheel bogie to be fitted. Early drawings of the Valiant Pathfinder show it with a fuselage length the same as the B.1, and the 4 ft extension ahead of the wing was not part of the original layout, being added at a later stage to counter a rearwards shift of the c.g. This was caused by the additional structure weight necessary to meet the specified diving speed, although by this stage it had been reduced to 500 kt.

On 24 April 1952 an order for 17 Valiant B.2s was placed with Vickers, covering two aircraft for development work and 15 to equip one operational

A composite view of the flight deck of a Vulcan B.2. (Tim Laming)

Victor K.2 XL191 suffered an undignified withdrawal from RAF service when the aircraft undershot the approach to Abbotsford's runway on 19 June 1986. (Roger Brooks collection)

pathfinder squadron. The prototype was the last aircraft to be constructed at Vickers' Foxwarren experimental shop, and after being taken by road to Wisley WJ954 made its first flight on 4 September 1953, subsequently appearing at both the 1953 and 1954 SBAC shows at Farnborough. The Air Ministry, however, finally realized that target marking was not a realistic proposition in a nuclear age, and the order for Valiant B.2s was cancelled, leaving the sole B.2 prototype to undertake a series of trials associated with the V-Bomber programme. These included rocket-assisted take-off flights and undercarriage braking tests, which continued until 16 October 1957. There then appeared to be no further use for the aircraft, so it was dismantled and transported to Foulness during July 1958.

Although the Valiant B.2 was a superb aircraft, the role for which it was designed could never really have existed, and it is all the more lamentable that the prototype was designed and built before the Government and the Air Staff realized this. It is even more unfortunate that, when Valiant production had ended, the RAF changed to low-level operations, for which the Valiant B.2 was specifically designed. With an airframe structure capable of sustaining speeds far in excess of those achievable by either the Vulcan or Victor, the Valiant B.2 proved its capability during a series of long-endurance, low-level flights around the UK, which were adjudged a great success. Had the decision to operate the V-Force at low level been taken just a few years earlier, the Valiant B.2 would have provided the RAF with an aircraft ideally suited to the task, and with deliveries of

Victor farewell as three aircraft overfly Marham on 15 October 1993, to mark the disbandment of No. 55 Squadron, and the end of Victor (and therefore all V-Bomber) operations.
(Roger Brooks collection)

XA900 was the sole surviving Vulcan B.1 until the aircraft was scrapped at the Cosford Aerospace Museum during 1986. Likewise, Cosford's Victor B.1 was also scrapped, raising the question of what purpose a museum fulfils, when unique aircraft are simply destroyed when their upkeep becomes expensive. (John Laming)

high–altitude Valiant B.1s already complete, the Vulcan and Victor might never have entered RAF service. Sadly, the Valiant B.2 was consigned to history, along with many other Air Staff projects which received huge amounts of taxpayers' money, before being abandoned in favour of other equally (or more) expensive solutions. However, in fairness to both the Government and the Air Staff, the RAF in the 1950s was entering a completely new age of aerial warfare, and at the time it was very difficult to establish what weapons systems could be made available, or which should be made available, and which might be necessary in the future. As Sir Frederick Handley Page commented in 1951: 'It would be a very brave person who would say they knew whether the Vulcan or Victor was the better aircraft. I do not think it is possible. If you ask what

I would order, I could tell you quite plainly, but I must declare my interest.'

He went on to say:

Nobody has ever won a war by trying to run it on the cheap. Nothing is so expensive as losing a war by saving money. If you want to have the cheapest possible air force today, it is very easy to standardize on a whole lot of aircraft which will be no use when a war comes.

His words of wisdom are more than 40 years old, but they are just as valid in the 1990s. The V-Force demonstrated the outstanding scientific and technical know-how which was available in post-war Britain. It also clearly demonstrates, in retrospect, just how close Britain and America have remained, in terms of military co-operation, from the Second

A rare shot of Valiant XD818 being rolled-out from a Marham hangar, prior to being installed at the station's entrance as a gate guard.
(Roger Brooks)

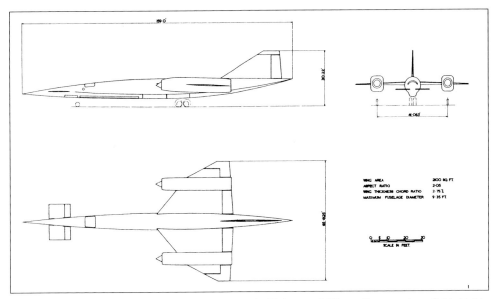

The Avro 730 was designed as a successor to both the Vulcan and Victor. Construction of this highly advanced design had already begun when the government opted to abandon the project.

World War right through to the present day. With the benefit of '20-20' hindsight it is very easy to see how many ill-founded and expensive decisions were made, but how, despite the problems of politics, finances, and the unknown intentions of a mysterious enemy, the RAF remained at the forefront of the West's striking power. Britain's present-day nuclear deterrent has permanently shifted to the Royal Navy, but the legacy of the RAF's V-Force lives on in the form of abandoned airfields and rocket bases, preserved aircraft and missiles, and hundreds of Service personnel who lived and worked through a fascinating era in RAF history, when British bombers literally led the way.

A Vulcan B.2 displaying weapons options in the shape of Martels, free fall bombs, laser guided bombs, Shrikes, and Blue Steel. Nuclear options such as WE.177 are not shown. (Tim Laming collection)

APPENDIX

Valiant squadrons

7 Sqn	Dec 56 to Aug 60	Honington	From 58 Blue Danube	B.1
	Sept 60 to Sep 62	Wittering	Red Beard	B.1
18 Sqn	Dec 58 to Mar 63	Finningley	ECM	B.1
49 Sqn	May 56 to June 61	Wittering	Grapple to 59	B.1
	June 61 to May 65	Marham	Project E (Saceur)	B.1
90 Sqn	Mar 57 to Mar 62	Honington	From 58 Blue Danube	B.1
	Apr 62 to Feb 65	Honington	Tankers	B(PR)K.1
138 Sqn	Feb 55 to Jul 55	Gaydon	OCU	B.1
	Jul 55 to Apr 62	Wittering	From 58 Blue Danube	B.1
148 Sqn	Jul 56 to Apr 65	Marham	Project E (Saceur)	B.1
199 Sqn	Jun 57 to Sep 57	Hemswell	Also had Canberras	B.1
	Oct 57 to Dec 58	Honington	Valiant Flt became 18 Sqn	
207 Sqn	Jun 56 to Feb 65	Marham	Project E (Saceur)	B.1
214 Sqn	Jan 56 to Mar 62	Marham	From 58 Blue Danube	B.1
	Apr 62 to Feb 65	Marham	Tankers	B.1
543 Sqn	Jul 55 to Nov 55	Gaydon	Strategic Recce	B(PR).1
	Nov 55 to Feb 65	Wyton		B(PR)K.1

The first aircraft was delivered to the OCU at RAF Gaydon in January 1955.

Victor squadrons

232 Sqn	Nov 57	Gaydon	OCU	
10 Sqn	Apr 58 to Mar 64	Cottesmore	Blue Danube Red Beards	B.1
	1960 to 1964		YS Mk 1 & 2	B.1
15 Sqn	Sep 58 to Oct 64	Cottesmore	Blue Danube YS Mk 1 & 2	B.1
55 Sqn	Oct 60 to May 65	Honington	Yellow Sun Mk 1 & 2	B.1
	May 65 to Jul 75	Marham	Tankers	B(K).1A
	Jul 75 to Oct 93	Marham	Tankers	K.2
57 Sqn	Mar 59 to Dec 65	Honington	Yellow Sun Mk 1 & 2	B.1
	Dec 65 to Jun 86	Marham	Tankers	K.1/2
100 Sqn	May 62 to Feb 63	Wittering	Yellow Sun Mk 2	B.2
	Feb 63 to Sept 68	Wittering	Blue Steel	B.2
139 Sqn	Feb 62 to Mar 63	Wittering	Yellow Sun Mk 2	B.2 (1st Sqn)
	Mar 63 to Dec 68	Wittering	Blue Steel	B.2
214 Sqn	Jul 66 to Jan 77	Marham	Tankers	K.1
543 Sqn	May 65 to May 74	Wyton	Strategic Recce	B.2(SR)

The first aircraft was delivered to the OCU at RAF Gaydon in November 1957.

Vulcan squadrons

230 OCU	Jul 56 to Jun 61	Waddington	Training	B.1
	Jun 61 to Aug 81	Finningley	Training	B.2
9 Sqn	Apr 62 to Nov 64	Coningsby	Yellow Sun Mk 2	B.2
	Nov 64 to Feb 69	Cottesmore	Yellow Sun Mk 2	B.2
	Feb 69 to Jan 75	Akrotiri	Red Beard	B.2
	Jan 75 to Apr 82	Waddington	WE 177	B.2
12 Sqn	Jul 62 to Nov 64	Coningsby	Yellow Sun	B.2
	Nov 64 to Dec 67	Cottesmore	Red Beard	B.2
27 Sqn	Apr 61 to Feb 63	Scampton	Yellow Sun Mk 1	B.2
	Feb 63 to May 69	Scampton	Blue Steel	B.2
	Nov 73 to May 82	Waddington	Strategic Recce	B.2(MRR)
35 Sqn	Jan 63 to Nov 64	Coningsby	Yellow Sun	B.2
	Nov 64 to Jan 69	Cottesmore	Red Beard	B.2
	Jan 69 to Jan 75	Akrotiri	Red Beard	B.2
	Jan 75 to Feb 82	Scampton	WE 177	B.2
44 Sqn	Aug 60 to Dec 82	Waddington	Yellow Sun	B.1 to 67:
			WE 177	B.2 66 to 82
50 Sqn	Aug 61 to May 70	Waddington	Yellow Sun Mk 2	B.1A
				B.1 to Oct 66/B.2 to 84
	May 82 to Mar 84	Waddington	Tankers	B.2(K)
83 Sqn	Jul 57 to Oct 60	Waddington		B.1
	Jun 60 to Aug 69	Scampton	Blue Steel	B.2
101 Sqn	Jan 58 to Jun 61	Finningley	Violet Club	B.1 to 61
			Blue Steel from 63	B.2 to 82
			WE 177 from 71	

The first aircraft was delivered to the OCU at RAF Waddington in January 1957.

Index

707, Avro, 62
A&AEE Boscombe Down, 45,
    123, 171
Aberporth, 138
Accident Investigation Branch,
    152
Advanced Bomber Project
    Group, 29, 53
Akrotiri, 175
Aldergrove, RAF, 33
Aldermaston, 20
Allam, Johnny, 92, 191
Allied atomic air operations,
    131
Amery, Julian, 141
Arado 234, 82
Armstrong Whitworth, 27
Ascension Island, 179
Ashton, Avro, 34
Atomic Energy Act, 109
Atomic Weapons School, RAF,
    49
Attlee, Clement, 15
Avon, Rolls-Royce, 39
Avro, 27, 30
AW.52G, Armstrong
    Whitworth, 54

B-2, Northrop, 26
B-29, Boeing, 16, 22
Backfire, Operation, 22
Bailey, Squadron Leader G. M.,
    108
Baker, Air Chief Marshal Sir
    John, 89
Ballykelly, RAF, 164
Bardney, RAF, 136
Bassingbourne, RAF, 43
Bedford, 164
Bermuda Conference, 131

Birch, Nigel, 118
Black Buck, Operation, 177
Blackbird, SR-71, 170
Blackburn, 83
Blackbushe, 73
Blue Danube, 50, 94, 111, 128,
    155
Blue Steel, Avro, 34, 111, 138,
    159, 163, 172
Blue Streak, 95, 136, 155
Bohr, Niels, 11, 12
Bomber Command
    Development Unit, 149, 158
Boothman, Air Marshal, 66
Boscombe Down, 87, 115, 126,
    164
Bracebridge Heath, 67
Brawdy, RAF, 164
Brazil, 181
Breighton, RAF, 136
Bristol, 27
British Aircraft Corporation, 40
Brize Norton, RAF, 190
Broadhurst, Sir Harry, 116
Brook-Smith, Tom, 35
Brooklands, 42
Broomfield, Duggie, 84
Brough, 84
Bruntingthorpe, 165, 189, 190
Buccaneer, 35, 162
Buffalo, Operation, 51
Burtonwood, 165
Bush, Dr Vannevar, 12

Caillard, Squadron Leader H.
    A., 108
Caistor, RAF, 136
Campania, HMS, 20
Canberra, 43, 166
Canberra, English Electric, 23,

    133, 170
Carnaby, 84, 136
Catfoss, RAF, 136
Catterick, RAF, 188
Chadderton, 53
Chadwick, Lord, 14
Chadwick, Roy, 54
Cherwell, Lord, 95
Christmas Island, 96
Churchill, Sir Winston, 12, 21,
    95, 109, 170
CIA, 170
Civil Aviation Authority, 189
Coleby Grange, RAF, 136
Colney Street, 85
Coltishall, RAF, 164
Coningsby, RAF, 23, 149, 164
Conway, Rolls-Royce, 144
Cosford, RAF, 191
Cottesmore, RAF, 126, 150,
    154, 158, 162, 175
Cranfield, 90
Cranwell, RAF, 165
Cricklewood, 78

Davies, Stuart, 61
Davis, Air Vice Marshal, 20
Defence Research Policy
    Committee, 26, 95
Derwent, Rolls-Royce, 62
Desert Storm, Operation, 189
Dickson, Sir William, 31
Dishforth, RAF, 136
Dispersal airfields, 157
Dobson, Sir Roy, 67
Driffield, RAF, 136

East Fortune, 107
Ecclestone, Ronald, 90
Eden, Sir Anthony, 73

Edwards, George, 29, 37
Eglin AFB, 158
Egypt, 47
Eisenhower, Preisident, 109, 131, 156, 157
Ejection seats, 41
Elvington, RAF, 165, 191
English Electric, 27, 31
Eniwetok, 94
Escape systems, 121
Esler, Eric, 63
Ewans, J. R., 56, 117

Falk, Wing Commander, 64
Falklands, 170, 177
Fatigue problems, 169
Feltwell, RAF, 136
Filton, 164
Finningley, RAF, 46, 113, 122, 149, 158, 164
Flying Wing, Northrop, 54
Folkingham, RAF, 136
Foulness, 195
Fox Warren, 37, 195
Frenkel, Yakov, 11
Frisch, Otto, 11
Full Sutton, RAF, 136

Gaydon, RAF, 43, 126, 154, 164
Gazette, 96
Geleypandhy, 87
General Aircraft Ltd., 83
Germany, 12, 82
Gibraltar, 187
Goose Bay, 121
Grand Slam, 110
Grapple, Operation, 96
Green Bamboo, 96, 111
Green Granite Large, 106, 111
Green Granite Small, 96
Green Grass, 113
Green Palm, 128
Groves, General, 14
Guided Weapons Department, 25
Gyron, de Havilland, 35

Hahn, Otto, 11
Hall, Sir Arnold, 72
Handley Page, 27, 67
Handley Page, Sir Fredrick, 77, 196
Harrington, RAF, 136
Harris, Sir Arthur, 22
Hastings, Handley Page, 43
Hatfield, 34
Hazelden, H. D., 88, 123

Heathrow, 116
Hemswell, RAF, 45, 136
Herod Committee, 49
High Speed Tunnel, Farnborough, 72
Hill, Geoffrey, 35
Hiroshima, 14
Holme-on-Spalding Moor, RAF, 136
Honington, RAF, 45, 133, 136, 155, 158, 164
Horten brothers, 54
Hound Dog, 157
Howard, Squadron Leader Donald, 116
HP.5 Yellow Peril, Handley Page, 82
HP.72, Handley Page, 78
HP.80, Handley Page, 78
HP.87, Handley Page, 83
HP.88, Handley Page, 83
HP.93, Handley Page, 85
Hubbard, Wing Commander K. G., 96
Hurn, 38
Hurricane, Operation, 20
Hyde Park Agreement, 13

Jacobsen, Roy, 189
Japan, 13
Joint Technical Warfare Committee, 13

Keith-Lucas, David, 35
Kennedy, President, 157
Kinloss, RAF, 164

Lachmann, Gustav Victor, 77
Leconfield, RAF, 136, 164
Lee, Godfrey, 77
Leeming, RAF, 136, 164
Leuchars, RAF, 164
Libya, 158
Lincoln AFB, 121
Lincoln, Avro, 22, 28, 49
Lindholme, RAF, 43
Lindley, Bob, 54
Lippisch, Alexander, 54
Llanbedr, 165
Lone Ranger, 121
Lossiemouth, RAF, 164
Ludford Magna, RAF, 136
Luqa, RAF, 47
Lyneham, RAF, 20, 164, 188, 190
Machrihanish, RAF, 164
Macmillan, Harold, 109, 131,

156, 170
Manhattan Project, 13
Manston, RAF, 164
Manx, Handley Page, 77
Maralinga, 51
Marham, RAF, 23, 49, 133, 171, 188, 190
Marshall Islands, 94
Marston Moor, RAF, 136
Martin Baker, 121
Maud Committee, 12
Maudling, Sir Reginald, 92
McMahon Act, 15, 131
Meitner, Lise, 11
Melton Mowbray, RAF, 136
Mepal, RAF, 136
Middleton St George, RAF, 164
Millett, Squadron Leader B. T., 107
Ministry of Supply, 14
Monte Bello, 20
Mosquito, de Havilland, 25 , 77
Muharraq, 189
Musketeer, Operation, 46

Nagasaki, 14, 16
NASR.1177, 159
Nassau, 157
National Defense Research Council, 12
North Luffenham, RAF, 136
North Pickenham, RAF, 136

O'Connor, Flight Lieutenant S., 108
Olympus, Bristol, 61, 126, 144
Operational Requirement OR.1001, 18
Operational Requirement OR.229, 27
Operational Requirement OR.230, 26
Operational Requirement OR.239, 28
Operational Requirement OR.1132, 138
Operational Requirement OR.1136, 110
Operational Requirement OR.1139, 136
Operational Requirement OR.1159, 138
Orfordness, 50
ORPs, 164

P.D.1, Shorts, 36
Park Street, 84

Pearl Harbor, 13
Peierls, Rudolph, 11
Pelley, Air Vice Marshal, 32
Penney, Dr William, 19, 49, 110
Pershore, 164
Plym, HMS, 20
Polaris, 155, 163
Polebrook, RAF, 136
Port Stanley, 179
Portal, Lord, 18
Prestwick, 165
Project 'E', 131, 167
Purple Granite, 106

Quebec Agreement, 13, 15
Quick Reaction Alert, 163, 172

Radlett, 85, 126, 171
RAF Germany, 134
Reconnaissance, 169
Red Beard, 111 155, 176
Red Snow, 138, 155
Red Steer, 78, 128
Refuelling, in-flight, 43
Riccall, RAF, 136
Richards, Elfyn, 39
Roosevelt, President Franklin
    D., 12

Saceur, 134, 156, 166
Sandys, Duncan, 131, 139
Sapphire, Armstrong Siddeley,
    37, 126, 150
Saunders-Roe, 40
SB1, Shorts, 35
Scampton, RAF, 113, 142, 149,
    163, 164, 175
Schmetterling, 26
Scorton, RAF, 136
Scott-Hall, Stuart, 27, 30, 78
Sculthorpe, RAF, 170
Sea Harrier, 162
Seletar, RAF, 20
Shawbury, RAF, 191
Sheffield, 187
Shepherd's Grove, RAF, 136
Sherburn-in-Elmet, RAF, 136
Sherpa, Shorts, 36, 55
Sherratt, J. J., 185
Short Granite, 96
Shorts, 27
Shrike, AGM-45, 182

Silyn-Roberts, Group Captain,
    78
Skybolt, 137, 142, 155
Slatterly, Air Commodore, 61
Slessor, Sir John, 25, 70
Southend, 189
Specification B.14/46, 28
Specification B.35/46, 27, 40
Specification E. 6/48, 83
Specification E.15/48, 63
Spectre, de Havilland, 140
Sperrin, Shorts, 29
Sprite, de Havilland, 39
Sputnik, 109
St Mawgan, RAF, 164, 190
Stansted, 84
Stentor, Armstrong Siddeley,
    138
Strassman, Fritz, 11
Strategic Air Command, 16,
    130
Strike Command, 165
Sturgeon, Shorts, 36
Suez, 47
Summers, Joseph, 37
Supermarine, 83
Sydenham, 33
Syerston, RAF, 121

Tanker conversions, 170
Tanker Training Flight, 172
Tarrant Rushton, 45
Tasman, Operation, 116
Tedder, Lord, 24
Tender Design Conference, 61
Thermonuclear bomb, USA, 94
Thor, 109, 135, 155
Tizard Committee, 17
Tizard, Sir Henry, 12
Tornado GR1, 178, 186
Tornado, RB-45, 170
Touch, Dr A. G., 119
Trimouille, 21
Truman, President H., 14
Tuddenham, RAF, 136
Tuttle, Air Marshal, 52
Tuxford, Squadron Leader R.,
    180

U-2, Lockheed, 144, 170
V-1, 22
V-2, 22

V-Class Bombers, 43
V-Class nomenclature, 70
V-Force, 14
V.1000, Vickers, 41
Valiant Tactical Bomber Force,
    167, 174
Valiant Vickers, 34, 128, 158,
    166, 194
Valley, RAF, 164
Vandenberg AFB, 136
Vickers-Armstrong, 29
Victor, 77, 79, 123, 179, 189
Violet Club, 112, 128
Von Braun, Wernher, 22
Vulcan, 53, 122, 175, 177, 185
Vulcan Restoration Trust, 189

Waddington, RAF
50, 67, 115, 133, 136, 158, 164,
    175, 188
Walton, David, 189
Warrior, HMS, 105
Washington, DC, 12
Wasserfall, 26
Wattisham, RAF, 164
Watton, RAF, 136
WE, 177, 162, 176
Wheeler, John, 11
White sands, 14
Whitehead, Gilbert, 70
Wideawake, 177
Wilson, Charles, 131
Windscale, 16, 20
Wisley, 37
Witchford, RAF, 136
Withers, Flight Lieutenant M.,
    181
Wittering, RAF, 43, 113, 143,
    154, 163, 164
Woodbridge, RAF, 34
Woodford, 63, 115, 173
Woomera, 51, 140, 159
Wyton, RAF, 164

Yellow Sun, 106, 110, 128, 155,
    159, 176

Yeovilton, RNAS, 164